D0513388

COUNTRY VOICES

CHARLES KIGHTLY

COUNTRY VOICES

LIFE AND LORE
IN FARM AND VILLAGE

* * *

with 35 illustrations

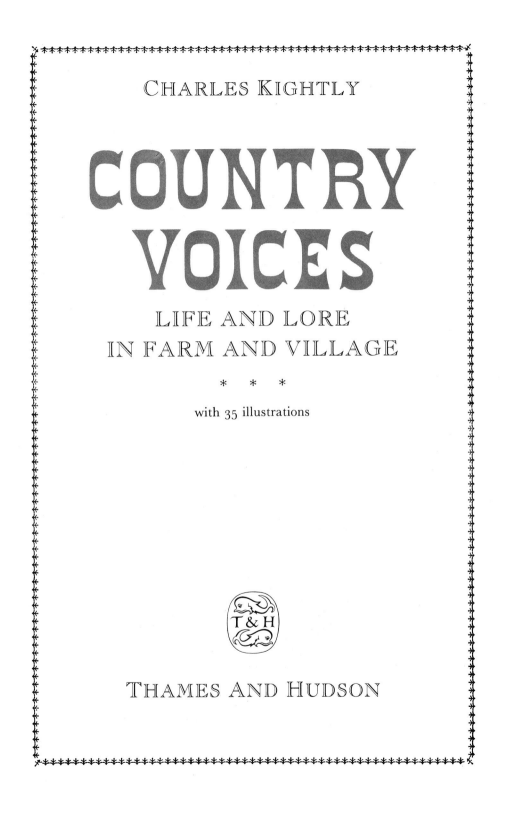

THAMES AND HUDSON

This book is dedicated to the memory of
Frederick William ('Fred') Brader,
Lincolnshire waggoner, shepherd, and
latterly landlord of the Jolly Farmer
at Leavening on the Yorkshire Wolds,
where he was well known and loved as
an authority on country matters.

The glossary at the end of this book provides definitions or explanations
of dialect words, technical terms and unusual ingredients for recipes
or remedies. These are marked throughout with an asterisk.

Printed and bound in
the German Democratic Republic

CONTENTS

ACKNOWLEDGMENTS

I should like to thank the following for their invaluable help during the compilation of this book:

Glynis Beech, Knighton; Miss Bell, Matron, 'The Limes', Driffield; Mrs Brewster and the staff, 'Ashfield', Malton; Mr Brown, Malton; Mrs Cadogan; Beryll Camplin; Debbie Cartmell, for 'quoils'; Mr Daniels, Malton; Mr E. J. Death, Stoke-by-Nayland; Francis Felix, OSB; Jack Gibbons, Coldred; the landlord, the Half Moon and Seven Stars, Preston, Kent; John Hayward, Ash-by-Sandwich; Paul Hicks, Harrietsham; Neville Hobson, York; Teddy Hogben, Ash-by-Sandwich; Mrs Hyde, Assistant Matron, 'The Cottage', Knighton; Mrs Jones and Mrs Watkins, Matrons, 'Cartref', Hay-on-Wye; Peter McDiarmid; Geoffrey Marsh, Ash-by-Sandwich; Bill Matheson, Llangunllo; Mr H. R. Owen, Knighton; Ronnie and David Pearcy, Heslington; Mary Price, Knighton; Mrs Edith Richards, Knighton; Mrs Sellers, Rudston; Miss Tarr, Malton; Christopher Tennant, Sedbergh; Rob Thomson, York; The Revd John Thorold, Spilsby; Rick and Erica Twyman, Llangunllo.

Thanks also, for their kind and patient assistance with research and the provision of photographs, to:

Stephen Ramm and the staff of the North of England Open Air Museum, Beamish, Co. Durham; the staff, Canterbury Central Library, Kent; the editorial staff, *Driffield Times*; Mr Brown of the Humberside Record Office; Catherine Wilson and Ron Cousins, Museum of Lincolnshire Life, Lincoln; the staff, Suffolk County Record Office, Ipswich; A. Lloyd Hughes, Archivist, and the staff of the Welsh Folk Museum, St Fagans; Richard Stansfield, the Castle Museum, York; Maurice Smith and the staff, Reference Library, York City Library; the Yorkshire Farming Museum.

And very special thanks to:

Mrs Bolam and Marian Lomax, Prudhoe; the Clements family, Northiam; Penny Crocker; Bill and Nora Denby, Heslington; Lawrence and Mary James, Sedbergh; Mike and Susan, Tregoyd; Robert and Judy Nichols, Askrigg; Mrs Gillian Stafford, Burgh-on-Bain; Mrs Dorothy Wallis, Eastry; Mrs Maudie Whymark, Lindsey; Mr and Mrs Williams, Lindsey; and Mrs J. Brooks, who did the typing.

INTRODUCTION

Within the living memory of the oldest surviving generation – which is to say within the last eighty years – the English countryside has changed out of all recognition. No longer do the 'farm chaps' gather in the market places for the hiring fair, or sit down to a breakfast of fat pork and skimmed milk. The stables which once housed the great farm horses have fallen into ruin; and the cunning, secretive waggoners have pinched their last corn and mixed their last, mysterious powders. The cottager's pig has gone, protesting, to the factory farm, and the cheese-press (with luck) to the museum. The scythemen and stook-tiers have left the harvest-field for ever; the mighty traction engines chug and clank no more from farm to farm at threshing time; and Kentish lanes echo no longer to the songs of London hop-pickers, warding off the country dark. All this has vanished as if it had never been, but it has not vanished without trace, for it lives on in the minds of the men and women who will share it with us in this book.

Most of them were born around 1900, into a rural world which was in many ways closer to the seventeenth century than to the last decades of the twentieth: and many were well established in work before the great cataclysm of 1914, which was to change that world for ever. I contacted them through old people's homes, through chance meetings in pubs or in country lanes or, most frequently, through their friends and neighbours. And though a few have elected to preserve their anonymity, not one single person whom I visited – even if he or she was a complete stranger – ever refused to talk to me. Everywhere, rather, I was received with kindness, patience and generosity – not to mention tea and cakes: and often I left, not only with invaluable information and treasured photographs, but also with gifts of apples, vegetables, home-cured bacon or country wines of formidable potency. Indeed, I now regard many of the people in this book as real friends, and I'd like to believe that they see me in the same way.

Their stories, sometimes shortened or rearranged but never altered or added to, were recorded on a pocket cassette tape-recorder, generally during two or three sessions. Among the many things I learnt while compiling this book, one of the most important was to listen to what people wanted to tell me – which was not always the same as, though it was usually far more interesting than, what I expected to hear. Thus the Flintons, expected to talk about milling, told me instead about geese, asthma cures and the life of a traction-engine driver; Maggie Joe Chapman, consulted about knitting, recounted in addition the saga of a hill farm family; and Ron Mills's story about the conjuror appeared in the midst of a conversation about cider. So if I have any advice to give to 'oral historians', it is to keep your mouth shut and your tape-recorder running.

The voices in this book came from seven areas, each with its own distinctive manner of speech – whose flavour I have striven to preserve in the transcription: Tyneside; the north Pennine Dales; the flat farmland of the Plain of York; the bare chalk Wolds of East Yorkshire and Lincolnshire; the secret hill-country of the Welsh borders; the rolling cornlands of Suffolk; and the apple orchards and hop-gardens of Kent. I should like to have travelled and recorded far more widely. But one must stop (or rather call a temporary halt) somewhere. So the reader must accept this as merely a sampler of the rich and varied material still to be found all over Britain in the memories of our older neighbours.

CAST OF CHARACTERS

BAINBRIDGE, Myles
b. 1900 near Mickleton-in-Teesdale, North Yorkshire. Crippled at an early age by bovine tuberculosis, he was unable to follow the family business of farming, and in 1915 became an apprentice clogmaker at Kirkby Stephen, Cumbria. In 1923 moved to Sedbergh, where he is still making shoes and clogs (see 'The Sedbergh clogger').

BATESON, Edward (Ted)
b. 1897 in Lancashire, but has spent most of his life in East Yorkshire, where as a boy he helped his stepfather, the Skipsea butcher (see 'To mend the pantry'). Thereafter worked as a farm labourer and waggoner. Served in the East Yorkshire Regiment during the First World War. Appears also in 'To be a farmer's boy' and 'Them old horse chaps'.

BIGG, Frank
b. 1915 at Milden, near Hadleigh, Suffolk, son of Cornelius ('Nelie') Bigg, horseman (see 'Them old horse chaps'). Tells of his experiences and training as 'The basketmaker': and also appears in 'The pig: the cottager's friend' and 'Recipes, remedies and beliefs'.

BIGG, Mrs Vinie
b. 1921 at Edwardstone, near Hadleigh, Suffolk. Daughter of the farmer of Owls Farm, Milden. Appears in 'The pig: the cottager's friend' and 'Recipes, remedies and beliefs'.

BRADER, Fred
b. 1916 at Belchford, near Horncastle, Lincolnshire. Began work as a farm labourer, waggoner and shepherd. Subsequently for many years the popular landlord of the Jolly Farmer, at Leavening on the Yorkshire Wolds. Appears in 'Them old horse chaps' and 'The pig: the cottager's friend'. Died 1983.

BRADER, Mrs Mary
b. 1918 at Heckington, Lincolnshire but brought up at Saltfleetby St Peter. Now lives at Burythorpe, North Yorkshire. Wife of Fred Brader. Appears in 'The village'.

CALVERT, Kit, MBE
b. 1903 at Burtersett, Wensleydale, North Yorkshire, the son of a quarryman. Beginning his working life as a farm labourer and shepherd, he became a tenant

farmer, and in 1935 formed a company which took over the bankrupt Hawes creamery, producer of the famous Wensleydale cheese. After running this successfully for many years, he sold out to the Milk Marketing Board in 1966 for nearly £500,000. Now keeps a second-hand bookshop in Hawes, whence he dispenses advice and tales. Appears in 'To be a farmer's boy', 'Hill farm' and 'Haytime'.

CHAPMAN, Mrs Maggie Joe
b. 1899 at Hill Top Farm near Muker, Swaledale, North Yorkshire, which she describes in 'Hill farm'. After marriage farmed in Bishopdale and Wensleydale, and now lives at Askrigg. Also appears in 'Haytime' and 'Church and chapel'.

CLARK, Miss Hannah
b. 1893 at Clyro, Radnorshire, Powys, the daughter of the head gardener at Clyro Court. Worked herself as 'The gardener' (see 'In service') during and after the 1914–18 war, and subsequently ran Clyro village shop. Also appears in 'The village'.

DENBY, Bill
b. 1905 near Doncaster, West Yorkshire, the son of a farmer and horse breeder (see 'Them old horse chaps'). In 1930 he and his father moved to Heslington, near York, as tenant farmers (see 'The village'): Bill subsequently became an agricultural contractor (see 'All is safely gathered in').

ELLIOTT, Miss Cissie
b. 1904 at Ovingham, Northumberland, where she still lives. Daughter of a mine 'deputy' who was also a smallholder and an hereditary tenant of the Dukes of Northumberland. Most of her working life has been spent in nursing. Sister of Mrs Mary Watson, with whom she appears in 'The pig: the cottager's friend', 'Haytime', 'The village' and 'Recipes, remedies and beliefs'.

FLINTON, Will
b. 1900, son of a Nottinghamshire shepherd. Moved in his teens to Burgh-on-Bain, Lincolnshire, where he took up the job of driving traction engines for an agricultural contractor. Appears in 'Them old horse chaps' and 'The engine-man'.

FLINTON, Mrs
b. 1900 at Burgh-on-Bain, Lincolnshire, the daughter of a farmer who also worked the village water-mill. Wife of 'The engine-man', she appears in 'To mend the pantry', 'The village' and 'Recipes, remedies and beliefs'.

FORMAN, Will
b. 1904 at Ash-by-Sandwich, Kent, where he began working with horses at the age of ten, and was still working (with tractors) when I talked to him in 1982. Appears in 'Them old horse chaps' and 'Hop-picking'.

FRIEND, Alf
b. 1899 at Minster-in-Thanet, Kent. Began his working life as a farm man and waggoner's mate. Now lives at Preston-by-Wingham, Kent. Appears in 'Them old horse chaps', 'Harvest' and 'Hop-picking'.

'GEORGE'

b. 1896 at Tetford on the Lincolnshire Wolds, son of a head gardener. He began working with horses in 1909, and the story of his progress from 'day boy' to head waggoner forms the basis of 'Them old horse chaps'. Eventually acquired a smallholding, which his son still farms. Also appears in 'To be a farmer's boy'.

'GIB'

Welsh-border farm man and forestry contractor. Appears in 'To be a farmer's boy' and tells the story of 'The War-Ag. pig' (see 'The pig: the cottager's friend').

GRANGE, Mrs Lizzie

b. 1906 near Durham of Irish-descended parents. Now lives at Prudhoe, Northumberland. In domestic service most of her working life. Appears as 'The tweeny' (see 'In service') in 'Church and chapel' (see 'The village') and in 'Recipes, remedies and beliefs'.

'JIM BUSH'

Welsh-border farm man, hedger, rabbit-catcher, etc. Appears in 'To be a farmer's boy' and in 'The War-Ag. pig' (see 'The pig: the cottager's friend).

LOW, Mrs Libby

b. 1902 at Brookside, near Knighton, Radnorshire, Powys; the daughter of a small tenant farmer. In domestic service until her marriage, after which she lived in Norfolk: she has now returned to Knighton, where she lives at the Old People's Home. Appears in 'In service'.

MEASDAY, Filmer

b. 1904 at Stodmarsh, Kent, son of a stockman. Worked for some time as a farm labourer before joining the Royal Navy. Now lives at Preston-by-Wingham, Kent. Appears in 'To be a farmer's boy', 'Them old horse chaps', 'The pig: the cottager's friend' and 'Hop-picking'.

METCALFE, Bob

b. 1905 near Bainbridge, Wensleydale, North Yorkshire. Horseman and farm labourer. Now lives at Askrigg, where he is captain of the bell-ringers. Appears in 'To be a farmer's boy' and 'Haytime'.

MILLS, Mrs

b. 1895 at Llaethdy, on the borders of Radnorshire and Montgomery in modern Powys, only daughter of a farmer. Now presides over the family farms and pony-trekking centre at Newcourt, Velindre, near Hay-on-Wye, Powys. Appears in 'Hill farm', 'Church and chapel' and 'Recipes, remedies and beliefs'.

MILLS, Ron

b. 1916 at Llaethdy, son of Mrs Mills. Worked for many years as a waggoner about the Welsh borders. Now helps run 'Mills Brothers' farms and trekking centre at Velindre. Appears in 'Them old horse chaps', 'Hill farm' and 'Recipes, remedies and beliefs'.

PARTRIDGE, Bill
b. 1900 at Lindsey, near Hadleigh, Suffolk, where he still lives. Descended from generations of farm men, he has worked on farms all his life, rising from 'back'us boy' to 'head horseman'. Appears in 'To be a farmer's boy', 'Them old horse chaps' and 'Recipes, remedies and beliefs'.

RECORD, Mrs Daisy
b. 1904 at Hunton, near Yalding, Kent. After a somewhat stormy career in domestic service (described in 'In service') she 'went on the farm' as a full-time labourer (see 'To be a farmer's boy'). Continues to do a daily paper round at Harrietsham, where she now lives. Also appears in 'Recipes, remedies and beliefs'.

ROBSON, Sam
b. 1912, Bempton, East Yorkshire, where he still lives. Farm labourer and (like his father and grandfather) a seasonal 'climmer', who scaled the three-hundred-foot cliffs of Bempton to collect sea-birds' eggs for sale. One of the last surviving practitioners of that craft, which he describes in 'To mend the pantry'. Also appears in 'To be a farmer's boy' and 'The village'.

SPOONER, Jim
b. 1903, in Suffolk. Farm labourer and donkeyman. Appears in 'To be a farmer's boy' and describes 'The old twizzler' in 'To mend the pantry'.

SWANSBOROUGH, Les
b. 1913, London, where he trained as 'The carpenter's apprentice'. After many years' service in the RAF, he came to live at Stackyard Green, Monks Eleigh, Suffolk, where he still works as a carpenter.

TINSLEY, Alfred
b. 1905 near Malton, North Yorkshire, the son of the travelling 'head lad' of a racing stable and the nephew of a racehorse trainer. After a brief period as a gardener's boy, in 1922 he became 'The gentleman's groom' (see 'In service').

WADE, Arthur
b. 1900 at Rudston, East Yorkshire, where he has now returned after farming for many years around Doncaster, West Yorkshire. The recounter of 'Rudston feasts and fights', he also appears in 'To be a farmer's boy', 'Them old horse chaps', 'Recipes, remedies and beliefs' and 'To mend the pantry'.

WADE, Mrs Violet
b. 1897, near Doncaster, West Yorkshire, daughter of a railwayman. Now lives at Rudston, East Yorkshire, with her husband Arthur. Appears in 'Recipes, remedies and beliefs'.

WATKINS, Mrs Edith
b. 1900 near Knighton, Radnorshire, Powys, the daughter of a shepherd. After working many years as a farmhouse maid in various parts of the Welsh borders (see 'In service') she became head dairymaid to Lord Rennell at the Rodd, near Kington, Herefordshire – near which she still lives. See also 'Recipes, remedies and beliefs' and 'The pig: the cottager's friend'.

WATSON, Mrs Mary
 b. 1898 at Ovingham, Northumberland, where she still lives. Eldest daughter of a mine 'deputy' who was also a smallholder and an hereditary tenant of the Dukes of Northumberland. Sister of Miss Cissie Elliott, with whom she appears in 'The pig: the cottager's friend', 'The village' and 'Recipes, remedies and beliefs'.

WILLIAMS, Mrs Elsie Hilda
 b. 1891 at Hay-on-Wye, Breconshire, Powys, where her father was postmaster and a town councillor. Her childhood there is described in 'May Fair blue' (see 'The village'). Subsequently gained a scholarship to University College, Aberystwyth (one of the first women to do so) and after travelling in France returned to teach in Hay, where she kept her own school.

Farmer's boy and farm labourer, c. 1930. The boy is wearing 'buskins' (leggings) and a 'mantle' (sack apron).

1

TO BE A FARMER'S BOY

'Can you tell me, if any there be
Who will give me employ
To plough and sow, to reap and mow
And be a farmer's boy'

THE FARM LABOURER

*I*t is only right and proper to begin this sampler with the man on whose shoulders the whole structure of rural life rested – the farm labourer. Labourer he was indeed, toiling for six days a week and often for twelve hours a day, or even longer at harvest and haytime. Yet his weekly wage, counted in shillings rather than pounds until the Second World War, was normally well below the national average: and in areas – such as East Anglia and the Welsh borders – where agriculture faced no competition from towns or industry, it was often scarcely above starvation level. Nor did he enjoy the dubious compensation of status, either in his local community or in the world at large. For in the first he was near the bottom of the social ladder, while the second rarely saw him as he really was, preferring either to idealize him as an 'innocent swain' or, more frequently, to caricature him as 'Hodge' and 'Bumpkin', the butt of innumerable 'yokel jokes'.

Many older farm labourers, therefore, were surprised that I wanted to interview them at all – 'Surely you don't want to talk to me, boy; I was just a farm chap.' But when they did begin to speak, I found them to be very far removed from their popular image: indeed, they were as a class the friendliest, wittiest and most interesting people I met on my travels. Admirable, too, for three special qualities: the endurance that carried them through the sheer drudgery of much of their lives; their pride in their hard-learned skills; and the versatility which enabled them not only 'to plough and sow, to reap and mow', but also to master hedging and thatching, milking and lambing, and the hundred other tasks required of the 'general labourer'.

I use the past tense advisedly, because farm labourers in the old tradition are rapidly becoming a rare breed. Farm mechanization and automation, gathering ever-increasing momentum during the last eight decades, have both transformed agricultural methods and drastically reduced the agricultural workforce: in 1900, more than one in ten of all British males worked on the land; by 1951, less than one in twenty; and by 1980, after the triumph of the tractor and combine harvester, scarcely one in a hundred. Neither do those that remain form anything like so recognizable an element in society as their forbears: for economic and social changes are destroying all but the last vestiges of the farm man's distinctive way of life – about which we shall now hear.

Bill Partridge ['I reckon I'm right a true Partridge, 'cause my father was a Partridge, and he married a Partridge: only o' course they wan't related'] is honoured as the oldest inhabitant of Lindsey, near Hadleigh in south-east Suffolk, where his remarkable memory is still consulted whenever boundary disputes arise. Born with the century, of generations of farm labourers, he has spent all his life working on farms in and around the village, rising from 'back'us boy' to 'head horseman' (see Chapter 2): so there can be few better qualified to remember the 'grass roots' of agriculture in this part of East Anglia during the decades surrounding the 1914–18 war. He did so in the broad Suffolk speech which is now rapidly disappearing in its native area (though it has left its mark in the modern accents of Australia and New Zealand). I make no apology for attempting to reproduce this. I do so not only in the hope of passing on some fraction of my delight in listening to it; but also because it helps to emphasize how little the country life of Bill's youth, now changed utterly, had itself altered since the days when Thomas Tusser based his Five Hundred Points of Good Husbandry *(1573) on his experience of farming at Brantham, not a dozen miles from Lindsey.*

Back'us boy

I've worked on a farm all me life – there wasn't nothing only farm work in this country,* you see. There wasn't no factories round here then. Well, I left school at tharteen, and I went to work in a farm right against me house. I went and helped the lady sort o' chop sticks and saw wood, and heat th' oven Sat'days to bake the bread and everything. We call it 'back'us boy' round here. It was helping the woman indoors, you know, the missus. Then the farmer used to keep some sheep, and when he wanted me I used to ha' to help him set the folds for the sheep to be in, with hurdles: that was at lambing time. But mostly back'us boy was inside work.

In East Anglia, the 'back'us' or back-house was generally a separate building immediately behind the farmhouse or cottage kitchen: it normally included a built-in copper and a large, brick baking-oven. The 'back'us boy' was specifically the 'missus's' servant, and his job was regarded by some as a fairly gentle introduction to the rigours of farm work, as Jim Spooner recalls.

I bin through the hup [hoop], boy, don't you worry about that. I started as back'us boy, hunting up eggs and cleaning fowl-housen [chicken houses] out, and cleaning the shoes. Back'us boy was all right: he used to be all grease. You'd git a fair bit o' good food, and you'd got a nice little place where you could set down, and they used to bring my dinner out. The back'us boy, his old meyther* [mistress] used to keep he up well. They used to keep *me* up well, they *did.*

What sticks in Bill Partridge's mind, however, is the long hours and low pay.

Sixty hours a week it was, for half a crown a week. That was six 'til half past five, Saturdays an' all. We never had no half-a-days Saturdays, we never looked for it. Only holidays we hed was Sundays and Christmas Day. Different from today, ain't that! Down Brent Eleigh 'Cock' [a pub], about six months ago, I was setting there, and they say to me, 'We'd like you to tell we what you earned when you started work.' 'Well', I sa', 'I can soon tell you, I earned a ha'penny an hour.' And they said, 'Don't come down here and tell we them lies: you'd better keep away.' So I say, 'I'm a-tellin' on you the *truth*.' Because I got a half-crown for sixty hours, when I was a back'us boy. That was a ha'penny an hour, wan't it?

And it wan't much better when you was a man. You never got man's pay 'til you was twenty-one: and when you was a full man, when you went to plough, like, it was tuppence ha'penny an hour, twelve shillings a week. And they what we used to call head horsemen, that used to goo bait* [go feed] them horses about five o'clock of a morning, so they were right ready when you got there at six: he got a shilling a week more'n another one to do that. He got thirteen shillings a week: and he hed to goo twice on a Sunday, too, to get that shilling.

Farm'd provide you a cottage, but you hed to pay rent, and about here you hed to buy your home milk too. That used to be about five pound a year rent, about two shillings a week. Wages was very low round here, and some used to goo off north to Yorkshire or Lincolnshire, where the money was a bit better – it wan't *good*, but it was better, a little. I had two brother-in-laws goo, and a brother. There used to be an agency at Stowmarket: you'd go see that agent, and he'd git you a job.

And it used to be worse still. My father-in-law – I dessay he'd be about 120 if he was alive now –, every Thursday, he used to take twenty or thirty pigs to Sudbury: drive 'em to Sudbury market [about nine miles]. Anybody wouldn't hardly think a pig would walk to Sudbury, would ye? And he wan't only thirteen. What d'you reckon he got for that day's work? Threepence! Eighteenpence a week it was, when he started work. I dunno how they fared to manage.

A bit o' extra money

Well, I do know, 'cause we had to pick up a bit o' extra money anyhow we could. We used to goo gleaning* the corn after harvest – the mother and all the children'd goo gleaning. Some o' the women about here, they used to git as much as a comb o' wheat – that's eighteen stone – and they used to git that ground into flour for their baking. They'd put it through th' old thrashing engine when that came round, and then they'd git it ground into flour. As soon as the field was clear, as soon as they'd carted the shocks [stooks] out o' the field, the women could goo in there and glean it: but some o' these farmers used to hoss-rake it afore they'd let 'em goo in, and they'd not get so much then. Or you'd goo gleanin' beans, and the pigs would have they.

I often went gleaning, yes, and I often went stone-picking too, dang it! Three shillings for twenty-four bushels* it was – that was what they called 'a load'. How long did it take to pick up twenty-four bushels? A long while, I can tell ye! You'd be gooing about and about the field, and you'd pick 'em in bushel baskets, or a pail: you soon got to know just what that pail held. That cleared the farmer's land a bit, see, and he used to git so much a load from the Council, to put 'em on the roads. All these roads were made up wi' them stones, and they wan't rolled in nor nothing. They'd just spread 'em on the roads, and then farm waggons and tumbrils* [carts] 'ould put they down as smooth as a steam-roller, after a time. They never used no granite on these old roads!

I'd be about six or seven when I started picking. All the children went stone-picking round here, *and* the mother: and father used to come out arter tea and help. O' course, you couldn't only pick 'em a certain time o' year. You'd ha' to goo in the springtime, 'cause when the corn got up you couldn't git in the field. A rotten job? I should think it was, a rotten old job. There ain't a-many liked it, but they hed to goo! They needed the bit o' extra money to buy clothes and that with.

Then there was sparrer-money, and rat-money. You'd git ha'penny a sparrer killed, and penny a rat-tail. Years ago, there used to be a lot o' straw stacks when they'd thrashed, and sparrers would sleep in there. And when it was gitting dusk, we used to go round with a big old sieve, and clap it on the side o' the stack, and they sparrers would come out into it: then you could put your hand in and get 'em. Or you could make a trail o' corn, and blast away wi' your old muzzle-loader. You took 'em up to a farm here, and farmer'd pay you: I expect somebody paid *him* – the Council, or the parish, or somewhere.

And moleskins hooly* sold [sold very well] sometimes. You could git six bob apiece for moleskins, one year. Oh yes, anybody would buy they, any o' these travelling chaps. We used to have proper mole-traps, and set 'em in a run: then we used to pin the skins out square on a board, and let 'em dry out. I reckon they went into moleskin coats: a moleskin coat was hooly dear wan't it?

Then you could sell rabbit-skins. When I went to school they sold about a ha'penny each, but when the Fourteen War got up, they went up to two bob a skin sometimes: then they went down again, I reckon. We used to sell they to the men that came round with bloaters and fresh herrings, on a pony and cart: well, they wan't *very* fresh sometimes, I can tell ye – they stunk! They wan't no proper fishmongers: they just used to buy a barrel o' herrings, and come round and sell 'em.

'We used to go gleaning the corn after harvest.' Children gleaning near Pinchbeck, Lincolnshire, during the 1890s: by the look of their sacks, the farmer has left them plenty of ears to pick up. Notice the girls' sunproof headscarf, and the various shapes of the newly thatched stacks in the distance.

Nineses and eightses, buskins and beevers

I used to help out round the kitchen and back 'ouse for two or three years. I'd be called there in the morning, and I helped until I went out in the fields. Then I'd mebbe go out hoeing. We used to hoe all the corn by hand them days, you know. We hed to hoe everything, beans an' all, and sometimes we hew the winter beans twice. I've bin in a field when there's been sixteen on us hoeing: and now there ent a man at all, hardly, on the farm!

And if there was some thistles come up, we used to goo through the corn with what we called a weeding hook. It was a long stick, about a yard long, with a little old hook on th' end, made like a crotch, so that the thistle just went in it. They was sharp as razors: the thistle was off in a minute, soon as it touched 'em: you could stand upright, with the long handle – you didn't want to keep bending, you see. Then, if it was docks coming, you used a dock iron. That had a split in the blade, that went round the roots and cut through 'em: it lifted 'em out, and you just bent down and put 'em in a bucket. You hed to put 'em in a bucket and take 'em off, do [or else] they'd grow agin: you couldn't leave 'em lying.

We never took no *sandwiches* them days. When I first started work afield, and I took me dinner, they used to put a whole big loaf o' bread in. They called 'em cottage loafs: there was a little loaf atop a big 'un, and we used to eat the little 'un for nineses, and the bottom bit for dinner. That'd frighten they today! We never hed no *sandwich tins*, we hed what they called a 'tommy-bag', a white bag they used to put the loaf in. They'd put cheese in, or a pork chop, or anything like that in with it, and we'd maybe take some home brew with us.

You needed it, you did, because you was working very long hours. We'd start at six, and when we hed a three o'clock dinner, we used to leave off ploughing about half past two, and you went home for dinner from three to four. Then we'd come back and feed the horses – fill their racks up with what we called 'stuvver',* (that was clover and hay, and all like that). Then you'd clean 'em down 'til it was time to leave off. And sometimes we hed a twelve o'clock dinner. Then we worked 'til four at ploughing, and we hed an hour at home with the horses to give 'em their tea and everything.

When we had three o'clock dinner, we always hed a break about eleven, and we called that 'elevenses', and when we hed twelve o'clock dinner, we used to hev our bit o' breakfasting about nine, and we called that our 'nineses' about here.

And we never used to leave off 'til eight at night in harvest time, you know. So we used to hev our tea afield at harvest time, and we called that our 'beever'.* You only called that beever in harvest time, and you hed that about five 'til half past. Some called it 'beever', and some called it 'fourses'. [Mrs Vinie Bigg: I used to take my father what we called 'beever', in the field, at about five o'clock. I'd take a steak-and-kidney pie to him, and a can of tea. I think 'fourses' was any time of the year, but we only called it 'beever' at harvest. 'Beever' was when you took a proper tea: 'fourses' was just a snack.]

Then there was your 'eightses'. Ever heard o' eightses? Ye never heard o' that, ha' ye? Eightses wasn't food, though. They used to tie their trousers up below the knee, so they didn't git muddy: everybody used to tie their trousers up with a strap or a bit o' string, and we used to call them straps 'eightses'. 'Half past eightses', we used to say.

All the trousers used to be thick old corduroy. There used to be tailors about here, and a lot used to goo there and hev cord trousers made – you know, made to measure. And they last over a year, because they was good stuff, I doubt [I'm sure] they was. You never see 'em worn today. They're mostly jeans today, 'cause they say they're easier to wash. They never washed them cords, no!

Then we used to wear boots, and a kind o' leggings – 'buskins' we used to call 'em. They was leather, and they'd got big buttons on: or some on 'em had a clip-spring at the bottom, and strap up atop. You'd wear them over your trousers and your eightses. You hed to wear 'em in winter-time, do [or else] you'd get pizened [poisoned] with all the mud and muck, and th' old horse keep poaching it about on you. [JIM SPOONER: I got *married* in brown leather buskins, corduroy breeches, and brown shoes. They wouldn't git married today in buskins, would they? (After a pause) Well, I don't think *I* should!] And d'ye know what a mantle is? Thet's an old bag tied round your waist for bad weather, we called thet a 'mantle'.

Everybody used to wear sleeved-weskits [waistcoats] too: that was cord a-front, and the back was made o' cloth-stuff. You could hev the cord brown or 'light': I always used to hev the light. You didn't want no jacket over thet, thet old sleeved-weskit was as thick as thet could be: you wouldn't git no jacket over it, thet you wouldn't. You'd wear the same summer or winter – sleeved-weskit, cords and buskins, and I generally wore a cap. But you'd wear straw hats summertime, to keep the avels* [sharp 'beards' of barley] out o' your neck, when you're loading barley!

And them days, no matter how they done it, they all always hed a lovely good suit. They wouldn't go out without they put a nice suit on for Sundays. You'd git a topping suit for thirty bob, that'd last you ten years, and just as good then as that was when you bought it. There was this tailor bloke used to live at Bildeston, his name was Prentice: he'd come round and measure you one Sunday morning, and bring your suit the next Sunday morning. You didn't want to go to his shop, he'd come right the way from Bildeston on his old bicycle: he didn't hev no pony and trap – they couldn't afford to buy one, such as they. Nor there weren't no motors. When we first seen a motor, we wondered what the devil it was, a-coming up the road. We'd never seen one afore.

THE HIRING FAIR

How did you get your first job? and how did you change jobs, if you wanted to? were questions I frequently asked the old farm men I spoke to. From Bill Partridge and others in the south of England, the answer would be that they'd 'seen a job in the paper', or 'heard that so-and-so wanted a chap'. But in the north, the west, and Wales, the reply would usually be 'I went to the hirings': for in those parts the traditional rural labour-exchange called 'the hiring fair' survived well into living memory.

Once, or sometimes twice, a year, countrymen and women seeking work would pour into the local market town during 'Fair Week', dressed in their best and often wearing some token to show they were 'hiring on': a reminder of the not-so-distant days when a prospective shepherd carried his crook, a horseman his whip, or a maid her mop – hence the alternative name of 'Mop Fairs'. Forgathering in a part of town established by custom, they stood on display until a would-be employer approached them, whereupon individual bargaining over the succeeding year's wage would begin: if agreement was reached, the deal would be clinched with a cash-down payment – 'fest-money', 'fastening-penny' or 'earnest-money' – which would usually be spent forthwith on the allurements of the fair.

The date of hirings varied from one part of the country to another, but they were normally held at the town's ancient Statute Fair – itself timed to coincide with a major religious holiday and, far more vitally, with a slack time in the agriculture year. The Yorkshire hirings, for instance, took place around Martinmas, on about November the 23rd. This puzzled me at first, because Martinmas, St Martin's Day, is actually celebrated on November the 11th: then I remembered that when Britain changed over from the Julian to the Gregorian calendar in 1752, eleven days were 'lost' from the year. But if the official calendar changed, the weather-dominated rhythm of farm life did not: and while the Londoners contented themselves with an ephemeral riot or two ('Give us back our eleven days!') countrymen registered a longer-lasting protest by obstinately sticking to the 'same' date for their fairs. Thus Yorkshire hirings continued to be held at 'Old Martinmas', now November the 23rd.

The legislation which fixed a national minimum wage for farm workers sounded the death-knell of the hirings: and in much of northern England they petered out during the 1920s or early thirties, though they lingered on into the fifties in parts of Wales and Cumbria. Some farm men remember hirings as a degradation – 'just like selling cattle really': while their middle-class critics (like that indefatigable anti-hiring pamphleteer, the Reverend John Eddowes of Garton-on-the-Wolds, near Driffield in East Yorkshire) complained that 'as the hiring day draws near, the servants become more rudely independent, more disobedient and impertinent'. No doubt this was because the fairs allowed the labourer some scope for bargaining with his masters, and it is surely no coincidence that agricultural wages in areas where they survived were far better than in those where they had died out. In the late Victorian period, for instance, the Yorkshire farm man – as Bill Partridge recalled – earned nearly twice as much as his mates in Suffolk.

Certainly 'the hirings' are remembered as a red-letter day in the labourers' year. To some, they might mean longed-for release from a hated employer – hence the East Yorkshire hiring rhyme recited for me by Sam Robson of Bempton:

'Good Morning, Mister Martinmas
You've come to set me free
For I don't care for Master
And he don't care for me'

while for others, like Kit Calvert of Burtersett in Wensleydale, they could bring a rare opportunity for bettering themselves:

I'd started work at twelve in 1915, and I'd started at five bob a week: and when I'd been there two and a half year, I'd got up to seven bob a week, and then he offered me sixpence a week rise. Well, I thought I was worth eight bob – a shilling rise: but me old boss said he couldn't afford it, so I came to Martinmas hirings here at Hawes. It was a law of the Medes and Persians that if you were already hired, you didn't git to t'hirings, but if you weren't hired, you could come. Well, I came to t'hirings, and there was a number on us standing just outside where we are now: this side o' t'street was considered the place for t'lads that was wanting hiring. And I was standing there when a cattle dealer came up from Bainbridge: and he looked us over, and picked me out.

'Is ta hiring?'

'Yes.'

'Work for me?'

'I will if you give me plenty.'

I was going to ask ten shilling, if I was to go away from me own home village.

'I'll give thee a pound a week.'

A pound a week! I thought that was a fortune beyond the realms of avarice.

'Aye', I said, 'I'll coom.'

I didn't enquire what sort of a home I was gan' to, for a pound a week. I could go through Hell for a pound a week!'

Not every 'hiring bargain', however, was as fair as it seemed, as Ted Bateson of Skipsea, East Yorkshire, once discovered.

First hirings is generally a fortnight afore you leave place you're at. 'Is ta stoppin'?', farmer'd say, and you'd say, 'Oh, I an't bin asked yit!' And if you warn't, you'd tell him. You'd not stay if he had a bad grub-shop [if the food was bad]. And then, at proper hirings on the 23rd of November, you all left and got paid. There used to be a hiring here at Driffield on a Monday, and then Martinmas Thursday was the main one – it used to be a real day here.

One Martinmas I never got hired until late on, until Saturday. And a chap comes to me and says, 'Ha' you bin hired, boy?' And I says, 'No, not yit' – I was only fifteen, mind. And he looked at me and says, 'What are y' asking?' 'Oh', I says, 'twelve pound a year and grub.' And he says, 'I'll tell thee what I'll do with tha, I'll give tha fourteen and half-a-crown fest.' They used to give you fest-money, to fasten' you, like – and I thought I was rich then, 'cause I hadn't a penny in me pocket, so I went straight into a shop and got a penknife for sixpence.

But this waggoner that hired me, he was a bad 'un. He thought I was a woman – he was trying to act with me same as he would with a woman. I wouldn't have it, of course. The foreman was a relation of his and all – I ought to have telled foreman. But I cleared off in the end, I ran away: and then this waggoner died.

And the *next* waggoner I hired on wi', 'e robbed me. I only had threepence, but he took it – he went into me box* and turned all me clothes upside doon to get it. But I got well paid for it! 'Cause they took him away, poorly, and he left 'is bike, with an acetylene lamp and a pump on. And I telled foreman 'e'd robbed me: so foreman said, 'Go and get his light and his pump.' And I hadn't got a good lamp, so I got his acetylene lamp. Now when this bloke comes back from being off sick, we were hoeing turnips in the field. And he comes over to us shouting, 'Where's my lamp?' And foreman shouts back, 'Where's that lad's threepence?' – and then waggoner turns and runs away, wi' the foreman chasing after him! And I had that lamp for years – it cost threepence!

Neither did the farmer always get what he bargained for, especially if he was lured into conducting a deal with one of the many young men – among them Arthur Wade of Rudston, East Yorkshire – who merely went to the hirings 'for a bit o' fun'.

Well, one year, at the last hirings I went to, in about 1918, I was wi' a pal o' mine, a school pal. Neither on us wanted a job: we was just there for a bit o' fun. And he'd spent up, had owd Bill. So I says, 'I can't help thee out while [until] we get hoom, Bill: but I'll show thee 'ow to mek some money.'

'Will yer?'

'Aye, if you'll back me up. Coom on up to Cross Keys corner yonder: there'll be somebody come across and see us.'

And a fella came across, and he's looking owd Bill up and down. And he says, 'Tha'll just suit me, thoo'll mek me a good thod* [third] lad.' And I nodded to Bill, be'ind fella's back, like. Well, they used to give you fastin'-money, to fasten yer, like, and mek sure you'd come for job: and you had forty-eight hours, by the law, to return that fastin'-money, if you didn't go. So Bill took the job, and fella gave him a quid fastin'-money: that was a lot, but it were gettin' hard to get men, and wages were gooin' up. And I says to Bill, 'Thoo better have his name and address', and he wrote it down.

And when fella had gone, I says to Bill, 'Tha's all right now: thoo can spend that quid now, while tha gets home.' And I hired for a quid too, so's I could keep old Bill up to sending it back, see. So when we got hoom, I says, 'Bill, goo in, and shove a pound note in an envelope, and address it to this farmer: I'm gooin' to do same: and we'll goo across and post 'em.'

And as long as you sent that fastin'-money back within forty-eight hours, they couldn't come onto you: lads used to do it all over.

Here, indeed, is a record of the selfsame dodge, recorded in a village pub not far from Knighton, a Welsh border town in the Radnorshire district of Powys. There the hirings took place during the third week in May, at a time not far off the 'old' date of May Day – which was also the Celtic spring festival of Beltane, when the new lambs were turned out to graze. A pleasure fair and a major stock sale are still held in Knighton during fair week, and men still 'come down from the hills' to sing in the Red Lion.

JIM BUSH: I hired out at the hiring fair many times. You went down to Knighton, if you wanner staying on where you was working. The boss'd say on the 17th of May, 'Are you gonna have another year with me?', and you'd say 'No'. So you went down to Knighton at fair time, and you'd be by the clock and down the street. And you'd put a bit o' wheat straw in your cap: I dunno why, just an old fad it was.

GIB: It used to be a big day in Knighton. The hiring'd go on as long as the fair was going – a week, that is. And some of them blokes never came down from the hills, only at fair time: the farmers and the farm labourers too. Fair day was their day, like.

BILL: They'd be lounging and leaning on the wall round the clock, and the farmers was weighing 'em up, looking to see which one he thought was the strongest.

JIM BUSH: The old farmer'd say, 'Dust 'ee want a job, boy? How much be you asking?' And you'd say, 'Twenty-six pound a year': and he'd say, 'It's too much, I'll give you twenty-two.' And you'd bargain with him: just like selling cattle, really.

BILL: If he took a liking to you, he'd beckon you across for a pint in the Red Lion, and strike a deal.

JIM BUSH: He'd try to get you half-pissed first! Then, if he liked you, he'd give you a shilling or two bob 'earnest-money'.

GIB: You'd get a few boys going down there as wanted a beer-up or summat, and they'd go and hire on theirselves for the earnest-money – and the farmers'd never see them buggers again, 'ud they? You could have a fair old huckin'* [bargaining] 'cause in them days you could get three or four pints for a shilling. So you'd hire on for one farmer, and then go on down the road and hire on for another. You'd do three or four of them. They never caught up with you – and if you got five bob, well you'm drunk, inner you? That was a big laugh, that was.

JIM BUSH: But if he give you half a crown, you'd *gotta* go. You wanner bound to go for two bob, but half a crown you'd gotta go, at least for a month. Then at the end o' the month, if you didner like it, you could give him a fortnight's notice or a month's notice – or go straight away and lose a month's wages! But if *he* didn't like *you*, he could only take you for a week, he could bloody soon send you going.

GIB: There was no job security, like – no such thing as that. If 'e found you lying on the hay asleep, 'e'd bloody soon send you down the road. You were tied to him, but he wanner tied to you. Nor there wasn't no set wage. You might hire on with one man for fourteen bob a week, and with another for fifteen. Our old chap, now, when he was working: there was four of us at home, and he was bringing home seventeen bob a week – and that wasn't so long before the [1939–45] war.

Rum do's at Driffield

Since farm men were generally paid their entire annual wage for the previous year during hiring week, this was the time for paying off tailors and bootmakers – who took care to lay in extra stocks of corduroy suits and leather gaiters for the occasion. And, in East Yorkshire at least, it was also the time for 'paying off old scores' of a different kind:

There'd be a lot drunk at hiring fair. They'd take their fest-money and drink it – and others' fest-money besides, if they could get it! And there was one couple always had a fighting-do every year, to see which was best fella. They used to get their collars and ties off, and go up agin' cake mill, and they'd have it out. Talk about blood!: and what with that and muck in road, they *was* a mess when they'd finished. But they went on while yan [until one] of them went down. And I think one of them got gaffer* [was the winner] every time. But t'other'd never give up. They used to meet a'purpose for it. There was rum do's Martinmas Thursday, I can tell you!   [TED BATESON]

And a lot of lads would put off a fight 'til Martinmas time – 'til Driffield hirings. Because, you know, in them days they used to have big flat caps wi' cane round 'em, to hold brims out – did you ever see 'em? Well, when lads were fighting, you'd see them spin right up in air! I saw that when two lads were fighting in Driffield street, over a girl: I shall nivver forget, because they were two brothers, and they were both ginger-headed. And what d'ye think lass said? 'What are you silly so-and-so's fighting for? I don't want neither of yer!' So they gave up, and shook hands.   [ARTHUR WADE]

And I've heard me father say, you could walk in through a pub door at Driffield hirings, and somebody'd knock you back out again. You'd nivver know who your enemy was – it was somebody getting their own back for summat what had happened during year. He said they were all wandering about three parts drunk, wi' black eyes and bleedin' noses. It was a natural thing! Only thing police could do was get out o' road, else they'd ha' got bashed an' all.

Why, me dad got pinched, 'cause him and *his* dad were there when they smashed a café up. They were in there, and a gang of hooligans went in and started taking mickey out on 'em. So they says, 'Right, you've asked for it, you can have it now!' Me grandfather chucked yan [one] clean through window, and they smashed t'spot up, everything.

Well, nowadays, if there's a fight or owt at one o' these disco-clubs, they say, 'They're nowt but a lot of vandals, youth of today.' But what I say is, what about them days, then? [SAM ROBSON]

It was this kind of thing, no doubt, that moved the Reverend Mr Eddowes – whose parish lay only too close to Driffield – to the following flights of indignation:

Hiring-day! The very name reminds us of scenes which we would willingly forget for ever – the reeling men and drunken women even early in the day, the profanity and blasphemy and profligacy unchecked.

Hiring-day! It would seem to be the signal for the suspension of every law of virtue and morality: every restraint seems loosened, and every feeling of shame forgotten.

Hiring-day! Its observance is a disgrace to the country that permits it – a disgrace, moreover, for which the country pays dearly ... For its natural effect is to increase the numbers of paupers in the poorhouse, and of prisoners in the house of correction. Paupers are not maintained for nothing, nor are criminals corrected at a trifling expense.

Hiring-day! Many a promising youth, now lingering in the felon's prison, may trace the first step in their course of crime to the temptations of the fair.

The worst of these, of course, were the 'beer-houses, those stagnant marshes whose exhalations are always dangerous, if not fatal': but the 'simple swain' also had to watch out for 'those ruthless and heartless harpies of every colour and shade, who flock to the hirings and rejoice to make the helpless and ignorant their prey'. On one occasion within living memory, however, the simple swains got their own back:

There was all sorts went on at Driffield hirings. I was there once, before First War, and there was one o' them what we used to call 'cheap-jacks', selling stuff cheap, watches and that. And a lad said he'd given this cheap-jack a ten-bob note, and cheap-jack swore he hadn't. So t'lad went down to t'George Hotel, where he knew his brother was, and he went and told his brother. God, everybody in George Hotel turned out when they heared it. Off they came, up street, straight to this fella's stall. Well, he wouldn't pay: and they said, 'Tha won't, won't tha?' And he had a stall wi' a lot of watches on – d'yer know wheer that went? A chap got hold of each corner, and it got straight up i' air and dropped in middle o' road. Well, crowd was all over him then – broke watches, just tramped on 'em.

First thing police did, they went straight to fairground and grabbed all t'rifles on rifle-range, and stopped all t'roundabouts. Because there was a riot on – God, and it *was* a riot. But police couldn't do much about it, they'd just wait until it quietened down on its own. And this self and same year – I saw it myself – there was an old policeman and a young policeman, and they were halfway down street wheer riot was starting. And th' young policeman says to th' old 'un, 'Coom on, we got summat to settle yonder.' But th' old 'un says, 'Look, tha's to coom wi' me, we're going down 'ere', and he teks him by shoulder and leads him down side-street, and he says, 'Coom on wi' thee. Tha'll learn. If tha goes up there, tha'll goo up i' air an' all. Tha can't stop them lads when they're like that. They'll cool off.' And he took him down street, away from it all! [ARTHUR WADE]

Sam Robson of Bempton, to whom I told this story, had heard a slightly different version.

That must have been year they read Riot Act at Driffield: I've heard me dad on about it. One lad had bought a watch, and it was replica watch, not a genuine one, like. Well, he played hell up, because he wanted his money back: of course, the cheap-jacks wouldn't give it 'im. They were all 'aled up', of course, and they started bashing stall up, and braying* [hitting] him with it, and all sorts. So they read the Riot Act, and they were for getting troops out from Beverley barracks! They didn't actually get 'em out, I don't think.

Under the impression that this 'riot' was an unusual event, I tried to establish its date by reading through the back files of the Driffield Times. *From these, however, it soon became clear that large-scale disturbances were such regular and commonplace features of Martinmas that the newspaper scarcely troubled to report them, or merely mentioned that, 'As usual, a miniature riot took place at Hirings'. The resultant court proceedings – where defendants vied with each other to amuse the onlookers and display their disregard for 'law and order' – were regarded as much more newsworthy. These typical examples occurred in 1905.*

ENJOYED MARTINMAS WEEK
Robert Gledhill, a young farm servant, was charged with having been drunk and disorderly, and with having assaulted Sergeant Chambers. On entering the dock, Gledhill, looking round the court, said, 'Good morning, friends. I hope you have enjoyed Martinmas week the same as I have.' Defendant was requested to pay proper attention to the court, and proceeded to eat a bun. An officer asked him not to eat the bun in court, and defendant replied that he could eat his breakfast in court if he liked. Fined 5s and costs for being drunk and disorderly, and £1 (including costs) on the charge of police assault.

COULD HAVE DONE WITH MORE

William Lawlor (17), farm servant, on being charged with drunken and disorderly conduct on the previous Sunday, said, 'I was drunk, but I could have done with some more.' (Laughter) 'I warn't so bad.' (Laughter) 'I could walk.' (Laughter)

Pag-rag Day and Rive-kite Sunday

Around Louth and Spilsby in Lincolnshire, the hirings were held on or about the 14th of May – near the 'old' date of May Day, which was also the feast of St James, the patron saint of the churches in both towns. But the late Fred Brader, once a Lincolnshire waggoner, offered me a more practical explanation of its dating.

There's a reason for it being the 14th of May. When you was a hoss chap, you'd got all the hard work done wi' horses then. You'd drilled all your spring corn, and a lot o' your roots, and you'd turned your horses out to grass. So that was the best time to leave. Because if another waggoner came when the horses was living in the stables, his feeding would be different to yours, and so therefore it'd throw the horses wrong. But if they was out at grass, they could be changed over when they was brought back in in October.

Be that as it may, hiring time was the farm man's one annual holiday, as 'George' of Halton Holegate in Lincolnshire recalls:

Well, when the 14th of May came, we always used to have 'Pag-rag Day'. And that was when the hiring markets were. If you wanted a job, you'd go stand in the market, and if a farmer thought you looked suitable he'd mebbe offer you a job. Louth, Alford, Spilsby, all the towns had hirin' markets, all in May. You'd see these hoss chaps, and they'd have a feather in their hats, or a straw in their hats, to show they were lookin' for a job. That was the end o' the year, and you packed all your 'rags' if you left: so it was 'Pag-rag Day', 'pack-rag day'. And it was always on May the 14th. And at that time you had a week's holiday: if you was goin' back to the same place, you had a week's holiday, and if you left you looked for another place in that time.

This was all very well when the hirings fell in May, but rather hard on the Yorkshire folk, who were forced to take their Martinmas holiday at the end of November, surely one of the dreariest times of the whole year. But the younger of them, at least, must have been somewhat appeased by the feasts laid on at the family gatherings which customarily took place on the Sunday of hiring week. Centred round some traditional dish – often a stuffed chine of pork in Lincolnshire (p.79), a rabbit pie on the Welsh border, or a goose in

Yorkshire – such meals were designed to allow everyone to achieve, for once, the state of repletion summarized in the East Yorkshire nickname for the day – 'Rive-kite Sunday', 'rive' being 'to split' and 'kite' being the stomach.

... AND THE GRUB-SHOP

These occasional 'blow-outs' were all the more valued because, during the greater part of the following year, the filling or otherwise of the young farm man's stomach would lie at the mercy of his employer. For in the areas where hiring survived, so also did the old system of 'farm service', whereby unmarried workers of both sexes 'lived in' at the farm for at least six days a week, receiving their board and lodging as a vital part of their wage. Only when they married – and not always then – would they set up in a rented cottage of their own. The system is (to say the least) scarcely recalled with universal affection, perhaps because – as Jim Bush remembers – it gave the farmer irksomely immediate control over every waking moment of his employee's life.

The farmer'd find your board and lodge, of course. You'd go and live in with the farmer – worse luck! 'cause he'd get you up at six in the morning, and you'd work 'til eight at night: oh yes, he'd be sure to get you out of bed at six! You'd have breakfast at eight o'clock, about: then you'd have half an hour for your dinner, and ten minutes for your 'bait'* [packed snack], and that'd be it – and your tea at night. He'd give you a lump of bread and cheese for your bait, and a pint of cider: outside, you'd have that, you wouldner go into the house. Then for your dinner you'd have fat bacon and potatoes – farmhouse pigs killed, in them days: you'd have fat bacon and turnip broth throwed at you, every day. Eat it or leave it, it's up to you. Some farms you'd be eating by yourself in the back kitchen, and some you'd be eating with the boss and the missus and the maid. A maid would hire on same as the boys, in them days. They'd never hire to go into service to a big place, of course: but for a farm place they'd hire on, and live in same as we did. Bloody hard life, wanner it?

But the aspect of 'living in' I've most often heard about – as here from 'George' – was the quality of the food.

All the single men lived in. Now, for breakfast we 'ad a basin o' milk: we 'ad no *tea*, them days. In the summer, milk was cold, and in winter it was supposed to be boiled, but it wasn't always: and it was always in a basin, never in a cup: and sometimes it was gone off a bit, a little bit sour. And then we'd bacon – it was chiefly bacon, for meat. Because they killed a pig for each of us, and there was three on us men, and the foreman: so they killed four pigs a year i' th' 'ouse, and they weighed thirty stone apiece! So we lived on fat bacon, and we got a nice few pig's heads, and chaps [cheeks] and that kind o' thing: but we didn't see a deal of *ham* – seemed like *our* pigs had no ham! See what I mean?

And the bacon wasn't *all* good, them days. I've ploughed bacon in, and eaten dry bread, it was that bad. And another chap I knew, if it was a piece o' bacon he didn't like, he'd chuck it to the pigs when he came out, and says, 'I hope that'll be bacon *next* time round.'

So we ha' bacon for our breakfast, and this milk. And then the waggoner was at the carving end o' table, and he'd cut us each a piece o' bacon off, and put it between two slices of dry bread, and maybe there was a little cake on the table, and that was your lunch. We used to have that about ten o'clock, and they used to let us unyoke* at half past two, and tek th' horses home and take their gear off: and then we'd goo in th' house for a good hot dinner. Then we used to feed our horses while seven o'clock, and we went in for our tea at seven. It was half past when you came out, and you had to be in again by nine, else the doors were locked! There was no stopping out after that. But you didn't say nowt: you was brought up to do as you was telled.

Thus a niggardly farmer would soon become notorious, and might well find himself shunned when it came to hiring time. As Ted Bateson put it – and as he himself proved – 'You'd not stay if he had a bad grub-shop.'

When I left school, they sent me off to Frodingham. Farmer there only had one old chap working for him, that was going onto pension, and *I* was only thirteen, but he was going to have me milkin' and doing owt. Thinks I, 'Well, he isn't, neither: he isn't going to have me under his thumb.' 'Cause coos was right away fro' th' house, right round stackyard and right again' t'other end: and I'd to goo and churn, and separate, and goo back and feed calves at all hours.

And the grub was bad – well, there wasn't any. Now they had a maiden there, and they called her Gladys Finch: and if I telled her anything, she used to goo straight into room and tell t'missus. *She* always had her meals with them, but *I* had to ha' mine wi' myself: and I just gat what they sent oot for my meals: just the leavings, if there was any. Well, this day, they'd just about had all the meat there was off the chine o' pig; and then Gladys comes to me and says, 'Ted, you aren't cleaning your bone very well.' 'No', says I, 'there's a dog there again' door, give *'im* it, 'cause there's nowt on it for me.' And then she says, 'I see you ain't gotten your box* unpacked.' 'No, and I dain't think I'm going tae unpack it, neither.' And I didn't: that neet I collared me box, and I was off!

In his next two 'places', however, Ted made up for his bad luck.

Next place I went to was as different as chalk from cheese. When I went to bed first neet, farmer says, 'Dain't get up while you're shooted [shouted] on, i' morning.' 'Oh', thinks I, '*that's* all reet.' Well, the next morning, he didn't shoot while Mary, the maiden, had got breakfast fit – and I was still i' bed! Then they'd shoot, and I'd be straight doon into me breakfast, *afore* I went out to work. I thought that was wonderful.

Then, after that year, I came here to Bempton Grange. Ooh, that was a cold 'ole i' winter-time, up there on them three-hundred-feet cliffs. They used to climb them cliffs for birds' eggs, you know [p.85], and by gum, they did sell a lot. And I remember the housekeeper there – Jemima Hatfield. By, she was a lump! But, by gum, she was a topping cook, she was. We very near knew what we was going to have every day. We'd a duck egg for breakfast, of a Sunday morning, and then Sunday dinner was roast beef and all t'lot. Monday was just cleanings-up fra' Sunday, wi' maybe a dumpling and gravy; then Tuesday was broth day; Wednesday was pie day – meat and tatie pie; next 'un was broth day again; Friday was pie day; and Saturday was anything you could catch, you might say! It was regular, was that. She had three joints a week, and any meat she had left ower, she used to stew that up, and we'd ha' that for tea. By gum, we did use to enjoy that, wi' a bit o' dry bread. I'll tell you, we didn't leave nain o' that!

But, by, she *was* a big woman: I dain't know what she weighed, but I wouldn't ha' liked to have her tumble on *me*. Foreman was a bit soft on her: he used to sit up wi' 'er, neets: and waggoner and me used to lay on wall-top and watch 'em through t'window. She was a topping cook, though.

Rumours of a 'bad grub-shop' did not always prove true, as Bob Metcalfe of Askrigg in Wensleydale discovered:

First place I went out to, at Bainbridge, the master had a hump on his back, and he was supposed to be very greedy, very mean. But this night, when I hadn't been there long, there was bannocks* on table – scones, you might call 'em – bread, butter, and jam or cheese, which you wanted. And master came in from front room, and said:

'Had thee supper, lad?'

'No, I'm just going to get it.'

Then he turned to t'housekeeper (she was a fresh housekeeper, she hadn't been there long) and he says:

'That's no good to a growing lad. He wants beef, bacon and eggs.' And he got carving knife, and he went into t'pantry, and he fetched the biggest chunk o' beef I'd ever seen: it was half-an-inch thick.

'Eat that, lad. That sweet stuff's no good to you. That's no good to work on.' He didn't believe i' sweet stuff. He once caught me eating a sweet: somebody had gone past and given me a toffee.

'What's tha eating, lad?'

'Nay, just a toffee.'

'Han't had plenty o' breakfast? Gan and tell th' housekeeper tha wants some more. Tha wants nowt wi' that stuff!'

And back I had to go. Oh, in his own way he was very mean – but not at the table!

For, living as they did in small and tightly knit communities, many farmers – like Kit Calvert's first employer – were careful of their reputation.

The people I started with, the five-bob-a-weekers – they were a family that had been brought up in the mining, over in Swaledale. And in their desperation, when the mines went down, they came over to Wensleydale and started work at the quarries, at Burtersett. They were very frugal savers, and by he was in his sixties they'd saved enough to take a bit o' land: but by the time he was about sixty-eight, the 'miner's cough'* had got him, that he couldn't do owt. So they hired me at five shilling a week.

And that family, they had 'tea-boily'. The tea that had been left from tea-table was warmed up with a drop of milk, and poured onto some bread. But they never would let *me* have any. For the simple reason that they were frightened that I went boastfully up into the village, and said I'd had a special supper o' tea-boily. And tea-boily, you see, was a stigma of absolute poverty, and I hadn't to have it, in case I set a rumour going up in the town, that I was fed on tea-boily. Because I'll give them their due, they fed me as good, or rather better, nor they fed themselves. But they *wouldn't* give me tea-boily. *They* were used to it, and they liked it: they used to put a bit o' sugar to it, and it was the kind o' supper they really enjoyed. But they wouldn't have it said they fed their farm servants on it.

One of the best ways to get the reputation of 'a good place' was to provide plenty of 'butcher's meat', even if this was not always cooked according to the modern standards of hygiene which Sam Robson scorns:

I've seen butchers stagger into farms wi' lumps o' meat so big, they could hardly carry it. Well, they only used to cook it *lightly*: then you'd cut off th' outside, and roast it again next day. They'd just roast th' outside, and you'd have that for dinner one day: what was left was weeping wi' blood, it was that raw, and you'd cook that *next* day, and so on – and then at end o' week, it finished up in stew. Was that sanitary? Well, I'm going to ask you this now: how many people was there took badly in them days? Not as many as there is now; there was not!

And another was to provide somewhere warm for 'the chaps' to pass their few hours of winter evening leisure – a rare enough luxury, according to 'George':

Because there was no drinking, we never 'ad no money for that. You 'adn't enough money, 'cause you only got paid once a year. But in the summertime we used to play quoits out in the fields; we used to put sticks up, 'cause we 'adn't a proper set of quoits, nor nowt o' that. And in winter we 'ad a saddle-'ouse with a fire in, and we could go in there; and the waggoner 'ad one o' these 'ere melodeons, and we used to sit there singin' Sankey hymns. They was a kind of a Methodist hymn, wan't they? but they was jolly good singing. And on the inside cover of my Sankey book was 'the Glory Song' – does you know that?

(sings)   O that will be,
                            Glory for me
                            Glory for me
                            Da Da, da-da

Now, I've forgotten the words – but I used to know it.

We used to sing these Sankey hymns, and write little tittle-bits on the painted wall. There was a bit I wrote on in 1912 or '13, inside the saddle-'ouse: and I wrote on it:

                            Mary had a little watch
                            She swallowed it one day
                            Now she's takin' Epsom salts
                            To pass the time away.

And the fella that was farmin' it up to three year ago, I used to see him in Louth market sometimes: and he said, 'I shall never have it rubbed off.' That was at Campaign Farm, South Ormsby, and that was the only place I was at that had a saddle-'ouse to sit in. In a lot of places, there was nowhere to go but bed.

Even in the south of England, where 'farm service' had virtually died out by the beginning of this century, a farmer would often provide some payment in kind in addition to his men's weekly wages. In Kent (where they make the best beer in the world), as in Bill Partridge's Suffolk, this often took the form of 'home brew', like that remembered by Filmer Measday of Preston-by-Wingham. (Mr Measday, incidentally, was named after his grandfather, whose unusual Christian name was said to be derived from that of 'a Sussex village': there is, however, no such village in Sussex, though there is a Filmer Hill in Hampshire. But could there be some connection with the knightly family of Filmer, lords of the Kentish manor of East Sutton?)

My father, he was the stockman at Newborns Farm at Grove: he worked there for seventy-two years, and he used to brew the beer. Every three months, he used to start at two o'clock in the morning, and brew. The best beer was used in the house, but the mild beer I used to have to take round to the workmen in the fields. I had two two-gallon stone bottles – those ones that were in a basket – and I used to hang 'em on a yoke across me shoulders. They might have that with their 'snap', what they used to call their 'proggins' or their 'progger' – that was their lunch. But in the winter, we used to put this beer in a stone bottle *without* the basket, and we always had a copper of boiling water just outside the back door of the farmhouse. We used to hang the bottles in the copper on a string, and when the men came for their wages on Friday night, they'd always have a great big mugful of hot beer. Only one thing I regret, I never got his recipe: 'cause that beer had some stingo in it!

Talking of 'proggins' – and as a last thought for now on the subject of farm food – a quite remarkable variety of local words survive for 'a packed snack'. We've already heard Bill Partridge's 'beever', 'nineses' and 'fourses' and Jim Bush's 'bait'; others include 'baggings' (Lancashire and Cheshire); the widespread 'snap' with its Staffordshire variant, 'snappings'; 'drinkings' (West Yorkshire) and 'nuncheon' (Hampshire, Berkshire, and Wiltshire) – all self-explanatory. 'Crib' (Devon and Cornwall) may perhaps be derived from the 'crib' or manger used for feeding animals; and the north-west Midland 'tommy' from a nickname for a loaf; while the East Anglian 'docky' and the Yorkshire 'jock' remain mysterious. But my own favourite, apart from 'proggins', is the south-western 'nammet' or 'nummet' – 'noon-meat'.

FARM WOMEN

What, finally, of farm women? Of course, women have always run farmhouses, and on occasion entire farms: they have always given vital help at busy periods, like harvest, haymaking, lambing and shearing, about which we shall hear in due time; and during the two World Wars 'the landgirls' amazed, outraged or delighted the locals by doing the work of the absent farm men. But during peacetime, all-year-round female farm labourers – already becoming unusual in Flora Thompson's (Lark Rise to Candleford) Oxfordshire of the 1880s – have been comparatively uncommon within living memory. I was lucky, then, to meet Mrs Daisy Record, from Harrietsham on the fruit-farming southern slopes of the Kentish North Downs. A tiny, cheerful and deeply tanned old lady – who, despite her seventy-nine years, still rises at four every morning to do her paper round – she 'came on the farm' after a somewhat tempestuous career in domestic service (p.151), and proudly declares: 'I could do everything a man could do, just about.'

Me and me 'usband used to work on the farm up at Ulcombe – nice place that. There wasn't no hops there, only fruit: there was raspberries, blackcurrants, blackberries and loganberries. There wasn't many women worked on farms then, and there was jest me and another woman there.

A Lincolnshire turnip-hoeing gang, c. 1914. The women's sun-bonnets (progressively more elaborate as their age increases) were worn against sunstroke, and also to prevent an unladylike and unfashionable tan.

We'd always work for the same farmer, but we din't agree on a wage like the men. There was never anything official said about us women. When the time came to goo to work, we jest used to say, 'Is it all right?', and farmer'd say, 'Yes', or 'I'll be lookin' for you': that's how it used to be. We 'ad to work from eight 'til four o'clock, an' 'e paid us fivepence ha'penny an hour – that's all we 'ad, though the men 'ad their eighteen bob a week: an' 'e wouldn't employ women by reg'lar agreement. But we 'ad to make the most of it, and take the good with the bad.

In the winter, when there wasn't no fruit about, there was all kinds o' jobs to do. Sometimes we used to ha' to goo up the wood with the men that was doin' the spiles and palings [for fencing] and git a shaver and shave all them. Then you'd be turnin' out yards, where the cows 'ad been in: and you'd goo spreadin' the manure on the fields – there was loads arter loads goin' out. But I din't used to mind at all, 'cause I'd 'ave a ride on the cart.

Then it'd be hoein' strawberries all up, and puttin' the straw underneath the fruit. Then we'd git the potaters in, and the swedes and wurzels. An arter that come hayin' – we 'ad five or six weeks o' that, an' I used to love it. First I used to goo out with a hay-rake, and rake that all in: then, when that was nice and dry, you'd cock it up into lumps. Then the time came you'd gotta pitch that up onto the hay-cart: or, if they was pitchin' too high for me, they used to say, 'You come up and load, an' we'll pitch up to you.' That used to make my arm ache at times! An' I used to say, 'Gawd, let's 'ave a blow [rest]!'

Well, we 'ad nine o'clock lunch – we used to call it our 'snap' – and one o'clock was your dinner. We all went to our place, an' 'ad a *really* hot cup o' tea, and a cup o' soup or whatever they liked. Or sometimes they used to bring their own food, long as I made the tea. Then I used to ha' to boil the kettle up agin: 'cause there was a bloomin' great ole white can I used to git the milk in, an' I used to fill that up with coffee, for three o'clock time. Then that used to be a little cool, and that was lovely! We was glad 'nough to 'ave that, when we was hayin': 'cause we 'ad to goo 'til half past eight at night. Cor, love-a-duck!

Then, between haytime and harvest, there was the 'wild white' clover to git in: and arter that was harvest – wheat and barley and oats. Then you're pickin' up your mangels and swedes. They used to say, 'Daise, are you wringing them wurzels?' I used to wring the tops off, and throw 'em in a lump, in a straight line: I used to like that, and so I did the swedes. And up there they used to 'ave some nuts, Kentish cobnuts, and we 'ad to go pickin' them: and then it was potatoing time.

Arter *that*, you come round to winter agin, and that was threshin' time. They used to thresh by steam: and did I 'ave a job to do then! I either 'ad to stand on the stack and push sheaves down to the thresher, or I 'ad to stand in the thresher and cut the bonds round the sheaves; or else I 'ad to build the straw stacks, and thatch 'em. So we bin real busy. 'Oh', I used to say, 'I dunno one day from another.' No more I didn't used to.

'Cause I could do everything a man could do, jest about: but they never give me no man's money! I used to say, 'Cor lumme, you want me to do all these jobs, but where's the extra money comin' in?' But I was very 'appy. I was never like 'arf of 'em are today, very moody – aren't they? I'd whistle me teeth out. They always said to me, you'll blow your front teeth out! Well, I said, as long as I'm happy!

Young horseman watering his team at Pinchbeck, near Spalding on the Lincolnshire Fens, c. 1890. Notice his stout boots, his billy-can fastened to the horse's collar, and his characteristic waggoner's 'sideways' seat.

2

THEM OLD HORSE CHAPS

THE WAGGONER

*U*ntil very recently, all farms ran on 'horsepower'. It was horses which pulled the plough, harrow and muck-cart, the mower for hay and the reaper for corn; horses which carted the crops from field to barn and stackyard; and horses which hauled the farmer's produce to market-town or railway station, returning perhaps with a load of coal, seed or fruit-pickers. So it is scarcely surprising that the man who supervised both their welfare and their operations should have been widely regarded – not least by himself – as the aristocrat among farm workers.

His title varied from area to area. In much of East Anglia he was 'head horseman', though he might be called 'the horsekeeper' in the Cambridgeshire Fens and 'the steward' in parts of Norfolk. In Lancashire and Cheshire he was 'the teamer' or 'teamsman', and throughout most of the south he was 'the carter', though in Kent – as in the northern Midlands, Lincolnshire and Yorkshire – he was 'the waggoner': somewhat misleading names, these, since the driving of a two-wheeled cart or four-wheeled waggon was merely the most public part of his many duties. In the uplands of the north and west, however, he seems to have had no particular title, if indeed he was differentiated at all from the other farm men: and there his prestige was least, for small livestock-raising hill steadings needed no more than a light horse or two to cart their hay and fodder crops. It was at its greatest on the large cereal-growing farms of eastern England, where he might well have charge over twenty or thirty heavy Shires or Suffolks and six or seven rigidly graded subordinate 'horse chaps', one for each pair or each team of four.

The aspiring waggoner (as I shall call him, since I was brought up in Kent and live in Yorkshire) would have to work his way up from the bottom of this hierarchy, accepting its unbreakable 'discipline' and picking up knowledge for himself as he went along: not always easily done, for horsemen (like many other craftsmen) tended to secretiveness about the tricks of their trade. Indeed, as we shall see, they were positively addicted to it.

It is thus characteristic that 'George', without whose more than generous help this chapter could not have been compiled, has asked to remain anonymous. But it will be clear from his reminiscences that his country is the Lincolnshire Wolds, the rolling chalk *hills that extend along the eastern edge of the county from the Humber to the margins of the Fens. Like their Yorkshire counterparts north of the river (the home of two of the other horsemen we shall hear from), these Wolds supported large-scale arable farms, where the waggoner was at his most powerful: and 'George' must be one of the last of the 'old-fashioned horse chaps' who rose to the top of their profession there before the tractor was much more than a rumour. Nor am I betraying any confidence by saying that he was, and is, a well-respected man. In the words of the late Fred Brader, who served his apprenticeship under him: 'He was a good waggoner, one of the best. They reckoned you were nearly qualified to go anywhere, when you'd had a couple o' year with "George".'*

I was born 1896: that's where we'd better start! I was born 1896, and I went to school when I was three year old. Wasn't that unusual? Well, *I* thought so: but they had a reunion at the school, and they brought the registers out, and there was my name, and me father's signature – me father used to write with a copperplate style – and the date 1899. Me oldest brother was seven at the time, so perhaps he used to take me.

So I was born at Tetford, and I went to school there when I was three: and then in 1902 we left Tetford for South Ormsby, and I did me schooling there. You've just been to South Ormsby church? I used to be in the choir there: and as you go up the church path, up the hill, there's a little grave of a boy that died about 1904 or '05. And I was bearer for him. He was only six or seven year old, and all his bearers was schoolboys. There was four of us, and we all had a white tie and a white armband – not a black one, a white one. That was strange, wasn't it? I can't remember what the hymn was, but the father and mother they broke down in the hymn, I remember that. And we was all young lads that carried him – two on 'em was killed in the First World War.

Now me father was head gardener at South Ormsby Hall: it was the Massingberd-Mundys that had it, yon man's grandfather and grandmother. It's a big walled garden, and it's hot in there, and there's asparagus beds. And when I was a boy, the squire – the old chap – used to give me a penny an hour for weeding asparagus beds – and they was all stinging nettles! And another thing. Before I started work, I remember, I used to ha' to go gleaning* in fields – picking heads of corn up after the reaper had gone round – after they'd led it all away. That was a kind o' privilege: the farmer'd say, you can come and glean today. And you'd keep that for your family. If we got a lot, they'd maybe take it to someone and let them thresh it, and sell 'em it: and if we didn't get so much, we'd keep it for chickens. We didn't grind it up for bread, we'd nowt to do wi' that.

There was me father and two more, and a lad, in the gardens, and they'd five girls in the house – the cook, housemaid, kitchenmaid, parlourmaid, and the lady's-maid: the lady's-maid, she had a room to herself and did all the sewing and all such like as that. And then they had a laundry, and they had two women out o' the village do the laundry, three days a week. Mother used to work at th' Hall: she went and did the cooking once, when they was wi'out a cook.

Everyone about was tenants of the estate: it comes from Tetford, Ormsby, Driby, Calceby, to Ketsby, and nearly to Worlaby: they farmed mebbe two farms themselves, and th' others was let. And I went to work on one of the estate farms when I left school.

I left school when I was thirteen – that would have been 1909 – for half time: you could git half time then, when you were thirteen. Me birthday was in March, and so I got six months o' work 'til October, and then went back to school for the winter.

Day boy

When I was on half time, I went for tenpence a day – six to six – as a 'day boy' on the estate farm. I did anything they wanted doing on the farm – pulling thistles, or leading the horse if they was scarrying* – if they was horse-hoeing: or any kind o' job. I was a 'day boy', because I used to go backwards and forrards from home: I used to ha' to git up in the mornin' at five o'clock, and git me breakfast, be there at six, and leave at six. But they didn't expect a boy to do a lot: they'd find 'im a job somewhere, maybe cleanin' chicken-houses out, or a bit o' tarrin': like, that he *could* do. We took our own grub in our basket: we used to have our lunch at nine and dinner at one. We'd 'alf-an-hour at nine, for our lunch, and then at one, we had an hour. And we went then while six at night, then home. But it *was* a long day, because I was only thirteen.

Then when I was fourteen, I left school: and the land agent – the agent belonging the estate – he put me on another farm that they was farming. And the first fortnight I had, the foreman only paid me eightpence a day, and I'd had tenpence a day before. 'Well', he said, 'that's all you can git here, eightpence.' But the next payday, he said, 'The agent says he'll ha' noo peace wi' your mother 'til I gi' yer tenpence. So you'll ha' to ha' tenpence again!' Well, I was there maybe a twelvemonth, and I was doing the same things as before. Me first job was tending crows. I'd several fields to go round, and they'd just got sown up: and I used to frighten 'em all off. I used to shout, and I had a rattle – it was like a piece o' wood, with a handle on, and two holes through it, and a flap that side, and enough band [string] to let the flaps go backwards and forrards. It was a good rattle: it worked well.

Well, I was there maybe a twelvemonth, and then they wanted a boy to help the gathman* [stockman] during the winter, at the place where I was at first. They wanted a boy to help the gathman with the beasts [bullocks].

They was breedin' beasts, and they was in a big crewe* [yard]. We'd two or three crewes, and we used to have a horse and cart to lead the straw into them, and I used to help leading this cart, and the gathman would lead me in, and I'd chuck it off into the tumbrils* [mangers] for 'em to eat. They was movable tumbrils, and as the manure grew up in the crewe you had to keep movin' 'em on.

Third chap

So I had that job for that year, and when May came, the third chap in the stable was leaving. They had twelve horses in a row: there was the waggoner wi' four, the second chap wi' four, and the third chap wi' four. And the third chap was leaving, so I asked me dad if I could go and be third chap. He said yis, so I went then to live in wi' the foreman, at ten pound a year. That was me first *man's* job: that was 1912, I think, and I should be sixteen.

I was lucky there, because they had a good 'seedsman'* there: the seedsman was a kind of second foreman, he was under the foreman but above the waggoner. They employed over twenty men on that farm, so they needed a seedsman as well as a foreman. He was a grand fella, that was: he was a good-living man, and he learnt me a lot, he was a good 'un to me.

He learnt me how to set me plough. Before I got in the stables, the foreman sent a man out wi' me, to learn me to plough. He says, 'Goo take that boy, and learn 'im to plough.' Well, they was ploughin' 'swing' – that is, without wheels on – th' other men was: and that was very hard for a beginner. So this chap took the wheels off, and he says, 'You want to sweat well, boy, you'll soon learn how to plough!' But, of course, *I* couldn't hold the plough, I was all over the auction wi' it! And I was roaring [crying] a bit, and all!

Well, this seedsman saw me, and he came over to me and says: 'Now, Dordie' – he allus used to call me 'Dordie', because my name's George – 'what are tha doing?' And I said, 'Foreman sent a chap to learn me how to plough, but he's codded off and left me.' 'I'll tell the foreman summat when I git home, he'll hear about this.' Then he said, 'D'you think you can manage to plough wi' *my* hosses? Go on, take mine, and I'll set your plough, and I'll put the wheels on.' And he put the coulter* [blade] straight, and then he hung the lines [reins] on the hales [handles of the plough] and he let the horses walk on; they was doing it wi' theirselves, he'd set it that nicely. 'You'll manage now while loosing time, I'll see you at loosing time.' And that's how he started to learn me to plough: he gave me confidence.

And another thing he learnt me was to be *regular*. For the horses' sake, you've got to be regular in their feeding and in their work. You don't want to be cutting and slashing at them with the lines, they want to go nice and steady. The man that went the steadiest got the most work done, and his work was more reliable. And in the end, I could time me rounds to half a minute: I could say at twelve o'clock how many more rounds I was going before half past two. The seedsman taught me that.

That was at Campaign Farm, South Ormsby: and the first year I was there, I wanted a bicycle, and in March there was a chap goin' abroad – they was emigratin' from this country [area] then, several people were, because they was beginnin' to go to Canada and different places – and he had a good bicycle for sale, and he wanted three pound for it. So I said to me father, could I have it. So he says, 'See the foreman, see if he'll let you have three pounds off your wages.' And I got it.

So when next 'Pag-rag Day' came, I'd 'ad a sub [advance], so I only had seven pounds left out o' me ten. And me mother says, 'Well, what you want to do is to go to Alford and put six pound o' that in the post office.' That left me a pound, and she said, 'Now I want ten shillings o' that for doin' your washing last year.' And that left me but ten shillings to manage for the next whole year! And I did.

The next year wasn't so bad, because with steppin' up one and goin' second chap, I got a little bit o' road work with me horses, taking corn in to Louth. And we used to get sixpence a load on all the corn we took out. That was extra, and he would pay you that every week: if you'd been two or three loads, you'd get a shilling or eighteenpence. Well, them little bits kept me going, you see.

But there wasn't a deal you could get. A few oranges, or anything like that, or bootlaces: but I never was in a pub, and I didn't smoke – you couldn't afford to. And we used to get rigged up for clothes at May Week, and that was for the year. The summer clothes used to be 'blewetts' – it was a kind of cloth that was all blue, and the trousers and jacket was the same [FRED BRADER: There was 'greyetts' as well: the trousers'd be lined, or half-lined, and the jackets wasn't lined at all. It was just choice, which you had]. And for winter-time you had corduroy. A lot on 'em used to wear cords for Sundays – I never did – and when they'd worn 'em a year for Sundays, they'd take 'em for weekday then, and git another suit for Sundays.

Discipline

Well, I was at Campaign three year: I was one year third chap and two year second chap. The second year I had £15, and the next year I had £18. And then I left 'im, because the farm was taken ower wi' a different man, a Mr Dale – his son's farming out Louth way now. He didn't want me to leave, and he said, 'Go to me brother at Walmsgate, to be waggoner.' I said, 'Oh, I couldn't manage that.' And he said, 'You easy can!' So I went to Walmsgate, at £25 a year, and I stopped with him all the [1914–18] war.

A Lincolnshire waggoner and his team, c. 1914, with a heavy load of corn. His distinctive 'Lincolnshire' waggon is notable for its pronounced up-sweep to front and rear and its high 'spindled' sides.

I was the head man then, and I had young chaps under me. I had nowt to do with their living, because I was still a single man, but they had to do as I telled 'em in the stables and in the fields. And when we went to plough, I took the lead, and they'd to do the same amount o' rounds as I did, but they *musn't* come in front o' me. No. It was 'discipline'. And they wouldn't put a [horse] collar on in front o' me, nor yit a helter [halter] on. Because I'd gone through the same routine. The waggoner would do everything first, then the second chap, then the third chap. As soon as the waggoner had put a collar on, then you could put a collar on: but you couldn't put a collar on 'til he

did. And he'd be first if you was doin' road work – you had to keep your place.

I had a young feller with me once, and he was a little bit clever, and he made me cross a few times. So I thought, well, I *will* learn 'im. So one day we was ploughing, and I drew out o' th' end: and he'd already drawn out and unlooped his horses. So I didn't say nowt, I just set 'em on again and I went another round: and he had 'em to yoke up again and come another round. And he swore and called me, but I said, 'I can stand that, mate, you've got to learn to keep in your place.' It was discipline!

Much the same kind of rigid hierarchy reigned in Suffolk, as Bill Partridge recalls:

Only we didn't use to call they waggoners, we called 'em 'head horsemen': I got to be one meself, about 1939. Perhaps there was six or seven horsemen on a farm: well, the one that'd been there the second longest, we called he 'second horseman', and all that. And when you went out to plough, you *dursn't* goo in front o' the head horseman. You hed to goo last, behind the lot, if you'd just started: you hed to stop 'til they all went by ye, whether you was a-gooing out to plough or a-coming hoam to dinner. You dursn't goo first, do [or else] they'd soon tell ye!

'Old-fashioned discipline', however, was naturally not so popular with those on the receiving end, like Arthur Wade.

Well, I'll gi' you some rough idea of what it was like. You got hired on a farm, and you'd be sleeping in the same part of house as the waggoner and the other hoss chaps. And that waggoner was out o' bed in t'morning at four o'clock, because you had them horses to do and git all ready, and breakfast was at six o'clock.

As soon as waggoner'd got dressed, he used to grab the storm-lamp and goo downstairs, and you were i' dark. And it was same downstairs: by time you'd got downstairs, he'd got 'is boots on, and he was off! – and the storm-lamp went wi' him, and you hadn't another light. That's how them old waggoners used to be. Anybody a bit slow – well, he was left i' dark.

Nor it didn't matter what sort o' mornin' it was. You could be taking a load of straw in for bullocks – i' dark! And I've helped to thrash on a mornin' when it's been pitch black, and they've had four storm-lamps on top o' thrashing drum, so's nobody got hurt. No matter about you at bottom, so long as it was lit up there.

O' course, First War knocked all that on th' head, because after that a lot o' farms round here hadn't them sort o' waggoners. They'd all gone in t'army. And after t'war, it got better and better, because there was very few old-fashioned waggoners left.

Many of them, like Ted Bateson, were no doubt driven to enlist by the virtually compulsory purchase of their horses – few of which ever returned, for over 500,000 died in government service and many others were sold abroad.

I' First War, they came and got all best horses, you know: all best 'uns there was. That's what made me 'list. I was driving two, and I couldn't ha' wished for a better pair – you'd just speak, and they'd go just as you wanted 'em. They were giving an hundred pound the pair – they were practically takkin' 'em, you know: farmer goes and sells these two, and we gets two 'screws' [poor-quality horses] instead. 'By', thinks I, 'I'm sick o' driving sike [such] things as these. I'm going to 'list.' Sae I did. One snowy day, the 12th o' February 1916, I 'listed i' Fourth East Yorkshires.

Such losses must have been particularly hard on head waggoners: because, 'George' continues:

The waggoner always had the best horses: of course he did, and if he could, he'd have a matched team. When I was at Walmsgate, I had three strawberry roans and an iron-grey, that's what I had.

And a waggoner'd have his own horse-brasses: they didn't belong to the guv'nor. I picked 'em up here and there. I had a loin-strap, and there was a lot o' little hearts on each side, and at the bottom there was a big brass heart: and then there was the face-brasses, and the martingales that went down the front. It looked a treat. But you wouldn't have them on for ordinary work, just if you was goin' waggoning on the road.

Down on the Fens

When I was at Walmsgate, at the end o' the First War, I wan't getting £50 a year, and me living, and there was plenty o' people getting £80. So I applied for a place down the Fens, they was giving big money down there: and this feller came and hired me, for £80 a year and me living. That was yon side of the river Witham, at Timberland [seventeen miles away]. And they'd no hedges, nor no shelter, nor nowt: it was all just flat. I'd been used to being up on the Wolds, and I didn't like it at all. And it was a rotten job, too.

There was two brothers, and they never knew what they wanted – they couldn't agree. The first mornin' I went, I sat in the stable while *nine o'clock* before anybody came and told me what to do! And there was a lot o' labourers and German prisoners waiting for a job. So I said to the boss at night, 'We want to do something different to this. I an't been used to this. You tell me what I've got to do, tonight, and I can git up in the mornin' and go do it. And if you tell me what the men wants to do, I'll tell them an' all.' Because they couldn't agree what to do.

One week I'd got three teams of 'orses, and three sets of harrows, and I'd started workin' some land. I was goin' to sow it with wheat, because they wanted the wheat in. Well, the boss came up, and he said, 'What are you doing?' 'I'm going to get ready to sow some wheat.' 'It's too soon for sowing wheat. I should loose off and ha' your lunch, and then rig some ploughs up and skim some twitch [skim off some weeds] and rubbish – just plough it shallow.' Oh, I was mad. And a bit after, th' other man comes down. 'What are you *doing*? Father said you was harrowing there this morning.' 'I was, but George fetched us off, and we had to get these 'ere ploughs ready.' 'You want to go back and start harrowing again.' So I said, 'Now look here, you want to go and see your brother. And you want to come and tell us what we got to do, or *he* does. You want to *know* what you want to do.'

And I said to th' other chaps that was helpin' us look for the ploughs, 'You needn't hurry boys, we're not gonna do a damn sight today. We'll learn them. We'll dodge about looking for these things, and I think we shan't be able to find 'em.' And I stuck that job while March time, and then I threw me notice in. I couldn't work like that. I'd been courtin' two years, and I come back up here and got married.

The waggoner's year

There was always plenty for the waggoner to do. We reckoned the year to start in May time – after 'Pag-rag Day'. And then we'd set off to work the land for the summer crops, for roots – turnips and mangolds and swedes and that. We'd be working the bare land, and getting the rubbish off with chain-harrows, and a horse and cart to fetch off the rubbish. But our land was fairly clean at Walmsgate, it just wanted working.

And then as harvest came on, you was binding. I had a binder [a 'self-binder', see p. 127], and the second chap had a binder, and there was somebody with some spare horses: 'cause we'd change horses, so we could keep the binder going all day. You'd have three to a binder, so you wanted six horses for one, to change: and the second chap had three, and he used to pull his binder out and take his home, and there was only one binder going while he fed his horses. That was at Walmsgate, but on the first place where I was, they kept two binders going, because they'd twelve horses there. And there was plenty of places on the Wolds where they had four and five waggoners, and they'd all have four horses apiece, so there'd be sixteen or twenty horses. But we only had nine at Walmsgate.

So we'd be binding, and the labourers used to do the stowking [stooking corn]. And we used to ha' to lead it in waggons: we'd ha' two horses in a waggon, so we could run four waggons, to lead it to the yard and stack it up.

When I was at Campaign, they was all blue waggons. And the waggon I had at Walmsgate was a Cooke waggon, made by Cookes of Lincoln – that was a good 'un: it was what they called 'out-runged' – the sides was turned over at the top. But at Campaign they were straight-sided, and you had some shelving to take off and put on as you wanted. But my favourite was this Cooke's waggon, a great heavy thing it was: it was a drab colour, and there was the date it was made an' all on a brass plate at the front. You used to fill the body up first, and then stack the sheaves on the out-rung: oh, yis, we used to get quite a load on, and then they had to be roped and tied on with the waggon rope.

The other kind of waggon they had round here was the ''maphrodite' [hermaphrodite] waggon: you could use it as a waggon, or you could take the front wheels off and use it as a cart. First of all you'd ha' to take the top off – because there's the cart at the back, and the flat top: then you'd have to take the shaves [shafts] off, and the front wheels off – and then you'd put the shaves back on the cart. And when you wanted the waggon again, you'd your undergear all to get right – you've a pole from the front wheels to the cart-axle, and then you've your front wheels to put on: and then you put the top on. Now there's some stays goes up, and there's a hole in that top, and these here stays go up and hold the top secure.

You'd use it as a cart most of the year: you'd only use it as a waggon for maybe six or seven weeks of the year, at harvest time and seed-leading time, that's all. You'd fill the cart body at the back, then you'd gradually load it on to the front, and build up 'til you got a load.

Before harvest, of course, there was haytime. It was all loose hay in those days, all raked up with a hay-bob. That used to leave a long trail of hay, and that would be heaped in round heaps – and we used to lead it out of them, loose. You'd stick into it with a fork, and pitch it up onto the waggon. It was

This ingeniously designed vehicle, once common in the eastern counties from Suffolk to Yorkshire, is a 'hermaphrodite' – so called because it is both a cart and a waggon. The rear portion served as a two-wheeled tip-up cart: but when the front portion was added, it converted into a four-wheeled waggon capable of carrying extra-large loads.

a job, because if you got somebody that wasn't really up to the job, half on it would flitter down again. Same if you was on the top, loading: the chap on the top, he wanted to put his fork *round* it, not stick into it and try to take it off your fork – he wanted to put his fork round it, and *pull* it off your fork. You wanted a bit o' skill to do it.

The winter job was ploughing, the biggest part of it. We had what they call a Hodgson Gem – they was made at Louth, and they was a double-furrow plough, wi' three horses. There was an art in setting them ploughs, you know, an art in setting that coulter. If you wanted your plough to run well and keep in, you'd edge that coulter just a little bit in to [unploughed] land, it kept your same size furrow all the way, and it kept you in to land.

And of course, there was a lot of rivalry about who could plough the straightest, and who could set it up the nicest. I had what they call a 'Premie' [Premier] plough, that was what they used to take to these ploughing matches: I got one of those reasonable from a merchant. It had a nearly like silver-steel breast, that wouldn't rust: and I bought it off him for six pound. My son has it now: it's a good plough.

We'd plough with three horses for a double-furrow plough, and we'd two strings [reins], one for each side: I've never ploughed wi' one string, but down the Fens they used just the one string. But when you got used to it, and you got your plough set properly, I could just wrap one line [rein] round the handles, and I could have a walk across and look at the other chap ploughin', while me 'orses was still goin' on their own: then I used to git back to them before they turned at th' head. But if it was set right, it would go on its own on the straight.

When you was turning 'em right at th' head, you'd say 'Gee': and 'Arve'* was turn left – I don't know where that word comes from, and I don't know what it means. But once, the Missus went to see some friends, her neighbour across the fields: and she wasn't sure of the footpath. And he watched 'er going, and when she got off the line, he shouted, 'Arve a bit, Missus, arve a bit!' – and *she* didn't know what it meant!

'That word' probably comes – not surprisingly in this heavily Viking-settled part of England – from Old Norse 'horfa', meaning 'turn'. It was also used by Yorkshire horsemen, though in slightly different forms: I have heard 'horve' on the Yorkshire Wolds and 'orve' round York. In Suffolk, however, completely different commands were used, says Bill Partridge.

We used to say 'woordie' and 'cappa-ree'. 'Right' was 'woordie' about here, and to turn left you'd say 'cappa-ree'. I dessay you've never heard o' that! What did it mean? Well, it meant 'turn left', that's what it meant. Th' old *horses* knew what you meant, they turned left soon as you said it. You didn't need to get hold of your cord [rein]!

Various versions of these have been recorded elsewhere in Suffolk: as 'cup-ee-weesh' or 'cup-ee' for left and 'wheesh', 'wurr-de-wish' or 'ree' for right. Their derivation eludes me at present.

WAGGONERS' WILES

Whenever and wherever I talked to, or about, 'them old horse chaps', it would not be very long before two subjects were sure to be mentioned. One was the waggoner's notorious secretiveness – about which more in a moment – and the other was his almost legendary ability to 'acquire' unauthorized extra feed for his horses.

First, here are Filmer Measday (a waggoner's son-in-law) and Alf Friend (a waggoner's mate in his youth) talking in the Half Moon and Seven Stars, at Preston-by-Wingham in east Kent.

FM: These old waggoners, of course, they were always rationed for their horses. But that didn't count, 'cause they'd pinch *anything*. My ol' father-in-law, old Fairbrass, he was a waggoner: and it didn't matter what farm 'e worked on, before 'e'd been there a month 'e'd 'ave a key to fit every padlock there was on the place.

AF: They used to have these big granaries, you know, and there was only one man that was supposed to have the key to the place. But they 'adn't bargained for the craftiness of the waggoners. They'd go to work with a lump of soap: make sure it was nice and soft, and then they'd get this key out when nobody wasn't looking, and they'd make an impression of it, and take it down to keysmith's and get one cut.

FM: Or they'd cut it themselves, more likely, a lot of 'em: so's nobody wouldn't know.

AF: And another stunt they used to 'ave. These granaries'd be raised up on what they called staddle-stones* – they was clear of the ground, so you 'ad to go up four–five steps to 'em. Well, these waggoners used to crawl underneath with an auger, at night: they'd drill an 'ole in the bottom of the granary, into one of the corn sacks, and they'd put a bucket underneath. And when they'd got a bucketful of oats, they'd stick a cork in the 'ole, 'til next time. 'Cause some of these farmers was a bit tight.

Some of the waggoners themselves – true to the secretive traditions of their calling – are more inclined to be reticent about 'extras', or (like Will Forman of Ash-by-Sandwich, Kent) to hurriedly change from the first to the third person when talking of them.

We put more time on them horses than we was ever paid for. And we'd do anything to get extra feed for 'em. You 'ad to be a bit crafty. Yes, it's a wonder some o' them ol' horse chaps wasn't locked up! 'Cause they'd go on out in the fields and pick beans out o' the neighbour's drill, and all that kind o' thing.

But others, including Arthur Wade, could be persuaded to reveal at least a few of their 'dodges'.

I'll tell you this little bit, but I mun't tell it all. In winter-time, we had a beastman [stockman], and he was bad i' eyes, they was allus watering. And as he was gooin' round taking cake to fat bullocks, *I* was behind him: and he nivver saw me, because you nivver made no noise on all that manure. I had me bag, and I'm fillin' it wi' cake for me hosses: I used to do it reg'lar every morning.

And then, another place, we had a right old-fashioned tractor stationary for grinding corn. Well, they had a hole cut in wall for a belt to go through, and this hole went through into granary. And I used to go in there when nobody was about, and I could tek me jacket off and git through into granary, and fill me bag wi' corn for me horses. They had an old groom, and he used to lock everything up at night: and he couldn't reckon up – somebody had been at his bags, and he couldn't reckon up how they'd done it: and everybody that ever went in that granary got blamed – but, of course, *I* nivver went in during day, I went in when he was in bed!

'George' does not regard his 'borrowing' as anything either to be concealed or to be ashamed of – and I must say I agree with him.

Because you'd do anything for your horses: you'd nearly die for 'em, sooner than hurt 'em. So of course we used to do a lot to get extra feed for our horses. Well, we used to pinch it!: but I don't know why they called it 'pinching', because it was only taking the boss's corn for his own horses. I tell you what I did do, at Walmsgate. The horses was down in this yard, and the yard where all the corn was was half-a-mile away. And I'd got a key that would fit – I could get through the lock, and I could go in the barn any time I wanted. Well, I knew the boss used to go to Louth on a Saturday night, and he wouldn't come home while about eleven to half past. So we had a spare horse, an owd mare – she was in a box to hersen' – and we used to use her for carting about. And one Saturday night I fetched her out about twelve o'clock, and I went up to the barnyard, and tied her in the waggon shed: and then I got the key, went in the barn, and I bagged a sack o' wheat up. And a sack of wheat weighs about eighteen stone – I tried carrying some of 'em once, and my shoulders ached for days: so I thought, this owd mare'll carry it on her back. So I bagged it up, and I swept the heap up again, so they didn't know I'd been, and I carried it out. I'd stood her on the wall side, and I'd got her too near the wall: and I'd got it partly on her back, and she moved, and it dropped on the floor. So I had to hick* [jerk, lift] it onto the waggon shaves wi' me knees, and I worked it up the shaves until I could get under it and get it on me back: I got it ower, and it balanced: and I'd a long string to her helter, and I walked at the side on her all the way home, wi' me hand ower the mouth o' the bag, so it wouldn't leave a trail.

And when I got home, I dorsn't take it in the stable, because I knew he'd find it: but the chap I lived wi', he had an empty pigsty: and I stopped and put it in this here pigsty. And I used to have a little tiny bucket, same but what these kids have at the sea: and every morning I used to take a little bit of wheat and give 'em it.

The Lincolnshire waggoners Will Flinton encountered whilst steam-threshing [p.132] had a rather more efficient – if less exciting – method of obtaining their corn:

And when we used to be thrashing, these old waggoners'd say, 'I want a couple o' bags o' wheat, for the spring.' So when you got started in the morning, and the boss'd gone for his breakfast or out o' the way somewheer, the waggoner'd take two bags o' wheat and hide it in the straw stack. Then, when we'd gone away, about a fortnight later, he'd go and fetch a bag o' wheat out o' theer for his horses. They used to put it in smaller bags, and put it in water-trough when they went to bed at night – when nobody couldn't see – and they'd take it out early in morning. So it would start to grow, and as soon as it got them little tiny green chicks [shoots] on it, then they'd give th' horses a ladleful each in the morning, afore they went to work. Because if they'd given 'em that wheat dry, o' course, it might have swole inside 'em, and mebbe killed 'em.

The dangers of injudicious dry-wheat feeding were indeed considerable, as 'George' recalls:

No, they don't want a deal o' wheat: and I came unstuck with that once, because if they get a bit o' water on it, it'll swell it up, and you're done. And when I was at Campaign – I was only a lad, but I should've known better – I had a horse get a stoppage with it. I knew what was the matter, because he wasn't very well in the daytime, and I'd kept him at work, thinking I might work it off. I didn't stop for any lunch, I ate me lunch as I was going, and kept him working. And it did work off him, but at night he was bad again – I'd give him some more, and I didn't ought to 'a done. And he was bad.

So I had to push-bike from Campaign to Louth [ten miles] to the vet: it was Eave, down James Street. I told him would he come and have a look at this horse that had a stoppage: he said, 'Noo, but I'll gi' you a drink for it.' And he said, 'Come in and have a bottle o' beer' – while he got the drink ready. But I told him, I said, 'I'll tell you what's the matter wi' it, but for

God's sake don't let me down.' 'I shan't let you down, boy, you tell me what you've done.' 'I've getten him some wheat.' 'I'll gi' you some medicine that'll shift that, and I shan't let you down.'

So I got ower that all right. But the chap that was exercisin' him saw the dung, and there was wheat in it. And he told the boss, 'Why, he's giving it wheat.' And the guv'nor came to me and said, 'I know you was giving it wheat, George; I know what it is, you want to look after the horses well. But be careful.' And I said, 'I will after this.' But a little bit of wheat would bring 'em in good condition, if you know how to use it.

Though I've known 'em killed by feeding dry wheat, too. I knew one place where the foreman's son was waggoner, and he killed a horse, feeding wheat. Well, that horse went to the cad-yard* [knacker's yard] to be opened, and it wasn't to be opened until the vet'nary was there to inspect it. But by the time he got there, the foreman had beat him to it: the horse'd been opened, and the foreman said there wasn't no wheat in it! It was a cover-up job.

THEY WOULDN'T TELL YOU A THING

If some horsemen are evasive about extra feed, the lips of most are firmly sealed when it comes to detailed information about the 'powders' and 'receipts' they used for conditioning, doctoring or controlling their horses. Even now, many waggoners refuse to admit that such things existed at all. Others confess to having 'heard of them' – 'but of course, I never used any of them sort of things': and on one occasion when I was so very foolish as to raise the matter in an East Anglian pub – even though nobody was present save myself and the otherwise helpful horsemen – I was told very firmly and repeatedly that, 'it wouldn't do' to talk about them. So I am all the more grateful to those who did: and most of all to 'George' who – albeit somewhat reluctantly at first – not only told me most of what follows, but also allowed me access to the 'receipts' in his private horseman's notebook.

Why all this secrecy? First of all, because the use of powders had to be concealed from the farmer – and no wonder, considering some of their ingredients. [Fred Brader: You wouldn't tell the boss, oh no! Because you wasn't allowed to use owt like that. If you'd lost any hosses over it, they'd have locked you up.] Secondly, it would be a breach of 'discipline' to divulge receipts to younger horsemen: partly, perhaps, because they might misuse them and partly, as 'George' here implies, because the obtaining of them was one of the necessary tests of apprenticeship:

You had to get the receipts for yourself. Because the older men was that secretive, they wouldn't tell you a thing, not even if you was working under 'em – well, specially not then. They'd never let you see what they was giving the horses, you had to find it out yoursen'. *They* know, but they won't divulge anything. Oh, yis, you can *ask*, but they won't tell you! You 'ad to git to know somebody that *would* tell you.

This could be difficult, for one of the most important functions of secrecy was to keep your hard-won knowledge from rivals on neighbouring farms – whose role in the horseman's game was to obtain it by any trick they could devise, said Fred Brader.

On a Sunday morning, you'd maybe git on your bike, and you'd go and look at somebody else's horses. Or maybe you'd go to town, to a station or a mill, some day: and the chap loading your waggon up'd say, 'So-and-so's been in today, and, by gum, his horses look well.' So you'd git on your bike next Sunday, and go look at *his* horses. And if they was better than yours, you'd wonder what he was giving 'em: but it wasn't done to ask, and if you did he wouldn't tell you.

And if I had a favourite receipt, I didn't write it down, I kept it in me head so nobody could git it. Because I can tell you how crafty they were. A waggoner'd go to the chemist, and he'd have this piece of paper with his receipt wrote on it: and he'd say to the chemist, 'Can you mix me this?' Well, if it was a waggoner you knew, and you knew his horses looked well, you'd maybe been following him, and watched him go in. And when he'd been and fetched his stuff out, you'd go into chemist's and say, 'Could I have same as that chap's just got?' It worked sometimes, you see: it'd work if you got a young assistant chemist, maybe, but not wi' the old chemists – *they* knew what you were at.

It also seems possible that some horsemen used secrecy – particularly concerning receipts for controlling wild or vicious horses – as a means of deliberately encouraging the growth of their reputation as men possessed of a mysterious power over animals. A reputation, in fact, such as was generally enjoyed by those who 'travelled entire' – the men who led the massive stud stallions (entires) which toured the farms covering brood mares.

Well, they're funny things, you know, they entires. And they used to take something on 'em to keep they quiet: but they would never tell you what 'twas. They had some sort o' bottle o' stuff in their pocket, to keep they quiet if they went to a show, among mares. But they wouldn't tell ye!

[BILL PARTRIDGE]

Sargent Tear was a clever fella wi' horses: he was cousin to my father. I think he used to 'travel entire' for Clark's of Maidenwell. He must've walked miles and miles on that job: because you never rode the horse, you walked and led it, and you bated [stayed overnight] at whatever farm you'd finished at that day.

He was a terror wi' horses, no mistake. Now some o' them there entires, they're brutes – they're real savage. But Sarge could take one in a pub, and walk him round a table, and the horse wouldn't touch the table – no. And if the stallion was going to serve a mare, he could leave him – just chuck the rein down on the ground: and that entire wouldn't dare move, even when he winded [got wind of] the mare. He'd say, 'Stop there', and there it would stop until he'd gotten everything ready: it wouldn't move an inch until Sarge shouted, 'Coom on!'

I'll tell you what he did do. Some fella had a pair o' horses, and they *would* stand right close together in the stables, so this fella couldn't get in between 'em to feed 'em. They wouldn't stand out and let him between 'em. Well, he told Sarge: and all Sarge did was to git a hay-fork, and stick a newspaper on th' end. And he stood behind 'em, and dropped this here fork between 'em: and God, they *flew* sideways then! He never had no more bother wi' 'em, after that.

And another thing. He broke a horse in for a man, that couldn't ride it. It was a hunter, and *nobody* could ride it. Well, Sarge broke it, and he rode through Alford on it, wi' an umbrella up! Aye, he did. He was a devil wi' horses.

['GEORGE']

Finally, it has been suggested that the English waggoner's continuing unwillingness to communicate his knowledge may be a relic of some secret horseman's fraternity or fraternities, analogous with the 'Society of the Horseman's Word' which survived until the 1930s (if it does not survive still) in north-east Scotland. There, novices could only be instructed in the arts of horsemanship (and given a 'word' that would control any horse) after they had passed through an occult initiation ceremony and sworn to 'hele, conceal, never reveal; neither write, dite, nor recite; nor cut, nor carve, nor write in sand' what they had been told. I have never yet personally encountered a single shred of evidence that such societies existed in England within anything like living memory – but perhaps that is a measure of their success!

We are on much firmer ground in stating that a majority of powders were used for nothing more mysterious than conditioning horses, so that they would 'work well and look well' – especially when on public display, such as at a ploughing match.

When I was at Minster, I went waggoner's mate when I was fifteen, and th' old waggoner there used to have some special things. He used to go to a chemist's shop in Sandwich, and get this perscription made up that had all kinds of things in it. One was from a shrub that growed in the woods, called 'tree of paradise',* and that used to produce a lot o' berries, and you could get oil from it. So there was this oil of paradise, and oil of cummin, and oil of cloves, and they all used to be mixed together.

Now the ploughing matches used to be the third Wednesday in October, and we used to start getting our horses ready about Midsummer – giving

'Some o' them there entires, they're brutes.' The Shire stallion 'Tivetshall Major', foaled in Norfolk in 1900, decorated for a Suffolk show. His smartly dressed leader looks distinctly apprehensive.

'em an extra clean-up, and looking after their diet. And about a month before the match, we'd start giving 'em this special tidbit. We used to get a lump of mangold-wurzel, and cut a chip out of it, and lift that out: then we'd put a few drops of this stuff in the hole, and put the chip back in, and then we'd pop it into their mouth. [ALF FRIEND]

And the key to conditioning, according to 'George', was:

You've got to keep 'em eating, that's the secret. The chap that told me the most, he said that if he had his way, he should weigh all their food, and give 'em the same every day. We fed in sievefuls, and he'd give 'em so many feeds a day: say, five sievefuls in a morning, between a pair, and seven or eight feeds at night. But on a Sunday, knock two feeds off: it just kept their appetites sharp. And when you're feeding in the crib [manger], *never* feed on top of feed: always let 'em make a clean plate, as you may say. That's what they wanted: you've got to keep 'em interested.

And, of course, a lot o' these powders was to keep 'em eating – to keep their insides cleared out, and their appetites going steady. This is one I had when I first went to service, in about 1912. And this here was the first powder I ever used: the chap that give me it, George Bark, he didn't get killed in th' army, but he died from the effects of the First War. He was in the Queen's Own Rifles. And that's a very good receipt for keeping them eating.

'8 oz. aniseeds*
8 oz. fenugreek*
8 oz. gentian*
8 oz. Brake's antimony
8 oz. saltpetre*
4 oz. Aethiopes mineral*
4 oz. crocus antimony.
Two spoonfuls twice a week'.
[Laxatives, diuretics and flatulence cures, with gentian for appetite, antimony against internal parasites, and fenugreek perhaps for its smell.]

You'd give 'em it in a little bit o' corn, last thing at night, before they went to bed, so they wouldn't get any water on top on it.

That used to cost me about five shillings. And I used to use a little bit of 'white hellebore'* with it. That's classed as a poison, of course. I went into a chemist's shop at Alford once, and asked 'im for some white hellebore: an' he says, 'You'll git it at the police station!' And I was soon out! Well, I should be about seventeen then: and I was soon out, I'll tell you, he put the wind up me. I wan't gonner give 'im me name nor nowt else: because he got the poison book out, and he said, 'You'll git it at the police station.' I bet he 'ad a laugh over it after, because I went out into the town, and I lit of [met] a pal o' mine, 'e was a year younger than me. An' I said:

'I shan't goo in theer no more.'
'Why, what's up?'
'I went for some white hellebore, an' 'e wouldn't let me 'ave it.'
'D'you want some?'
'Aye, I do.'
'I'll fetch you some.'
And he goes into another chemist, an' gets it and brings it out. It was sixpennyworth, that was all I wanted.

Well, we was leading wood with these horses, with a wood-cut* [timber-tug]. And they was full o' life, they was buckin' an' jumpin' on the way home: they was full o' flesh. And we had the carpenter with us, 'cause he went to show us which poles to git. And he said to me, 'I think you must be giving 'em some white 'ellibore.' I said, 'White 'ellibore, what d'you mean?': and I turned as green as grass. And he made me stay for a minute, and he said, 'Don't yer know what 'ellibore is?' An' I says, 'I don't, nivver heard on it.' But I was, you know, and 'e just struck the nail on the 'ead!

I had a team of horses when I went to Walmsgate, and they'd been 'done': by, they *had* been done ['powdered']. I knew the last chap had been giving them something, but I didn't know what it was. An' I used to git up 'alf past three in the mornin', and yoke out at six. An' I *couldn't* get 'em t'eat: they wouldn't eat. They'd just eat as if they was 'alf asleep: and if they won't eat, you're done, aren't you?

And one day I was goin' to Authorpe station, and I was goin' down Cow Deg Road, a near cut to go to Authorpe. And there was a chap ploughin' in the field opposite, an' 'e looked at me, and 'e said: 'Aren't they eating very well, Waggie?'

'You *know* they aren't, you know what's a matter wi'em.'

I knew 'im because he used to keep the chaps where I was working then, and 'e'd left. So I said:

'I'm coming to see you one night.'

'All right, you can come.'

'Will you see us square?'

'I will. I'm goin' to Candlemas Market on Wednesday. Come down on Wednesday night, and I'll see you square.'

So I went down Wednesday night, and 'e'd got these 'ere powders and put 'em on the table, and put a newspaper out. And 'e'd got 'em all separate. There were some juniper berries* in, I remember that, and he got an old beer bottle and rolled it over, to crush 'em. Well, I'd never been used to that. I'd always been used to the chemist mixin' 'em for me: putting 'em in the bowl and mixin' 'em. Well, *he* mixed 'em up, and 'e said, 'Give 'em a teaspoonful o' that, twice a week. And now I've some more stuff 'ere: give 'em as much as'll lay on a sixpence. How you want to do it, git a little drop o' water on the palm of your hand, put it in theer, mix it up, and put it in their drinkin' water. They'll not find it then: but if you put it in dry, and they git some water on it, it'll maybe currick* 'em [cause diarrhoea]': I'd to start with these powders on the 1st of March, and if it come snow, I wasn't to give 'em any.

And it was arsenic: that was arsenic. Did it work? It *did* work. The second chap had gone to the [1914–18] war, and the fella I lived wi', the labourer, he was doin' these other four horses. And 'e said to me, 'By gum, you've oiled their jaws!' Because you know, when they stopped eating, it woke you up. After dinner, I often used to give 'em a feed and sit and 'ave a sleep on the bin: and they was eating that ravishly at it that when they stopped eating, it woke you up. He said, 'You've oiled their jaws!' And I says, 'Aye, I don't understand it: they suddenly started to eat.' *I* knew what was the matter! And from March to May, you could *see* them horses mend: they was as fat as seals by 'Pag-rag Day', May the 14th. You see, these horses was already habited [addicted] to it, to arsenic, and they'd do no good wi'out it.

Now after I was on me own, I could goo and buy anything from a chemist, because I wasn't frightened of anybody knowing. So I went to a chemist and asked him for some white markberry – that's what they called arsenic – and he gave me some. And I said to him, 'D'you think they get habited to it? That if they've once had it, they'll always want it?' 'Oh, no', he says, 'they wouldn't get habited to it.' 'Well', I says, 'I can tell you different. I *know* they will.'

They do. If they've once had it, you'll never do no more good wi'out you give 'em it. You'd give it 'em twice a week: and when they'd 'ad it a year or two, and they suddenly ain't it, you *can't* git 'em to eat. They'd never look that fresh, and have that shiny skin. You see these race'orses wi' shiny skin: well, they're giving 'em something – it's not all corn. Noo, it isn't. And they find 'em out at times, don't they?

And, of course, the waggie'd never let the farmer know 'e was giving 'em owt. I was out o' this stuff, the last year I was at Walmsgate, and I wanted some. And I knew another waggoner from further up the Wolds, up Kelstern way, and he said he could get me some. It was on a Saturday night, and the silly devil went and got drunk, and he was telling everybody that he'd some white markberry for me. He was saying, 'I've got some white markberry for George, and I can't find him.' Another fella had heard him, and he came to me and said, 'For God's sake git off 'ome, git out of 'is way. 'E's telling everybody 'e's got markberry for you, and if your boss gits to know, you've had it.' And of course I slithered off, and I never did git any. Well, the horses was poor when I left off, but I couldn't give 'em any: I couldn't get it. That was the finest stuff out.

Cures good and bad

I had quite a few other receipts to make horses eat, though. This one was give me by Joe Caldron – he was an old gentleman at the time:

'2 oz. gentian*
2 oz. saltpetre*
1 oz. aniseeds*
2 oz. liver antimony
2 oz. madder*
One dessertspoon twice a week.'

And this was a good recipe:

'2 oz. saltpetre*
2 oz. black sulphur*
2 oz. aniseeds*
6 oz. black antimony
2 oz. juniper berries*
2 oz. Dragon's blood*'

Isn't that a poison? I give a chap that – it's years ago – and he sent me ten bob! And I've another here, it was Bob Oliver's:

'2 oz. black antimony
2 oz. green coprose (copperas)*
2 oz. fenugreek
2 oz. tartar emetic*
As much as would lay on a sixpence.'

Now that was as cheap as anything: it didn't hurt 'em, and they worked well and they looked well.

And then there were ointments: we used to make this 'Mother's ointment':

'½ lb. mutton fat
4 oz. yellow resin
3 oz. sweet oil
Render down fat and strain, then simmer a few minutes with resin and sweet oil, and stir until cold.'

You must use lump resin, not powder. That's for any kind of cut or inflammation. And then there was this blister ointment, white oil:

'½ oz. oil of ragrain
4 oz. turpentine spirit
3 oz. hartshorn*'

And this is an embrocation:

'4 oz. white vinegar
2 oz. methylated spirit
2 oz. spirits of turpentine
2 eggs
Beat eggs well and add the rest: shake well in bottle.'

Then there were all sorts of horse-balls. Have you ever seen 'em ball a horse? You hold the ball between your first three fingers, and git the tongue out o' the mouth in this hand. And you shove your hand down as far as here, put it in their throat, let go o' the tongue, and pull your hand back. And you'll see it go down the gullet. But you've got to have the right action to git it theer. You see, you don't want to be *nervous*: and a lot on 'em would be.

Some of the Kentish waggoners remembered by Filmer Measday and Alf Friend apparently fell into this category – though it must have taken some 'pluck' to apply their last remedy.

FM: Some horsemen – the ones who'd got most pluck – would get 'old of its tongue, and put their arm right down his throat with this pill. But some of the windier ones used to 'ave what they called a popgun, like a child's popgun made from a bit of hollered-out alder, and they'd *shoot* the pill down.

My late father, a cavalryman during the 1914–18 war, remembered blowing balls down a horse's gullet with a kind of pea-shooter: many apocryphal tales were told of occasions when the horse blew first.

AF: And others used to have a frame – that was a round bit of metal you could put your arm through, into the horse's mouth: he couldn't bite you then. Then you'd hold the physic-ball in your hand, and push it over the horse's gullet. I've done it meself.

And some of these waggoners, if their horse was off-colour, they wouldn't just ball it, they'd bleed it as well. They'd get out their pocketknife, and they'd bind a piece of tarred string round most of the blade, to about an inch from the point. They'd get the horse's mouth open, with his tongue out so he couldn't close it, and then they'd dig that knife right down into his gum, and they'd bleed two–three pints of blood out o' that horse. They'd keep that quiet, 'cause they wasn't allowed to do that sort o' thing, but that was their old-fashioned way: and next day you wouldn't be able to hold that horse!

And now back to 'George':

You *could* buy horse-balls, of course: but we generally used to make our own, with soap and such to bind 'em together. These was Jack Ellis's horse-balls:

'4 oz. green coprose (copperas)*
4 oz. sulphur*
4 oz. Castile soap
2 oz. black tobacco
2 oz. resin
2 oz. ginger
4 oz. Venice turpentine
2 oz. saltpetre [Mainly purgatives]
Make into one-ounce balls.'

And then there was a powder 'to follow': to give 'em after you'd balled 'em:

'4 oz. cream of tartar
4 oz. liquorice powder
4 oz. mint
6 oz. gentian root
6 oz. steel-filings [!]
4 oz. crocus antimony
6 oz. saltpetre
4 oz. Arabic mineral
6 oz. fenugreek
6 oz. ground ginger
2 oz. tartar emetic
One tablespoonful, twice a week.'

That would be for conditioning 'em, keeping their blood right, and keepin' 'em from being greasy.* And if you wanted to help them slip their coats, you could give them 'a dessertspoon of common gunpowder twice a week'. At the back-end o' the year, your horse'll grow his coat, and then at spring-end they'll slip it. Well, if you wanted it off early, you'd give 'em some gunpowder.

Or if they'd picked up lice, you'd rub 'em all over with derris root,* twice a week, until they were clean.   [FRED BRADER]

The most sought after receipts, however, were those for controlling unruly horses: and these, for reasons stated earlier, were usually a particularly closely guarded secret – like the contents of the horse-bottle used by the horseman father of Frank Bigg, the Suffolk basketmaker:

I can remember Dad's horse-bottle well. We'd got an old clock on the mantelpiece, and it always used to lay in the bottom of there. And if you got a horse which was a little bit funny, all he used to do was just damp the cork, and he'd put that on his shoulder or somewhere, and the horse was never any more trouble. You could do what you liked with that horse. And I remember there was a chap came in, and he was having trouble with some young horses. Dad said, 'You don't want to worry about them horses – you come in with me.' And he put a little drop o' that on the clothes he was wearing – just rubbed the cork on his shoulders: and he said, 'They won't be no more trouble to you.' They wasn't! Nobody ever knew what was in that bottle. I never asked, and I don't suppose I'd have been told if I had!

It probably contained some such mixture of aromatic substances, irresistible to horses, as made up 'George's' drawing oil. The 'business' with the handkerchief was perhaps as much for the benefit of human spectators as for the horse:

'18 drops oil of rhodium
3 drams scented sorrel
3 drams oil of paradise
3 drams oil of caraway.

Mix and place a few drops on a handkerchief, and if possible rub the nose with it, or swish on a handkerchief pretending to make it stand back. The first time. After that put a few drops on the cap or coat-sleeve, will make it follow you.'

Aye, it *would* follow you. I bought a young horse from a field o' horses, and I had some o' that on a handkerchief – I got it a-purpose – and she followed me out!

'The bottle' may also have included a preparation made from the 'milt' or 'false tongue', a lump of fibrous matter which lies on the tongue of a foetal colt. This, according to George Ewart Evans (The Pattern Under the Plough) was used by East Anglian horsemen in the manufacture of their 'drawing' and 'jading' (temporarily paralyzing) oils. But I have only heard of it – from a Welsh-border waggoner, Ron Mills of Velindre, near Hay-on-Wye – as a good-luck charm:

A colt has a false tongue, did you know that? When a mare has a foal, if you're standing by there when the foal starts to struggle to get up on his feet, you might see this false tongue drop out of his mouth. It looks a bit like an ordinary tongue. And it always used to be the custom to pick that up, take it home, and nail it on the stable door. I seen it on there for twelve months or a couple o' years. They reckoned it was good luck for the horse, like. I've nailed plenty up myself!

Finally (and lest anyone should be tempted to try the receipts given here), the home doctoring of horses was fraught with deadly danger. Some receipts – like this one from Ron Mills – had to be used with great care:

If they had a horse they wanted to sell, some used to get this old yew tree, and cut it up real fine, and dry it: and once it gets real dry you can rub it up in your hand, 'til it comes out like dust. Now if you put a *very little* of that in their feed, that would give 'em a nice shiny coat, and it'd give 'em an appetite as well. But it could be real *deadly*, if you gave 'em too much.

And tragic mistakes – like that remembered by Filmer Measday – could destroy whole teams:

I had an uncle, and he poisoned the only team o' grey horses there was in Kent, at the time. Because the foreman on his farm, he used to give the chaps some brimstone to give to their horses, but one particular weekend, the foreman wasn't there. Now my uncle knew where he kept the stuff, so he went into the granary and got it: but instead o' brimstone, he got Cooper's sheep dip instead. You see, he couldn't read, so he couldn't tell what was on the box. So he gave them what he thought was brimstone on Sunday morning, and when he went to feed 'em on Sunday evening, they was all laid in the stable, stone dead. And he could never work with a horse afterwards: he couldn't bring himself to go near 'em.

And so too could dosing by inexperienced or over-enthusiastic horsemen, says 'George':

But there was a lot of things I'd never use. I'd never use liquid stuff, like this here:

> '1 oz. oil of vitriol [sulphuric acid]
> 1 oz. white spirits plus vitriol
> 1 oz. (five to nine drops) red lavender.'

A chap gave me that, he used to 'travel entire' – he used to lead the stallion round to cover the mares: but I wouldn't use it. It was too dangerous. Now I had a lad live wi' me at Walmsgate, and he was using bottled stuff. Well, them horses was as wild as wind. If he wanted to do a job for hissen', he's got to keep hold o' the lines – he can't leave 'em, else they'll gallop away. And I said to 'im, 'You want to stop using that bottled stuff, or I shall tell the boss on you. It's not safe. You'll ha' your horses gallop away, and mine'll gallop wi'em. Then we shall be nowhere!'

Because you've got to be careful. On that Ormsby estate they had four grey horses on one farm, and a chap killed three o' them with powders. He'd given 'em some strongish powders, something he shouldn't ha' been doin' – or else he didn't use it properly. Anyhow, he killed three. And he got the sack, and he didn't get any wages – they turned him off adrift!

BUYING AND SELLING

Extreme caution also had to be used – as it still must – in buying and selling of horses. The buying was usually done by the farmer himself, who liked to think himself a better judge of horseflesh than his men: but the disposal of 'queer 'uns' was often left to waggoners like Will Forman of Ash-by-Sandwich:

Canterbury was a rare place for 'orses, Saturdays. They was always sellin' 'orses there, them days. I've sometimes gorn up with three and come back with two, or gorn up with one and brought three–four back. They'd trot 'em up and down in the market, and that's the way they used to sell 'em. You'd stand there and bid on 'em.

I've 'ad some queer 'uns, I 'ave: they ain't all been good 'uns. These ol' Shires, they take a bit o' handlin', they do that. Some 'ave been rough 'uns, and some 'ave been kickers. I 'ad one up there at Drew's, a little black 'un: that could kick, tew. I took it up Canterbury one Saturday, and they wouldn't look at it – wouldn't give a bid on 'er. They knew 'er name: they'd got 'er name reckoned up.

So I brought 'er 'ome, and we 'ad 'er another couple or three months. Then the ol' guv'nor says, 'You know what, Will: we got to get rid of 'er.' So I took 'er up Canterbury, an' she did sell that Saturday. And I took the bridle off it, and left 'er in a halter. And the bloke what bought 'er said, 'Hey, leave that bridle on.' So I said, 'That's mine, that don't belong to yew: the horse is sold with a halter.'

There's a pub by the old market, by the double iron gates: and I went straight in there to git a drink. I 'adn't bin in long enough to jest git a drink out the glass, and a bloke come running in and said, 'Is Drew's chap in 'ere?' And I sez, 'Yes, I'm 'ere, what's up?' 'You come and catch that 'orse you just sold: he's broke that 'alter, and 'e's running up and down the market. We can't git near it.' So I went out, and she came galloping down the road: and I says, 'Whooah!' an' I pulled 'er up:

'You gonna put that bridle on 'er now?' 'e says.

I says, 'I'll put that on, 'til you git something to tie 'er up with. I'm not leaving it on, and if you don't git something, I'll take it off.'

'Where the devil'll I get anything?'

'You go up by the pub there: there's a stable up there, they'll lend you a bridle.'

And then they brought a van-bridle back with blinkers, so's 'er eyes was all covered up. An' I put that on and tied 'er up. And they see'd she was gonna break loose agin, so they put 'er on the scale where they weighed bullocks, and they put wattles all round, up to 'ere. But that thing scratched up and smashed them wattles, and got out! She was a real devil.

But by then I'd got on that bus, and I was gorn! And didn't I hear all about it tew! Next mornin' guv'nor says to me, 'You 'ad some antics up Canterbury, didn't yew?' 'Antics?' I says, 'When that horse was sold, it was out o' my 'ands, wasn't it?' 'I suppose it was', 'e says, 'but d'you know what, it kicked its way out o' the weigh place, and they thought it was going to break its neck.' 'Well', I says, 'that was the best thing it could 'a done!' 'What time did they get it away?' 'Six o'clock that night,' he says, 'They didn't get it 'til then.'

And that wasn't the end of it, 'cause we heard that on Monday they put it to a water barrel, a water cart, round about Hougham way. And as soon as they got that shafted up, that bolted – water cart an' all: that would, tew!

Horse-breeders had their own methods of dealing with 'kickers' and other vicious animals, as our final tales show. They were told me by Bill Denby (b. 1905) of Heslington, near York, whose father's business centred on his farm at Askern, near Doncaster in the West Riding of Yorkshire. I have not yet tracked down 'Professor Smith', but presume him to have been one of the professional 'horse tamers' who abounded in late-Victorian circuses.

When we lived about Doncaster, Dad used to breed high-stepping horses. We had a breed of our own, all high-steppers: they was trap-horses and waggonette horses, and they'd come in as farmer's outfits, to look smart to go to market in. One of our horses was bought for an ice-cream cart, to go in a tradesman's outfit for the Royal Show; and Dad used to show them himself in one o' them four-wheeled waggons.

There was a lot attached to training a hackney-horse, you know. Of course, you had to groom 'em and stable 'em right, and they was always fed on the best of food and rugged up in horse-boxes. Because they was very valuable: a high-stepper would fetch a hundred pound, a good one, when an ordinary horse might only cost you ten or fifteen. And then you had to train 'em to step high and step even. Dad used to put 'em in fetlock-straps – that was an elastic strap that went between the foot and the girth so every time they picked their feet up, the elastic strap would pull it up a bit higher. And to get 'em into even strides, we used to put sleepers down on t'road, all spaced out at same distance: then we'd walk 'em over these, and they *had* to step evenly.

They was very high-bred, and some of 'em could kick a midge's eye out! If we got a kicker, we used to put him in a special long-shaft trap we had. That kept him away from the trap front, so when he kicked he'd be kicking at nothing. Because a horse won't kick above once at fresh air: but if it hits the cart front by kicking, it'll kick again and again, and it'll kick the trap front out. But with this trap he could kick himself while he threw himself down, and if he dropped on one o' the shafts, they was made so they wouldn't break and hurt him. These shafts was made o' what they called lancewood: the horse could lay on 'em, and they could bend nearly double or split from end to end, but they'd never break. Or you could have kicking-straps on. That's a strap that went over behind the horse from one shaft to t'other: and as soon as it lifted its back end up to kick, this strap would check it on t'way up.

And Dad had another thing for a horse that was a bit vicious. He called it a 'Professor Smith', and whatever horse it was – even a really wild horse – you could put this thing on it and make it stop. I suppose this 'Professor Smith' invented it, and he must have been a clever man. There was a girth round t'horse's middle, and then there was two straps round its fetlocks – that's its front feet – and you had a rope that was laced in a certain way from

Bill Denby's father Fred (right), breeder of high-stepping hackney horses, proudly exhibiting his stud-stallion 'Drewton Masher II' at Maltby Show near Doncaster, West Yorkshire, c. 1912.

each fetlock to this 'Professor Smith' on the girth. And then there was a long rope from the 'Professor Smith', and you used to take hold o' that: when you pulled so hard, it pulled one leg up, and when you pulled so much harder, both feet came up, and horse was on its knees.

So you'd take the bridle off, and the horse would go: and if you pulled this rope, a man could easily take horse clean off of its front legs. Dad used to let horse run, and he'd shout, 'Whoa', and then he'd pull this rope and throw horse down: and it wouldn't be very long then before it'd stop as soon as he shouted, whether he pulled or not. We've fetched horses out of a grass field that's never been ridden or had anything done to 'em: and when he put 'Professor Smith' on, I've just gone on their backs and ridden 'em. But you had to watch out when he pulled rope, because it would drop straight down on its knees, and you used to go over its head!

Now say you had one you was riding, and it was always rearing up. You could cure that if you got a bottle of water, and carried it with you when you

went out. As soon as horse reared, you'd hit him between his ears with this bottle, and break it, and the water'd run down over his ears. He'd never rear up again! The only thing about that was, you might cause a sore place on his head, and nobody'd buy him with a sore place there – they wouldn't entertain him, 'cause they knew he was a bit of a rearer.

Oh, it was an art, buying horses then. Dad's was always kept in top shape, for if there was a buyer happened to come past. And I'll tell you a fake-up he once did – I oughtn't to tell tales, I suppose, but it's a long time gone now. Anyway, he had one horse with a long tail, and he sold it to a man: but the man didn't like it some way or another, and Dad got it back again. It was unusual, then, was a long-tailed horse. So when we got it back again, all me dad did was to cut its tail short. And a few days later, along came the same man again: 'You've a nice horse there, Denby, is it for sale?' says he, and Dad says, 'Yes' – and he sold it back to the same man that'd had it before! The man didn't know it with its short tail, you see, and he didn't recognize it while he took it out of trap at his home – and then, of course, it went straight into t'same place in stables, and it knew where t'water trough was. Then he realized he'd got his own horse back again!

There was all kinds of tricks and dodges for selling. They'd often bandage the legs, to make 'em look nice and thin, and make the hair stick down – people didn't like the leg hair to stand off, and that made 'em look better for selling. They used to bandage the tails as well, to make 'em look more slimmer. Of course, they'd take the bandages off before they sold 'em, but the hair would still stick down. And another of my dad's receipts – it's rather rude – was to stick a lump o' ginger up a horse's behind: it made 'em real frisky!

Dad stopped breeding in the 1914 war, when the army took away his two stallions: we never saw 'em again. And after the Fourteen War nobody wanted trap-horses any more: everybody wanted cars. My father, though, he never took to cars. He never could drive, and he was always dead agin' motors.

3

To Mend The Pantry

THE PIG: THE COTTAGER'S FRIEND

From the great horses which powered the farm, we move on to the humbler but equally necessary creatures which powered its workers. The chiefest of these, as we have already heard, was the pig, with its unrivalled talent for converting odds and ends into meat: almost the only meat, indeed, that a 'living-in' labourer might taste from one year's end to the next and, for the poorest cottagers, the one bright spot in a diet which might otherwise consist of bread, potatoes, cabbage and weak tea.

> *'Make [your pig] quite fat by all means. The last bushel, even if he sit as he eat, is the most profitable. If he can walk two hundred yards at a time, he is not well fatted. Lean bacon is the most wasteful thing that any family can use . . . The man who cannot live on solid fat bacon, well fed and well cured, wants the sweet sauce of labour, or is fit for the hospital.'*

So William Cobbett advised readers of his Cottage Economy *(1822), and similar doctrines continued to prevail until after the Second World War, when 'the housewife' – 'educated' for reasons of their own by the butcher and wholesaler – began to demand 'lean meat', which neither the old methods nor the old breeds were designed to provide. Thus the pig began its move from the cottager's sty to the factory farm.*

But until then, as I have been told time and again, 'Everybody kept a pig or two, in the country.' Nor is 'everybody' much of an exaggeration: certainly everyone who could scrape together the money to buy one – even if they had to mortgage half its meat to the butcher in advance – did so, provided only that they could find a corner to keep it in. For the modern bye-laws prohibiting pig-keeping as 'a nuisance' would have been regarded as an insupportable piece of tyranny, and reforming landlords provided their village tenants with 'model pigsties' to go with their 'model cottages' – and in some cases with the pig as well. 'Fatteners' were also most sought-after prizes at village 'sports', as Arthur Wade remembers: and anyone who has tried to catch even an ungreased piglet will applaud his mother's tactics.

They'd always have a greased pig for people to catch, at Rudston Feast. One o' farmers would give a pig, and if you caught it, it was yours. Me

'Jesse Lily', champion Lincolnshire Curly Coat sow, at Carrington near Boston, c. 1905. The hardy Curly Coat was an ideal cottagers' pig, famous for its ability to convert a diet of scraps and grass into prodigious amounts of fat pork and 'solid fat bacon'. But such qualities did not appeal to modern producers of factory-farmed 'lean meat' and the breed became extinct in the early 1970s.

mother caught it one year, and I've never laughed so much. She got dressed up ready for it, and she was a big strong woman, you know: and they all shouted she was cheating, because she waited while they'd tired pig out, and when it came for her way she just knelt down in front of it and wrapped her apron round it! They were chasing it all over, and grabbing it, but their hands slid off, and pig kept squealing: and she just saw it was tired, and she dropped on her knees and flung her apron over. And so she got it, and it was just right for feeding up for pork.

The cheapest piglet to buy was the runt, the smallest of a litter, which could nevertheless do well with careful feeding. In Kent, this was called the 'ant'ny', in memory of the pet pig which allegedly kept St Anthony company during his long years of desert meditation: and there it commonly formed part of the perquisites of stockmen like Filmer Measday's father:

My father was stockman on the farm, but he always kept pigs of his own. When they had a litter o' pigs at the farm, there was always one small 'un they called the 'ant'ny', and he always had that. That was part of his pay, and I've known him have as many as five in the sty. And the butcher in the village here used to buy them off him when they were big enough to kill: but he only let butcher have 'em on condition that *he* never had any o' the meat.

He was not the only one to regret the passing of 'one of the family', as the cottager's pig so often became. One Welsh family (the Millses of Newcourt, Velindre, Hay-on-Wye) broke into song at the memory of

> 'Oh how sad and grieved was we
> When we killed the Mochyn Dee'

('Mochyn Du', 'little black pig': sung to the tune of 'Crawshay Bailey'.) But hearts had to be hardened, for most 'family friends' were both killed and eaten at home, as the Elliott sisters (p.173) of Ovingham, Northumberland, recalled:

CISSIE: We always had two pigs, to serve for bacon and ham. We used to feed them on peelings and such, and we had to boil their food in the wash-boiler, in the wash-house. We'd boil twice a week, and then we'd mix it with 'boxings' – that was a special kind of bought pig-meal, and they loved it. And then we used to get the 'drains', the old barley, from the brewery, sometimes: then the pigs were drunk! You'd see them go wobbling away into the sty, to lay down. The neighbours used to give us peelings, as well, and then we'd give *them* a bit sausage and a bit black pudding, when the pig were killed.

MARY: Oh yes, killing day was a great day! It was November we generally killed the one, and January or February the other: they were always killed in the cold weather, the dead of winter, because they had to keep. The butcher used to come early morning, and we'd have all the pots and pans full of boiling water ready, for when he scalded it. He'd have to scald and shave the pig as soon as he'd killed it, to get all the hairs off. Mother or Father would stand over him, pouring on the boiling water as he was shaving: he shaved every inch of it – a black pig would be pure white when he'd finished.

CISSIE: Then they had what they called sheer-legs: that was three very long poles, tied together at the top. And they'd fasten the pig's back legs together, and pull it up on a thing called a 'camron':* it was like a coathanger, hooked at both ends, and it used to be pushed through the pig's legs. Then it would be hauled up on the sheer-legs, and there the pig hung all day, out in the frost: it used to hang from about nine o'clock in the morning until six at night. And in the evening, the butcher would come back and salt it down. He'd cut it in two pieces, straight down the backbone: the backbone was what we called the 'chine', and we used to roast that – it was lovely.

MARY: He'd lay the two halves of the pig down, and inject into the joints with saltpetre: then the halves were covered all over in coarse salt and a special kind of sugar – covered all over, like snow. The second side was laid on top of the first, and they'd put a bit more salt on, and then a sheet – a good linen sheet – was laid on top of the whole 'corpse'. The whole lot was put on the pantry floor, and the brine used to *run* off it, into the kitchen: we had to dry that up each morning. *We* got used to it, but if ever the little ones were naughty, they were always told they were going to be put in the pantry!

CISSIE: It took three weeks to cure, and halfway through the three weeks the butcher would come back and turn the pieces over. After the three weeks were up, it was taken out of the salt, well rubbed-down with a coarse towel, and then hung up on great big hooks in the kitchen. The hams were hung on two hooks, the shoulders on another two, and the sides on four hooks. We'd hang it until it got dry, and then we'd start to use it – it was gorgeous! But my father would never have bacon cooked in a frying pan, oh no. It had to be roast in a Dutch oven,* in front of the fire. The bacon piece was hung on hooks inside the Dutch oven, and then you shut the oven door. And when you'd got the fire red-hot bright, you stood the Dutch oven on a grid thing that slid onto the fire-bars, and the bacon cooked beautifully.

Bacon was not always cured by dry-salting. In East Anglia, it was generally cut up and pickled in brine:

'Take two gallons of boiling water and pour onto two pounds of salt and one ounce of saltpetre, in an earthenware jar. Put the bacon to soak in this, and it will be ready in a fortnight.'

A Suffolk speciality is 'sweet-pickling'. This produces a dark-brown bacon with a delicious sweet-salt flavour, which I first tasted by courtesy of Mr and Mrs Frank Bigg of Kersey:

You can pickle the chaps, the cheek-pieces, of a pig; and that's one of the sweetest pieces on the whole animal. Put it in an old glazed sink, and mix up a pound of sugar and half a pound of salt for every twenty pounds of meat. Then you just rub that into the bacon, and baste it with the liquid that comes off, every day for three weeks. When it's ready, you can boil it, but you usually cut it into rashers and fry it: only you *must* fry it slowly, or the sugar burns off, and you don't get the taste. It's best left for a while, though, and we generally keep ours for eighteen months. Mind you, that sweet-pickle bacon will keep as long as you like: my uncle's got a piece of ham

Pig-killing day at Crookhall, near Consett, Co. Durham, c. 1914. 'Mother' poses with a kettle of the hot water used for shaving off the pig's bristles, and the neighbours await their share of black puddings, 'fry' and sausages.

coming up for twenty-one years old, truly. I keep asking, when he comes, when he's going to cook it and give me a piece: but he won't!

Not all the pig's meat, however, could be cured, and in pre-refrigeration days there was no other means of preserving it. So any momentary sadness surrounding the pig's departure was soon dispelled by the prospect of plentiful fresh food, and the rush to manufacture the extraordinary variety of dishes that could be produced from pieces now normally thrown away.

MARY: Then there were all kinds of things you made on the actual pig-killing day. You hadn't to waste a thing on a pig but the squeak!
CISSIE: The squeak and the tail.
MARY: Well, I don't know, *we* used the tail to torment people: we used to tickle them with it! And there was an old gentleman used to get the feet, as well – the trotters. *We* didn't eat those, because Father didn't want them, and what he didn't like, we didn't like, of course: but some people considered them a delicacy – Uncle Fred used to love them, by Jove, yes!

You cooked them and let them go cold, and then they were full of jelly, and people thought they were beautiful.

CISSIE: Then there was black puddin's, and white puddin's. White puddin's was offal, innards and all sorts, all put together and minced. They'd boil it first, and then take it out and put it in a big bowl, and then season it with peppers and salt. After that it was fed into skins, like sausage skins – that was all done by hand – and then they were dropped into boiling water, to what we called 'leep'* them: that was to cook them for three or four minutes.

MARY: The black puddin's, they were made from the pig's blood. We used to run away while the butcher was killing the pig, but when he'd killed it we used to have to come back and catch the blood. Because as soon as he'd killed it, he used to slit its throat, and you had to catch the blood in a kind of a ware* jug, and you *must* keep stirring it to keep it from congealing. Well, you'd already cooked the barley that you were going to put in the black puddin', and you'd shredded the suet and bread and got the new milk ready – it had to be *new* milk. So you'd get all that, and your sage and mint and peppers, and you'd mix them all thoroughly with the blood. Then you fed it with a funnel – we have that funnel yet – into sausage skins made from the pig's innards: they'd been scraped clean and salted, and left in salted water overnight. You had to tie one end with linen thread, feed the skin of the other end onto the funnel, and pour the mixture in: and when the skin was full, you had to catch it closed and tie it onto the other end with the thread – and there was your ring of black puddin'. And then it was dipped into boiling water, to leep the blood.

Mother used to very often just butter a pie-dish, and fill it with black pudding, and put it into the oven for tea: and it was so light, you could blow it off your plate! Then there were sausages. Our sausages had nothing in them but meat, pure pork and sage: they had lumps of meat in, like what they call a Cumberland sausage. The pork came from the rib side of the pig, which the butcher would trim for us: there wasn't any offal in our sausages, and we never got as many as we got black puddings and white. We used to fill all our sausages by hand, 'til we got a sausage machine ('the Universal Food Chopper'): we have that machine yet.

CISSIE: All our neighbours would get a bit sausage, and our doctor from Ovington always used to turn up at pig-killing time. 'I knew you'd be killing, I knew you'd have the things ready by now.' Ee, the old devil, *he* had to have his share – his black puddin' and his white puddin' and his sausages – and away he would go.

Black puddings, still popular in the north, seem to decline progressively in favour the further south of the Humber you travel. Many midlanders and southerners have told me that 'they never could fancy the blood': and some – like Mrs Edith Watkins, who was brought up on the Herefordshire–Powys border – used simply to 'dig a hole and pour it away as quickly as possible, so the sheepdogs couldn't get it'. The pork dishes she particularly remembers were 'faggots' and chine.

And then there was the liver and the heart: we minced those up and made *faggots* of those, with sage and onion. The fat off the inside of the belly would be a huge leaf: and we used to use that for putting round our faggots: put the faggot meat onto a piece of this lard, roll it up, and then put them in a big roasting pan.

And the chines were lovely – that was the backbone. There was about three big bones on it, and we'd roast it. And there was one big chine, what they used to call 'the christening chine'. We used to have such fun with that. The butcher used to say, 'Well, I've got to ask you a question now: d'you want this christening chine?' And Mum used to laugh and say, 'No, we don't need it this time!' And if it wasn't needed for a new addition to the family, the butcher had it.

In Lincolnshire, the butcher would certainly never have got his hands on the chine. For there, as the late Fred Brader recalled, stuffed and boiled *chine was virtually the 'national dish':*

We used to call it 'christening chine', because you'd have it when there was a big family gathering – for a christening maybe, or for when all lads and lasses came home on holiday on May the 14th, 'Pag-rag Day'. 'Pag-rag Day' was a good time for it, because the parsley was ready then, to stuff it with. You'd make cuts in the chine every few inches, right down to the bone – but you wouldn't cut it *off* the bone: then you'd stuff these cuts with parsley, as much as ever you could get in – a big chine could take a whole tin bathful of parsley, and that's quite a lot! Then you'd put the stuffed chine in a cloth, and boil it in the copper: you wouldn't roast it, you'd boil it, and then you'd let it go cold, and cut it in strips *along* the bone, so it was green, pink, green, pink all the way along. That was lovely.

Oh yes, we always had a chine when there was a 'do' on. They'd have one at a village feast, and they always had one at Saltfleet Fair – that was a horse sale, with races and all. You can still get it in some of the old-fashioned butchers round Louth, but it isn't the same as home-made! [But even 'boughten' chine is excellent, as I myself can testify.]

And they used to make haslet in Lincolnshire, too. That was made of minced up liver, and a bit of fat pork, and seasoning, onions and that. It was liver and a bit o' red meat, the sticking-bit as they used to call it: that was the bit in the throat where they stuck the pig, and it always looked a bit bloody. They used to form it into a ball, and mix it up wi' seasoning and a few breadcrumbs, and then they'd wrap it in a piece of the lining of the stomach – it was just like a piece o' lacy net-curtaining. Some people called it 'the veiling', and some 'the apron'. And they cooked it in that, in the oven, and they'd eat it cold. You could buy some in Louth now, I expect.

'Pig's fry' was another favourite killing-day dish, as Sam Robson of Bempton near Bridlington, Yorkshire remembers:

At one time o' day, when everybody knew everybody, they used to have what they called 'pig's fry'. All the liver and small bits, sweetbreads and such. Well, there'd be too much for one family, and of course you couldn't keep it long, so you'd share it out with the neighbours. You used to give one a bit o' this fry, and th' other a bit: and you remembered who you'd gi'en a bit to: and when *they* killed, *you* got a fry.

And even the unpromising 'odds and ends' of the pig's exterior could be made into brawn – or 'pork cheese' as it is called in Suffolk, where Mrs Vinie Bigg told me:

You put all the bits and pieces in a big saucepan. The head, the bones, feet, ears, all the odds and ends, you boil them up with whatever herbs and spices you like. Then you let it cool, and you get all the bones out with your fingers: pick out all the bones and gristly pieces – anything you feel solid in your fingers, throw it out. Then you pour what's left into pots, and they set solid: you can turn them out onto a plate like a blancmange.

The 'War-Ag' pig

Finally, a pig story told to me in a certain Welsh-border pub – which had perhaps better remain anonymous, along with the surnames of the teller and his 'victim'. One thing, however, needs to be explained. During and immediately after the Second World War, the 'War-Ag'(ricultural) rationing laws forbade farmers to slaughter more than a set quota of their pigs, and ruled that part of each of these should go to the government. But it was by no means unknown for farmers to covertly kill far more than their quota, and to sell the carcasses at a fat profit on the black market.

'G': That pig as we found up in the quarry, now. Well, we was having our bait.* We was felling some timber up – well, I won't say the name of the place, but 'twas down below here. An' me and my mate 'ad a bit o' bait, like, an' we got an aal' lurcher-dog there – 'e always catched 'arf-a-dozen rabbits during the day, to mend the pantry. An' there was 'e in these nettles, in the quarry there: an' I said, 'There's a rabbit there, Griff'.
J: I knows where it was, too.
'G': And 'e said, 'Ar, we'll 'a that bugger out from there.'
J: You 'ad a bloody pig instead!
'G': So I was down there, and there was nettles up to 'ere: an' I could see

there was a tar barrel in there. An' I said, 'All I can see in 'ere is a tar barrel
– I can't see no blasted rabbit.' So I walked in there a bit, an' th' end o' the
barrel was loose, see. So I takes the end out o' this tar barrel, and I starts to
dither: 'cause there was a bloody pig in there. There was two 'alves – two
sides – and two hams: an' 'e was cured. Well, I scratches my head, an' I
said, 'Well, I dunner reckon this belongs to anybody, do it, now we found
the bugger?'

J: Ah, but they couldn't own [to] it, could they? You'd got 'em.

'G': It's sure to 've been a mile-and-a-'alf from the farm, see. An' the farmer
were a bit of a rum bugger – he were a Birmingham chap, a know-all
bastard, see. Anyway, I said, 'I'm goin' to take one of them sides down the
road now – I amna' gonna do no more work.' You know Norton Ruck, 'e
goes down by there. An' I said, 'I'm going down Norton Ruck home' – an' I
tell you what, it's a bloody long walk. Now I hadner bin long out o' the
army, an' I got me army greatcoat on. So I gets this aal' overcoat, an' I
wraps 'im up in there, an' I was goin' down the road: an' just now I looks
round, an' Griff was coming the same effort – 'e'd got 'is jacket round it,
wrapped round the bit o' pig, on 'is shoulder.

An' I said, 'Dunner worry about the hams, let's have the sides' – boy, it
was good bacon, too. So we took the buggers home – an' I tell you what, it
was bloody hard work. Then I said to Griff, 'We inner goin' to leave the rest
– we'll 'ave a walk up there after tea.' We went up in the dark: 'cause we
knowed the ground, didn't we? An' we took the rest. An' then we went down
the pub – down the back way, through the gates, an' down the garden: an' I
said to Griff, 'We'll drop 'em in 'ere, in the green 'ouse' – those hams, see. So
we went in an' called landlord to one side – we was broke, see, as we was
always, like. 'Cause that landlord'd 'ave anything, anything that was going.
An' I said, 'Arthur, come you 'ere a minute.' An' 'e said, 'I warrant you
want a bloody sub [loan], do yer?' – 'e shouted it out in front o' everybody.
An' I said, 'No, I dunner want a sub, I want to see you a minute.' So I took
'im up the garden, an' 'e got a light. An' I said, 'What about them there,
now: there's two hams there. You can 'ave em cheap.' 'Cause, well, they
didn't belong to us, exactly. So we made ten pounds on the deal – that was
pretty reasonable, wan't? 'Cause we 'ad to carry the buggers a long way,
like!

Anyway, the side I kept, it came now that I cut 'im in 'alf, an' I cut 'im up
in the larder and hanged 'im up. An' I sez to myself, I'll take some o' this to
work – I'll cook it in the wood, start a bit of a fire and 'ave a frizzle-up. An'
bugger me, we was cookin' this bacon on a bit o' stick, when that bloody old
farmer came riding by. The farmer that'd left it there. An' 'e never said a
bloody word – 'e just give us a look, but 'e never said a bloody word.

But 'e got done in the end. 'E 'ad two pigs hanged down the well in 'is
yard – hanged on the well chain. An' 'e was goin' to Birmingham every wik

and selling 'em. But they got onto 'im, and it cost 'im I dunno 'ow much. ——, 'is name was: lousy old bugger 'e was. Well, you'd ha' done the same as me, wouldn't you? O' course, I wouldn't pinch money nor nothin' like that: but anything t'eat, I'd eat – I'd gotta 'ave it, see. You got to. 'Cause it was illegal, what he was doing, wasn't it?

Now then, Charles, dunner you tell 'em 'up there' as we told you that, or we'll ha' the Min. of Ag. down on we!

RABBITS

Another animal which helped to 'mend the pantry' – as well as to provide both sport and pocket-money – was the rabbit. Properly cooked, it could even provide a fine Christmas dinner, as Edith Watkins remembers:

When I was a little girl, at Cwmgilla, we used to very often have rabbit at Christmas – stuffed rabbit, it would be stuffed with sage and onion. We've often had a rabbit for Christmas: two rabbits, often, on a long dish.

Some people kept 'hutch rabbits', but the majority of those eaten were the wild variety – as often as not poached, says Arthur Wade:

I'll tell you what I used to do, when I was down on a farm other side o' Burton Agnes, down in t' 'low country'. I used to goo poaching rabbits. I used to sell 'em to our carrier, and he used to tek 'em to Driffield. I used to get ninepence a couple, but mind, they'd got to be good big rabbits. Would they be shot or snared? Noo, I'd catch 'em in me hand! Because down in that low country, they had hedges, and wheerever there was a gap in hedge, they used to put thorns and a couple of stakes to fence it up: well, they'd rot down, and you could go under there then, and d'you know, the bank was as dry as snuff, even in t'middle o' winter. And I used to goo down there, and I used to tek farmer's dog, when they didn't know, like – poor owd Nell, she got to be a bigger poacher nor me! She'd snuff 'em out, and when I knew where they was, I used to get on me hands and knees, and I used to scrape it out – because it was all loose stuff under them hedges – until I'd got one.

But, I made biggest mistake o' my life, first time I did it. I'd grabbed rabbit out, and I was that thrilled – and then two more ran out! But they never did it again on me: because after that, I always used t'have an old bag with me, and when I got hold of first rabbit's legs and pulled him out, other hand was shoving this bag in: then I could get 'em when I liked. They couldn't get too far down th' hole, you see, because those holes was in hedge bank, and hedge bank was only so thick. We kept ourselves in wi' pocket-money that way.

In one Suffolk village – Lindsey near Hadleigh – rabbits also provided the basis for an indoor sport. Jim Spooner (b. 1903) recalled it for me in the White Rose pub (a haunt of his for over sixty years) where 'The Old Twizzler' – a species of roulette wheel, with a centrally pivoted needle which spins until it comes to rest opposite a number on the disc – is still fixed to a roof beam.

But I've seen some changes here, thet I hev. I can remember th' old boys a-coming up here wi' their short clay pipes in their mouths. Little old short pipes, clay pipes. Doctor Grange at Bildeston, he used to say to me, 'Jim, what you want to smoke thet wooden pipe for? Why don't you smoke a clay pipe, that's more healthier. You'll git more comfort out o' a clay pipe than you do a wooden one.' They used to gi' they clay pipes away: when they old boys'd git a half ounce o' baccer, there'd be a clay pipe chucked in wi' it, free.

A wet day like this 'un, when they couldn't work, them boys'd git up here dinner-times, and they'd git on thet 'ere Old Twizzler. You'd twizzle that 'ere thingummy round – you ha' three goos each – and the highest take the prize. Perhaps some on 'em bring in a brace o' rabbits, and then th' old baker from Hadleigh, he raffle off some bread or cakes: or they used to raffle off beer, or baccer, or cigarettes. But it was mostly rabbits was the prizes.

They used to kitch the rabbits theirselves. They'd set the snares in the arternoon, and goo and look round at nights, and they'd mebbe git half-a-dozen rabbits. We was allowed to kitch rabbits where I worked, and there was thet many rabbits them time o' days, three on us got so many once, we had to tek a horse and tumbril to git 'em home, look. We weren't allowed to kitch hares – thet's game: but o' course we *used* to kitch one now and agin.

Them rabbits made sixpence each then, and a penny the skin. My wife used to skin 'em, and I used to say, 'Here y'are, you can ha' thet penny!' You break the hind legs at the joint, and poke that through the coat, then that all came off clean as you like. But I couldn't flee [flay, skin] one now, no, not if you was to arst me!

Old Beckett from Hadleigh used to come and buy they skins. He used to be an old fish-man, he came round wi' bloaters and herring, two bob a dozen. He used to take a lot o' skins, that old man. And Jake Garden o' Bildeston used to take our rabbits: he used to pay me sixpence apiece, big 'uns or little 'uns. And beer was fourpence a pint, in them days!

GEESE AND PIGEONS

Fowls, too, were a vital element in cottage and farmhouse economy. Where there was space and feed for enough of them – as on the mill-cum-farm where Mrs Flinton of Burgh('Bruff')-on-Bain, Lincolnshire was brought up – they could indeed provide 'mother' with all her housekeeping money, as well as a bit extra for Christmas. It had better be explained that 'scalding' (steaming) the newly killed geese makes plucking immeasurably easier: 'otherwise', I've heard it said, 'you'd have to feather 'em with a pair o' pliers.'

The wife had the money from the eggs and butter to keep the house, and she didn't touch nothing of the other money. And if you sold a chicken or a goose, that was mother's money too. We used to keep thirty or forty geese, and we'd dress 'em and take 'em to Louth market, for Christmas. We used to fit the wash-house up wi' trestles, and there was Mother and Mrs Cook – her we used to call 'Mother o' Burgh', [p. 223] – and the waggoner and his boy. They used to start just after twelve on a Sunday night, and they'd be at it while about four next day, scalding and plucking all these geese, and Mother drawing 'em all. Dad would kill 'em all wi' a little penknife: and he got the goose between his legs, hold their heads tight and just make a hole behind the head, and let the blood run out: well, now they reckon that's cruel.

Of course, Mother wouldn't start anything before twelve on a Sunday, because she believed in keeping the Sabbath day; but after midnight, that was Monday, wasn't it? So when they'd finished, they'd pack 'em all in baskets and take 'em to Louth market. And Mother's geese was very popular, because she had a special way of blanching them. She used to put 'em all round the pantry shelf, then she'd mix a boil of salt and water, and soak some nice bits o' linen in it. And she'd lay this here linen on their breast, and that fetched all the red off them that had got there from killing and scalding 'em, so they was all beautiful and white. And the woman on the next stall, her's was all red, and nobody would buy 'em when they saw them next to Mother's. 'Get 'em sold, Mrs Smithson,' she said, 'Get 'em sold, and then mebbe I can sell mine!'

The once widespread keeping of pigeons and doves – for their flesh, eggs and manure rather than their ornamental value – was already becoming uncommon by the beginning of this century: which is surprising, for (at least as practised by the Smithsons) it represented nearly a hundred per cent profit.

And the money from the pigeons, *that* was Mother's. They was wild pigeons really, blue rock-doves. We had this dovecote, and these blue rocks would just come in from round about: and we always kept a big mirror in the cote, to 'tice [entice] them in. Because they'd get in front of a mirror, you know, and they'd go in like anything: you'd hear 'em cooing like mad. Well, they'd get in, and they'd breed. And every so often, when the cote was full, a man would come with some crates, and he and Dad would climb up into the cote and catch them all. Then we'd clean the mirror and we'd start off again: they'd just come in, and we'd feed 'em with the chickens, and soon enough the cote'd be full again. So man would come again, and take mebbe forty or fifty off to Louth market, to sell for food.

And not just for food. From what I've heard elsewhere in Lincolnshire, it seems probable that some of these 'blue rocks' were bought for the 'sport' of live trap-shooting. At a given signal the birds were either launched into the air by hand or released from their coops, and the assembled guns would compete to see who could shoot the most. Rock-doves were considered more sporting for this purpose than wood-pigeons, because their swifter flight made them harder to hit.

In at least one part of the country, moreover, sea-birds contributed – albeit involuntarily – both to 'the replenishment of the housewife's larder' and that of the farm labourer's pocket.

CLIMMING

Bempton, near Bridlington, where the Yorkshire Wolds plunge sheer into the North Sea in a sweep of chalk cliffs over three hundred feet high, is the site of one of the largest sea-bird colonies on the British mainland, now owned by the Royal Society for the Protection of Birds. In May and June each year, hundreds of thousands of birds congregate there to nest, and ornithologists flock with equal enthusiasm to observe, among them frequently myself. As a sufferer from hereditary fear of heights (my father claimed to be nervous of pavement kerbs, and my grandfather used to take formal farewell of his family before tipping his hansom-cabbie to drive over London Bridge as quickly as possible), I find it a stomach-turning experience merely to peer over the cliff edge. So I was appalled to learn that the iron stakes still to be seen there were once used by egg-collectors, to secure the ropes upon which they deliberately descended into the horrid abyss.

'Scoot-egging' or 'climming', as it is known locally, was probably already an established Bempton industry by the sixteenth century. It suffered a severe decline in mid-Victorian times, due to the popular holiday sport of shooting massive numbers of sea-birds from boats; picked up again after this was banned in 1869; and then went into a further decline after the 1939–45 war before itself becoming illegal nearly thirty years ago. So I was fortunate indeed to meet Sam Robson (b. 1912), the son and grandson of 'climmers' and one of the last survivors of 't'old kids that went scoot-eggin''. To him and his 'gang', it seemed neither romantic nor particularly intrepid. Nor did they see themselves as wanton despoilers of wildlife; and those inclined to condemn them as such should perhaps consider the words of the Bempton vicar of 1946, who commended them

*by name 'for the assistance they have given in the replenishment of the housewife's larder,
which at times during recent years has suffered from depletion owing to war conditions'.*

It's been going on donkey's years, the climming. Long before my time, it
started: me dad used to do it, and me grandad a-front on 'im. They'd start
off with *their* dads, when they were about twelve, I should think: me and me
brothers all started together, and Grandfather came with us, to show us all
how to carry on. At one time o' day, men used to tek their wives, two men
and two wives together: the men would be climmer and anchor-man, and
the two wives'd help to pull up. But in them days they didn't go so far down
as we did. There was more birds about then, and they only climbed top half
of cliff, 'cause it was too hard work for women to pull 'em back whole
distance. In my time birds had dwindled down, and *we* had to go right down
to bottom, more or less three hundred foot, to get owt at all.

Four chaps would get together to make up a gang: you'd have to have
four, because you needed three to pull climmer up. We'd mostly be farm
chaps, who'd arranged to have the six weeks of the season off: or often it
might be young married blokes that were out o' work, or short o' money.
Because there was no dole for farm workers then: if you'd no work, you'd no
money, and that's all there was about it – you had to do owt in them days.
There might be as high as four or five gangs working here, and there was
some more at Flamborough.

First of all, you had to rent your patch of cliff off the farmer who owned it.
You'd maybe take the length of a field, and you used to barter with eggs for
it – you'd promise to give him so many of the eggs you collected: you
couldn't pay money, you hadn't any. I've heard me dad say that in his time
one farmer would only let 'em have his cliff on condition that they knocked
off at turnip-hoeing time, and then they'd go and help hoe his turnips: he
wanted to make sure they went to him, because you couldn't ever seem to
get enough hands for turnip hoeing in them days.

When we started depended on weather to a day or two, but it'd probably
be about the 8th or 9th of May: we'd start then, and we'd maybe go on for
six weeks, though that would vary, too. We'd pick out best spots on our
patch, and we clumb those spots every three days. You had to do that, to
make sure eggs were fresh: otherwise you'd be getting so many dicky 'uns.
Say you went down on 8th May, and collected all the eggs from that spot:
well, when you clumb that spot three days later, you'd know all the new
eggs couldn't be more than three days old. We'd climb all those spots in
strict rotation, in strict order, every three days.

When we'd clumb all lot twice over, we called that a 'fling': and we'd
have a first, second and third fling during season. You see, we were mainly
after guillemots' and razorbills' eggs, and they only lay the one: at least, the
young birds only lay the one, but the old birds would lay one, and if that was

Scoot-egging. Sam Robson (second from right) and his gang after a successful egg-collecting 'fling' on Bempton cliffs, East Yorkshire, c. 1947. Sam's brother Harold, the gang's 'climmer' (second from left), is still wearing his collecting bags and in the foreground is the rope on which he was lowered.

taken, they'd lay another, and they'd lay a third one if you kept taking 'em. And young birds always laid a fraction earlier: 8th of May, if it was good weather, you'd have the young birds' eggs, and by about the 12th the older ones would start.

So first fling wasn't so good, because you were only getting young birds' eggs, and only getting *them* in bits and bats: you might be climbing almost for nowt when you first started. We always reckoned second fling was the best, because then you'd be getting all t'lot: all the old birds, and some of the later young ones as well. That was when we made most of our money. First and second flings were only about three days apart, but you used to reckon about twelve or fourteen days between second and third flings: of course, we used to get oddments in between flings, because they didn't all lay at same time. Third fling wasn't so good as second, because you only got the old birds then, and not all of *them*, because they wouldn't all lay again. And after that it would be whittling down to where it wasn't paying you, so you'd knock off and go back on farm. At latter end, if any collectors came round and wanted some to blow, you might go down just the once and get 'em, because it didn't matter if they were a bit off, a bit bloodshot-like.

The gang

There'd be four in a gang, and of course you had to have your 'climmer' – that's broad Yorkshire for 'climber'. That was always the same fella, and climmer in our gang was my brother Harold: I went down meself a few times, of course, but he generally liked me to stay up top and be his anchor-man. He wouldn't trust nobody else to do it: he wanted somebody he could really trust, and who knew what they were doing.

Climmer didn't get more money than t'rest: no, it was all fair shares. Naturally, he had all the proper gear: he had a proper harness on. He had a real strong belt round his middle, with two loops on it, and you tied the main waist-rope he was lowered by to that with a figure-eight knot, one that won't slip. That belt was more or less round his bottom, and he used to sit in it: he had two straps that went between his legs, and held him in. Then he had a little brace across his chest, wi' two spring clips on it like a dog's lead, and two bits o' rope going from there to his waist-rope. That was in case of him getting knocked unconscious or owt, and it kept him right end up – otherwise he might hang upside down. That was biggest danger, was falling rock: because a little pebble from top has gained a lot o' weight before it's halfway down cliff, and it can knock you out. That's why climmer in our gang always used to wear an old army tin hat. But I never remember anyone badly hurt, in my time.

Most important part of climmer's job was knowing his ground: he had to get to know every bit o' that cliff face. It's absolutely different when you get ower top, you know. You look from a distance, and you think it's just a straight face – but, by Hell, it's deceiving: it goes in, it goes out, it goes all ways. You'd go over, say, thirty foot, and then you'd find it was all underneath, all concave, so you can't touch cliff. So you'd strike off wi' your feet, and swing *out*, and by the time you swung back in again you're over that bump.

You had to use your feet a lot: you aren't stood up, you're more or less sat in your breeches, with legs straight out a-front of you, and you use your feet to beat in and out o' cliff. If you didn't, you'd maybe start to spin round, and come with your back into cliff. You'd got to keep plumb. That was why it was very difficult if there was a bit o' wind on cliff face: then, if you swung out, and you didn't know your job, by the time you came back in again you'd ha' swung round and hit your back on the cliff. You'd *got* to do a lot o' swinging, because it's no use just covering that little area where you got straight down. You'd got to swing in and out, and you'd got to swing sidewards on both sides: you'd swing right, and then you grabbed hold o' cliff to hold yoursen' there while you grabbed two or three eggs, and then you'd swing back. But in lots o' spots there was ledges, and that's where you got majority of eggs.

The birds showed a bit o' display, but they wouldn't trouble climmer a lot. The worst 'uns were fulmar petrels: they didn't like you, and they used to spit all their substance at you – it does stink, an' all! That was when they were reluctant to come off nest: so climmer'd maybe take his hat off and gi'em a swipe wi' it, to shift 'em. He had a leather cuff on, to stop his hand from chafing on rope, so they couldn't hurt him much.

How long he'd be down would depend on the ledges, and the number of eggs there was: it'd maybe be half an hour from start to finish, and of course he'd go down as often as he could. There was one spot we used to climb, they call it 'Cat Nab', and that took you an hour. There was a big nab* stuck out to sea, and there'd be iron stakes stuck into cliff top. We used to put us ropes round that, go down one side, come back up, put 'em the other way ower and go down t'other side.

Climmer would have two ropes, you see: he'd have his waist-rope, and he'd have a hand-rope as well, a guide-rope. Ropes were three hundred foot long, and we used to have three sets, one set for each spot, to save carrying 'em: when we'd finished that spot, we used to bury ropes in a hole under turf, so nobody could find 'em while we needed 'em again. We'd renew one set every year: the old waist-rope would go for a hand-rope, and the old hand-rope – well, that would be getting a bit tired, so we'd flog that for waggon-bands [ropes used to secure loads on waggons] or owt.

Of course, climmer was no use wi'out rest of gang. The rope for his waist-belt was sort of fed over an iron pulley on an iron stake on cliff top – that was to keep it from chafing on cliff edge – and then it went round *anchor-man's* waist. That was generally *my* job, anchor-man: I lowered him down, and in my mind I went down *with* him, and I took all his signals on that waist-rope. Climmer knows what I'm doing, same as I know what he's doing. He'd give one pull if he wanted to be up, and two if he wanted more hand-rope down. Another chap would be hand-rope man: he sat by a stake wi' the hand-rope round it, tied wi' a clove hitch. Then, if he wants to lower some rope down, he takes clove hitch off and runs it round stake 'til climmer signals he's got enough: so I say stop, and hand-rope man ties it up again wi' another clove hitch.

We had to have another man, too, to help us pull climmer up: because it takes three to do that. When I got the signal for 'up', all three of us would pull together on waist-rope, because that's where his body is. You all pulled in rhythm, and you don't jiggle and jerk: you pull, hold what you've got, and pull again, slow and steady. You leave hand-rope tied while he gets nearly to top, because he pulls himself up on that. The younger the climmer was, the more work he did for hisself: a young chap would do a lot of his own pulling, but an older one would leave you to do it.

* * *

Scoot-egging

We used to get guillemots' eggs, razorbills', kittiwakes', fulmar petrels' and puffins' – we used to call those 'sea-parrots': but best eggs to eat were guillemots' and razorbills', what we called 'scoot eggs'. 'Is ta going scoot-egging?' we used to say. The guillemot actually was the 'scoot' – but that was only, like, the common name for it. The guillemots and razorbills used to go about in droves, and they had a leader: and if they found a shoal of fish, you could see 'em all dive down together. That's why we used to say they were like a lot o' scoots* [scouts]. We never touched gannets, though, because they were put here in Bempton to get established. And gulls' eggs were no use to us, they were all bitter. We used to jump on *them*, or owt, because there were too many of 'em, and they were driving out all the other birds. Them common gulls would pinch guillemots' and razorbills' eggs, and they'd hatch three or four of their own eggs to a guillemot's one, so they were gradually outnumbering all other birds.

Climmer had a bag on each side to put his eggs in: they'd be slung round his neck. There was two pouches on each bag: one was a little 'un at top for the tender eggs, and there was a bigger 'un for the stronger-shelled ones. The top one was for kittiwakes' eggs, because they're tender, or for owt that was a bit special. Because in them days you'd get quite a few egg collectors come round, and if you could get a clutch of sparrowhawk's eggs – it was usually four or five – you treasured them, because you could get a bit more money for 'em. They might pay, say, two quid for a clutch of sparrowhawks' (mind, you had to have the whole clutch) and when you reckoned that up, it was ten bob to each of gang.

You went by colour a lot, for collectors' eggs: if you saw an unusually marked one, you'd take care o' that, and wait 'till these collectors came. In them days, eggs was same as coin-collecting or summat: they'd get the set, and they used to trade 'em or flog 'em. They used to come all together, did collectors: you'd get as high as four or five staying in the village. It was their profession to collect eggs, and sell 'em: a lot of 'em was dealers for other collectors.

So it was more or less like an auction when you got to cliff top, sometimes. There'd be dealers there, and young kids collecting for theirselves, and you couldn't get eggs into baskets before they was all crowding round, turning over eggs to see if there was any better what they hadn't got. 'How much is this, mister, how much is that?' they'd say, if you'd any out o' the ordinary. It was a gamble, what they would pay: you demanded so much, and they'd barter you if they could, to beat you down. We took what we could get, because we wanted rid on 'em: we didn't want eggs, we wanted money.

We'd sell what we could at cliff top, and rest we used to bring in to village. Because most of our eggs, people used to buy 'em to eat: they used to cart

The birds that produced the most appetizing eggs: the guillemot and razorbill – the 'scoots' –
(centre and right) and the kittiwake (left).

'em to market at Brid[lington] and sell 'em, and some went further, to Leeds, or owt. There was wheelers and dealers in that, too. They'd come and fetch 'em, or else they'd have a confederate in village, like: we never bothered, as long as we sold 'em.

'Scoot' eggs were best for eating: you could boil 'em or fry 'em and if you kept 'em vertical they'd keep for a month or two. Kittiwakes' was nice, too, but they used to crack very easy. When I used to come home on a night – I was a youngish bloke then, and I was always hungry – I used to bring all cracked 'uns, and we used to break 'em all into a saucer first, to make sure they were fresh, and then tip 'em all into a basin. I remember we had a dozen in, yar [one] night, and we put 'em all in frying pan wi' salt and pepper and vinegar on, and a rasher o' bread: and we ate the lot. They were very nice, but the whites were thicker than an ordinary hen's egg. The yolk was just the same as hen's, but the white was more rubberified – you had to champ 'em.

The end of climming

All through my time birds was dwindling and dwindling: because the guillemot and the razorbill have a lot of enemies, and gulls and kittiwakes was driving 'em out. So towards the end it wasn't worth taking time off your job, and we just used to go evenings and weekends. Then, of course, it stopped altogether by law, in 1954: they stopped it altogether.

When birds had really started dwindling, some gangs used to give demonstrations to holidaymakers, to make a bob or two. And sometimes odd people used to want to go ower themselves. 'How much is it?' they used to say. And we'd say, 'It's nowt to go ower, but it's ten bob to come back!'

Some would actually manage it, but a lot backed out when they got to cliff edge and looked ower! So we'd take their ten bob first. Well, we were there to make a bob or two, and you couldn't take gear off climmer and put it on

'You just walk backwards over the cliff, and don't think about it.' Sam Robson about to descend the three-hundred-foot cliff at Bempton, equipped with egg-collecting bags and a 'tin hat': he holds his hand-rope, and the waist-rope on which he is raised and lowered is firmly attached to his body harness.

this other bloke, and then he gets to cliff edge and doesn't want to go. Because all that time we aren't earning nowt: we could have had two spots clumb, the time we were messing about wi'em.

Like we had some miners come one day: they'd been pubbing, of course, it would be a miner's outing. And they said height of cliff was nowt, they went further than that down t'pit, and all this that and th' other. So I said, 'Why, it's different down there to what it is in pit: you're in a cage there, just getting lowered down.'

'Na', he says, 'this is nowt': and he *would* have a go. Well, we wanted his ten bob first. And when we got him to edge, his face was as green as grass. When I asked him was he going or not, he just shook his head – he couldn't speak, for fear o' vomiting. No, he *didn't* go!

I suppose it seemed like suicide to him, and it probably sounds dangerous to *you*: but it was only dangerous if you didn't know your job, and know your cliff. I don't think there was ever a Bempton man badly hurt in my time, or in my father's, or my grandfather's: them that did get hurt was always outside people messing about, that didn't know what they were at. But if you know your job, its safe enough. You just walk backwards over cliff, and don't think about it: and it isn't policy to look down too much, you always keep your face to the wall. The blokes that was climming thought nowt about it: we needed the money, and it was just a job. And that was it!

THE VILLAGE BUTCHER

However plentiful the home-fed bacon, rabbits or sea-birds' eggs might be, those housewives who could afford to bought 'butcher's meat' for Sundays, and many regarded 'a real butcher's meat dinner every *day' as the apogee of prosperity. But unlike some of their descendants, who insist on their meat being neatly and impersonally packed by the supermarket, they preferred to see their joint 'on the hoof' before they bought it: and being without refrigeration, they needed to fetch their liver and kidneys direct from the slaughterhouse. So a village butcher had literally to* be *a 'butcher', and neither he nor his customers could afford to distance themselves from the animals they ate. Though when it came to killing fully grown bulls with a pole-axe, Ted Bateson's stepfather must sometimes have wished he could!*

Ted comes from Skipsea in Holderness, in what is now known by officialdom as 'North Humberside', but by its inhabitants as the East Riding of Yorkshire. Bounded to the north and west by the Yorkshire Wolds, and to the east by the North Sea, this flat coastal plain is closer in spirit to Lincolnshire than to the mines and industry of the West Riding: for it is an entirely agricultural region, whose nickname of 'the back o' nowhere' sums up its feeling (at least away from the caravan-infested seaside) of remoteness and timelessness. The distinctive accent and many dialect words used by its older country-folk – as well as their commonly ice-blue eyes – are a reminder of their Danish Viking origins: and the story goes that Scandinavian servicemen stationed there during the Second World War could easily communicate with them – 'They didn't speak English, but they could understand East Riding.'

Well now then, I'm going to tell you the honest truth – I've never known who me father was. But I've heared this tale, like, that he was a 'bullocky', a beast-man on a farm: and when me mother wanted to marry him, her parents wouldn't let her. So I've never known who he was, and of course I've never bothered. I was born very near against Blackpool, in Lancashire: but I just forget what the name of the place was – it comes back to me sometimes. That was in 1897, the 12th of June.

And when I was three year old, I came to Skipsea. I think we had some family at Skeleton Farm at Skipsea, and Mother had sometimes come to them, and that's how *she* got to this country. She married a Skipsea man, they called him Morris Hawkins: and I always went [by the name of] Hawkins when I went to school. But I took me t'other name when I finished, and I've had it ever since – Edward Bateson.

When my father – well, I always called him me father, though he wasn't – married me mother, he was butchering at Skipsea. He'd taken over from *his* father, who'd been the Skipsea butcher afore him. I used to go round with him while I were holidaying, so's I could look after his horse and cart while he was in the houses and farms. They was all horsed, butcher-carts in them days. And I remember there was one butcher at Beeford, they called him Biglin: and we were once at Dunnington at same time as he was, with his cart. And he went into the houses on business, and he left his cart-hetch [the hatch of his box-cart] down – they used to let hetch down, and hang steelyards on to wire the meat – well, he left that down to tek his meat into doors, and afore he came back, his hoss set off on its own. Set off down road, and his meat was all dropping in the road, and we set off after him, picking his bits of meat up!

My father'd kill one bullock a week. He killed Wednesday morning, and he went out Thursday, Friday and Saturday, while me mother looked after butcher's shop. He'd buy the bullocks off the farmers, and me and me pal'd have to go and fetch them. My father'd say to me on a Tuesday, when I went back to school after dinner, 'Bring your pal home for tea.' And he used to get a penny and his tea, and he thought he'd gotten the world! Then, after tea, we used to go to some farm to fetch the bullock we were gonner kill.

And I mind one day, when we'd had our tea, Father said, 'We aren't off while [until] it's dusk to fetch that bullock.' And he went with us and all that night, which he didn't usually. Thinks I, 'What th' heck's all this for? What's on here?'

Well, when we got it, it were a little heifer, all skin and bone. And d'you know, it were that poor that it never said 'Baw' – it never bealled [bellowed] nor nothing – 'til we were turning right by church corner at Skipsea. And there was a farm just t'other side there, and there was a bullock bealled there. And when this bullock bealled, our little heifer started to beall too, and it bealled all the way up the street – and when folks heared it, they kept opening their doors to see what it was. And when they *did* see it, they didn't want butcher-cart *that* week, 'cause it was all skin and bone. And I thought, no wonder he wanted it fetching after dark.

Christmas bullock was just the opposite. It was always from the one farmer – they called him Crozier – he fed it every year, and it was always fed tied up. By, it were always a good 'un. And we used to take it and bray [drive] it round Skipsea, for all the folks to see. There was some money on Christmas bullock.

Killing the bull

We used to kill bulls, too. There was only me father and me mother and me to do it: and I was only ten year old – no, I wasn't that. I had to stop at home the morning he was killing a bull, and we all three had to get up at four o'clock, afore it was daylight. First Father'd go to pinehouse* – it's where you kept them, just afore you killed them. And some bulls were that wild, he had to get up on top of roof to get rope on it, to get it out into slaughterhouse. And when he'd got rope on, he'd drive it through to slaughterhouse, and Mother and me'd pull on rope from outside through a hole in slaughterhouse wall, down near ground. And just outside the hole was a great post. And Mother and me pulled this rope through, while bull came right where he wanted it to stand, to knock it down: then we had to keep rope wrapped round this here post while he struck it.

He'd strike bull with a patent affair – you know, a pole-axe: they wain't let you kill 'em that way now, you know. It was like an axe at one side, and just like a spike on t'other, as thick as thy finger. And he'd strike the spike into bull's head, right in between th' eyes, and down it would go. It wouldn't get up again! And as soon as it dropped, he used to shout out: then Mother and me – we were still outside in th' open – would slacken off rope and rush in. And then he'd cut its throat, and bleed it, and skin it, and of course I had to help.

When they knew he was killing, folks used to bring sixpences in a basin. And when bull got opened, he took out guts and put them on a table. Then I had to run puddings – as you called the guts – through, and fetch fat off them. And if he just happened to look behind when he was tending to bullock, and I'd just made a mistake and nicked puddings – up came his foot in my behind! When all stuff was ready, me mother'd come in and put bits of all sorts into these basins – lungs, kidneys, liver, brains and skettins:* and when they was filled, I'd take them out to them that wanted them, and they used to have it for dinner. And there was as much as would feed four, at anyways, for sixpence. By gum, killing day were a big day!

And, of course, he'd kill pigs, for labourers in cottages: 'cause in them days nearly all folks would keep a pig or two. He used to kill them at Monday, and cut 'em up at Tuesday, for eighteenpence or two bob apiece. I think some Mondays we had nearly twenty pigs hung up in slaughterhouse. And there was them that'd come and bring a jug or a basin, to get blood out of their pigs to make black puddings on. It had to be got as it came out of pig, when Father cut its throat: they used to bring a jug and a great long wooden spoon, and stir it while it went cool. They had to keep stirring, 'cause if it went stiff afore it got cold, it was no good for black puddings.

He'd kill them at the Monday, and cut them up of a Tuesday, all for eighteenpence. They used to come with their barrows to fetch home the meat, and a lot would ask him to go salt the hams for them, which he did.

* * *

4

HILL FARM

A SWALEDALE WOMAN

So far, most of our 'country voices' have come from lowland farms. But now it is time to go up into the high hills, and our principal guide there will be 'Maggie Joe' Chapman, born in 1899. She now lives at Askrigg in Wensleydale, North Yorkshire, a village recently made famous as the television setting of James Herriot's All Creatures Great and Small. *Surnames here are still in short supply – a call for 'Mr Metcalfe', they joke, would be answered by half the village – and there were once so many Chapmans and so many Maggies that:*

I needed a name to myself. My husband's sister was Maggie, and I was Maggie, and I remember eight of us being sat round table, having this party. Somebody said, 'Pass that to Maggie', and youngest daughter said, 'Which Maggie?' So they said, 'You're Joe's wife, so we'll call you "Maggie Joe"', and it's stuck ever since: I really like it.

Though she has farmed for most of her married life in Wensleydale and its offshoot, Bishopdale, Maggie Joe's early life was focused on Swaledale – a mere five miles north of Askrigg, but linked to it only by a mountain road which is even now often impassable during the long snows of winter. In this region of east–west communications along river valleys, the two dales are therefore quite distinct in character, and proud of it.

Yet they have much in common. Both are emphatically hill-farming areas – even the valley bottoms are seven hundred feet above sea-level – and both share a jigsaw landscape of small fields and dry-stone walls, rising via vertical rocky 'scars' to sliced-off tops and heather-covered moorland plateaux. And, like all the north Pennine dales, both bear the

---

Hill-farming country: dry-stone walls and field barns at Thwaite, near Muker in upper Swaledale, North Yorkshire. Each field barn accommodated four cows and a 'mew' (hay store) and is carefully set so that the liquid manure flowing from it will fertilize as much as possible of the adjacent pasture.

---

imprint of the Norwegian settlers who came here in the tenth century by way of Ireland and Cumbria. From them originated many of the place-names Maggie mentions – like Gunnerside, Burtersett and Satron, all derived from the Norwegian saetr, *'hill pasture' – and the dialect words she used when she talks of 'heughing' lambs or knitting 'lofrums'. That such words have to do with sheep is no accident, for these dales have always been primarily sheep country – though the black-faced Swaledales have long shared the lower-lying pastures and 'inland' fields round the farms with the dairy cattle which produce the famous Wensleydale cheese.*

Kit Calvert, also from Wensleydale, adds a tale to this chapter: and Mrs Mills (b. 1895) and her son Ron (b. 1916), of Newcourt, Velindre, near Hay-on-Wye, will be telling us something of sheep-farming ways among the Welsh border hills. But now, as she herself said to me, 'Sit quiet and listen to Maggie's story.'

I'm really what you'd call a Swaledale woman, from Muker: but I've got a lot of connections here in Askrigg. I married an Askrigg man, of course: and a lot of my mother's family used to live over here. My mother's auntie – that was Sarah Banks – started the firm of Bankses [now a large animal-feed concern] here at Askrigg: I remember her very, very well. She was left a widow with three children, and there was no Social Security then, nothing of that as we have today: and she was left without very much money. Well, they were building the railway up Wensleydale at the time [1869–78], so she started baking bread for the navvies, because there was no bakeries around in them days: and then she started cooking a bit of meat for them. And then, at Easter time, she used to boil up a lot of eggs and dye them for the children – that sort of thing. She struggled and struggled, and she opened this shop: and when her son left school, she sent him away to be taught the business proper. And that son was the great-grandfather to young Billy Banks that's here today. So that was how the Bankses business started, from nothing at all, until it's a big business today.

A real goer-ahead: Granny Scott

Now this old Sarah Banks's sister was my grandmother. She came from Muker, and her name, before she married, was Hunter: that was a very familiar name in Swaledale, and there's quite a lot of Hunters left there yet. Well, my mother was born before Grandmother was married – which was a *terrible* thing in them days, you know, though it's nothing thought of today. The boy responsible didn't suffer, it was only the girl that was shunned: never thought of any more, you might say. My granny was a wonderful woman, a real goer-ahead sort of woman: but wi' her having Mother, no other young man would look at her – they'd never think of such a thing. So she went home, back into Swaledale. And eventually she married an oldish man, which *we* called Grandad, though he wasn't really: he was an old man

'A very charitable woman, but as hard as iron.'
Maggie Joe Chapman's 'Granny Scott':
unpaid midwife, layer-out and district nurse of
Muker in Swaledale, c. 1905.

on two sticks when *we* knew him. But she did have four children to him – he managed that all right! *His* name was Scott, but my mother's name was Hunter, because she kept her mother's name. Being illegitimate went through life with her: people didn't look down on her, don't think that, because she was a well-liked woman – but she always felt it. There was always that little bit of a chip on the child, which was all wrong. And when what we called wir [our] grandad died, Mother didn't get any of the bit of money he had.

My *real* grandfather, my mother's *real* father, became biggest horse dealer in the north of England. And when it came Askrigg Hill Fair, he always used to come to Hill Top and have his lunch with us. But me mother never liked him coming, because she never got over being illegitimate, you know. So she was always in a bad temper when he came, and one time she snapped at him about something: and I'll always remember how he walked up to her and put his hand on her shoulder, and he said; 'Belle, I always owned you were mine, and you *are* mine: and I've never run off it.' But me mother, she didn't want to know, and she'd never be friends with him. Us kiddies thought he was grandest fella living, though, because he always gave us a shilling each!

He never *had* run off it, mind. He would have married me granny, but she wouldn't have him, no. In them days lads like him had no money, you know: they worked at home, and they didn't get a wage, they never got a penny. So he had no money to marry with, and *daren't* tell what he'd done, at first. Because Grandmother was a servant girl in the house, you see, and *he* was the son of the family: and it was a big let down for the son to marry the servant girl, in them days. But when it did come up, his two old aunties that lived here with him said, 'You'll get her married!' And he says, 'I can't marry her, I've nae money.' So they gave him a hundred pound (which was a lot of money in them days) and set him off walking over to Muker to marry me granny. But *she* wouldn't have him. Because by then she'd got stout with me mother, and she says, '*I'm* not going into no church a disgrace!' She never did have him: and afterwards he went over to Reeth, and started taking horses to fairs, and he became biggest horse dealer in north of England. Woodward was his name. And it's so funny, none o' my sons is really horse-minded, but me youngest daughter knows horses from A to Z, and one of *her* daughters has gone into horses, and wins all sorts o' prizes.

So me granny married an old man, which she would never have done normally: because she was a very smart woman, my granny. She did very well for herself, because the man she married had a farm of his own, he was a landowner: but all the same, they never looked man and wife. She was a very smart woman, a thrifty woman, and he was on two sticks.

I remember me 'grandfather' and grandmother very well, because us children often used to stay there, until they died. Grandfather died first, and then she died a few years later, when I was ten: so that would be in about 1909. She died in her fifties, but she was an old woman to us. She was a real goer-ahead: I had curly hair, and she used to get comb and go straight through it, until tears was rolling down me face. And t'old grandfather, that was on two sticks, used to get hold of me, and say, 'Cum here, me lass, she hasn't a bit o' sense!': and he used to brush away at me hair so quietly. You know, them's lovely things to think about when you get old.

But Grandmother was a very clever woman this way: she was a good nurse. Which they didn't train nurses then, but Granny went when every baby was born in Muker, and when anybody died, she'd go and lay them out. It was usually the same person who brought people into the world in a village, and who laid them away, and Muker was her place. And when the children wasn't well, people used to send 'em to Granny's: 'Mam's sent me to see what you think *this* spot is', or t'other spot. She was very clever with herbal remedies, too, but I really don't remember what they were.

I know *we* used to have treacle and brimstone – ugh! We had to have that every morning in springtime, when we'd been through winter: they started in March giving us this brimstone and treacle, to clear all badness out on us that's got into us in winter. It was horrible! Then there was Epsom salts: Mother used to mix 'em and put 'em in a three-gills bottle, and come up with a wine-glass for each of us to have in bed. We used to have a fern plant halfway down t'stairs: and it was wonderful it didn't die, 'cause it used to get half o' mine!

Yes, Granny was a very clever woman, and very clean: but she was as hard as iron, nothing affected her. I remember hearing me grandad say, when she'd been called out to a confinement, 'What have you got, Margaret, this time?' And she just stood and said, 'I've got a bouncin' lad', she said, 'but it's deed.' Just as if a cat had lost kittens! 'It's deed', she said, 'and thoo nivver saw sike a set* [such a fuss] as she's makkin' in thee life – Lord, it's a repairable loss!' That's what they thought of losing babies, 'a repairable loss'. I should be only a little girl, and I didn't know what it meant, but it stuck in my mind.

Mind, she was a very *charitable* woman. As I say, she married financially well: they were on their own farm, and considered fairly comfortable, wealthy even. And on a Sunday morning – I can see them yet – she used to put a great big pan onto t'fire, wi' a big hunk o' beef and a great square o' bacon in, and boil that. And then the soup off that (we called it broth) she put into basins, and us children took it out to all the poor people of Muker – and that was their Sunday dinner! They were ready wi' *their* basins, and some were coming nearly to meet us. Old David always met us and took it back hisself: he was ready for it.

Because there was no pension then, you know, there was nothing, and there were quite a lot of poor people in Muker. I think they'd be old lead-miners, mostly, because a lot o' lead mining was taking place over there. One couple I remember, the father was an invalid, and he couldn't work, so we used to take quite a lot of stuff to them. Grandfather and Grandmother were comfortable, and they didn't gather a lot of money together and bank it, like we do today: they did that sort o' thing *with* their money – it was much better. They didn't crave for money, same as we do. As long as they could carry on, they were just as rich as we are, that has two or three farms and all sorts.

Tragedies

Us children used to stop wi' Granny to be near school, because we lived right up at top, two-and-a-half or three miles away: so we used to stop wi' Granny during week, and go home Friday night. But after they died, we walked to Muker school every day, wi' a sandwich in wir pocket, a drink o' water to wash it down with, and walked three mile back, wi' a good dinner to come back to. There was four of us, two boys and two girls: well, there's three of us still living, and the youngest is eighty, so it didn't kill us, did it? And you know, we knew every flower and bird's nest on way to that school!

We used to walk from our farm, Hill Top; it was right on the top, and it was the first house you came to after you left Askrigg on the road to Muker. My grandfather – my father's father – had been tenant there before my father: his name was Guy, and in them days Muker was full of Guys, same as Askrigg was full of Chapmans. Now my grandfather Guy was killed with a bull, one he'd brought up himself. It was a Sunday morning, and me grandfather used to play the bass fiddle in Muker church. There was an orchestra in the church, them days: me grandfather played the bass, and there was a fiddle, and I wouldn't know whether they had drums or not, but they had four or five in orchestra. Well, me grandfather had put his best Sunday clothes on to go, and he passed this pasture where the bull was: and there was some heifers there, and he heard one of them in service, and he wanted to see which one it was. That was why he climbed over the wall, they think. And they always think that the bull didn't know him in his Sunday clothes, and that was why it gored him. Me father said he hadn't a rag left on him when they found him; it had gored him to death. He was a real good man, my grandfather, one of the best-living men there was: everybody said he wouldn't play a dirty trick on anybody. But the bull didn't know him in his Sunday best.

We never kept a bull after. We used to bring bulls up, and keep 'em one year to service for calves, and then off, it was sold. We never kept an old bull after that – me father never would.

So after that, me father took over the farm. And he'd bought all his stock in before he married me mother. He was born about 1865, so he was seven years older than her: but he was a wonderful man, and they were very happy together. My mother would have been married before. She was a Muker woman, and engaged to be married, but her young man died with consumption a few days before they should have married. A lot died with T.B. then, you know, they died like mice. And they said she went into deep mourning, and never went out at all for a long time: it was a big shock for her. But two years after she lost Jim she was introduced to me father, and he was badly wanting a housekeeper: so they married, and they were very happy together.

Dry bread for the Misses Clarkson

Now Hill Top Farm was on an estate that belonged to two old ladies, the two Miss Clarksons that lived at Satron: there was five or six farms belonged to them, which was considered quite a lot in them days. They were born at Hill Top, was Miss Barbara and Miss Mary, and they used to often get their manager to fetch 'em up in a cart: he had a terrible set,* because she was twenty stone, was old Barbara! He used to have to get his shoulder to her, to push her into cart! So they used to come up, and they'd never knock – we'd just be messing about in t'house: they'd open front door theirselves, and open gate at bottom o' stairs, and go up to bedroom where they were born, to have a look: they always did that – as though it was going to do them any good!

They'd never *ask* to go, and of course you couldn't say anything. Landladies and landlords were strict in them days: you had to knuckle under them, because they could push you off any minute, there wasn't a law to stop them. You had to courtesy [curtsey] to 'em, if you saw 'em, and lads would take off their caps. I remember the Mayor coming up from Richmond, in first car there was at Muker, and we had to courtesy to him.

Well me father, evidently, had lived with these Miss Clarksons as servant boy: he'd been their man, their manager. So he knew all their whims and fancies, and they thought a lot about him: he was their pet. And when me mother married him, when she was a blushing bride, he said that old Barbara and Mary would be coming up to see her, to look her over. So of course she primmed herself up a bit, and put a cloth on, and laid a very nice table: she buttered the bread, and had cheese and jam and the rest, and a nice cake. But when they got sat to it, old Barbara said, 'Tha knows, Bob, thoo can't do with baith bread and butter *and* cheese: thoo'll nivver pay thee way if tha's getten a wife that does that.' And me mother sat there, and she didn't know what to do: and old Barbara said, 'Tha wants nowt wi' all these cakes and stuff. I'll tell thee what, me lad Bob, there's been some butter put into that cake. Thoo'll nivver get t'rent paid, if tha's getten an extravagant wife. Dry bread's what tha should be having.' Well, Mother was furious, and she never forgave them. But she cured 'em: because when they came up ever after, she just gave 'em dry bread. She really did.

It must have annoyed her all the more, because she really was a marvellous housekeeper, and very frugal. We hadn't to waste one *crumb* of bread, not one crumb was wasted. We were brought up very carefully, but there was always plenty to eat: we always had a big dinner *every* day, not just on Sundays. It was there for us when we came back from school. We always had roast beef on the Sunday, and we used a lot of rabbits – we had plenty of our own rabbits – and we reared our own chickens.

BUTTER AND CHEESE

Yes, Hill Top was a good farm. It was the best farm the Miss Clarksons had, and it was a lovely house, very well built in 1852 – so it was really quite new. And it was considered a big farm, then, though it wouldn't be now. We had about 180 lambing ewes, which was quite a lot, and then we used to milk 14 cows, and we'd generally have about 80 cows altogether, counting calves. They were Shorthorns, because there was no black-and-white cows [Friesians and derivatives] about then: in fact, if there was a *bit* of black on a cow, it was a disgrace to a farmer! We brought our own cows up, we didn't go to market and buy them, as they do today: we'd bring them up from calves, and keep them until they had their first calves at the three years old: then they might have two calves with us, but then we'd sell 'em off. You see, we didn't go in for milk selling like some: we had no old cows with great big bags [udders], tottery old cows that can hardly stand. No, *we* had lovely young cattle.

We didn't sell milk, but of course we made a lot of butter and cheese – that was a good part of our income. We'd make butter in t'old-fashioned tumbler churn: which Father churned, because Mother always said that if she churned the butter, she couldn't *make* it – her hands would be too hot from churning, and you *must* have a cool hand to make butter. We used to make a hundred and some pound of butter a week. That was done *before* the cattle went out to grass, which was in the last week in May – they wouldn't go out before that. Because the cows didn't calve i' autumn-time, you know, same as now: they started calving in January, and went on until April, and then finished: so's there'd be plenty of milk for the summer, for the cheese.

Then, when they got turned out, Mother would start to make cheese: she'd start at end o' May, and she'd go on maybe 'til end of October – because after that they wouldn't have much milk. They were lovely cheeses, ·*real* cheese – I can taste them yet: they were a crumbly cheese, like a Wensleydale but a bit different.

To make cheese, you have to start by getting the milk to blood heat: it's got to be warm, but not hot, *not* hot. Mother used to stand it in buckets in hot water, in the side-boiler. Sometimes people had cheese kettles, but we never had one – ours was a sort of tin. It had to be at blood heat, and then you put your rennet in: we always bought Fullwood's and Bland's, and I suppose they'll be making rennet yet. And then you put a lid on, and you draped rugs or something on to keep it warm – because your house could be like an iceberg sometimes, you know. It stood for an hour, and you took and opened it, and then you had to what we called 'break it down'. You didn't stir it hard, you just stirred it very gently with a kind of round wire grill on a wooden handle – I think they called it a breaker – and it just helped to separate the curds from the whey.

So the cheese curd went to the bottom, and the whey came to the top. You'd let it stand like that for perhaps three-quarters of an hour, until she'd settled right down, and then you took the whey off, and that went for the pigs. When the whey was off, we had a big wood to put on top of the curds: that was a weight, to weigh as much more of the liquid out as you could. Next she used to cut curd into slices, and carry it into a lead bowl (you couldn't do without a *lead* bowl), and she'd spread out slices there to drain as much of the liquid away as could. Then, at night, she crumbled it into the cheese vat with her hands, very gently: she didn't squeeze it, just crumbled it with her finger ends. And then it went out into the cheese press.

We had them old-fashioned presses, built onto the house – they're still yonder at Hill Top – where you had a great big stone to press the cheese. Well, you put it in there at night, and pressed it all night: then next morning you went and shook it out, put a clean cloth in the vat, turned cheese over, tipped it back into vat, and pressed it again, and next night it was ready to come out, and go into pickle. We always pickled our cheese, we didn't salt it. You made this pickle of salt and boiling water, and it had to cool two days before it could be used. Cheeses would swim in this pickle a day, then you turned 'em over and left 'em another day, and then they were ready. They were different altogether from these modern cheeses. They were fourteen- or fifteen-pound cheeses, and when they were pickled they kept right 'til back-end [autumn] if you wanted.

Some people would let their cheeses go to Gill, the grocer that used to come once a month, in exchange for flour, or ground rice for making puddings, and such. But we didn't do that. Once a fortnight, in summer, my father used to get up at four o'clock in t'morning, pack his cheeses in his trap, and go to Barnard Castle market with them, which was twenty mile. He went down to Low Row, then up Peatgate and over into Arkengarthdale, and then over the Stank to Barney Castle. I've gone with him often, when I was a little girl. He'd put cheeses out on flags in marketplace, and that's where we used to stand, and pit people from up north came down to buy 'em. There was one old lady came, from up Durham, and she was buying for the Co-op[erative Stores], and she used to take as many as Father would let her have, because of course he had his other customers to think of.

Well, after that'd gone on for twenty years, this lady arranged to buy all the lot, and we never went to Barnard Castle again. We just used to pack two big boxes of cheese and put 'em on train at Askrigg, on a Tuesday morning, and they went to Durham, and on Friday morning a cheque came by post. That's where all wir cheeses went, for the mining people. So that was ready money, and it was very important to us: because you'd sell a cow when it was new-calven and you didn't need it, and you only sell your sheep once a year.

The manufacture of sheep's-milk cheese – such as the famous French Roquefort – has long since been forgotten in the Dales. But it survived well into living memory in Wales, where Mrs Mills remembers making it on her parents' farm at Llaethdy (appropriately, 'milk house') on the borders of Radnorshire and Montgomery.

After we'd sold the lambs in June or July, we used to milk the ewes and make cheese from the milk: you could only do it for a few weeks, because after that the ewes'd go dry. I used to mix a lot of cow's milk with the ewe's milk – you wanted more cow's than ewe's – and then get it warm, but not hot: and I'd get some rennet from the chemist's, and put that in to make it curdle. Then I'd press it in a cheese press that we had in the house. You didn't have to do nothing with it: once you'd put the curds in and scrow [screwed] the press down, what we called the whey would come out underneath. And after it'd been in there about a week, it'd come out real firm, like a shop cheese.

But I couldn't eat it myself, I don't know why: I did never like home-made cheese. Anybody came to the house and asked you for some, I'd just give 'em a lump to take home. I did often give some to the man that came to do the thrashing. You don't often hear of people using ewe's milk now: when they milk the ewes, it mostly goes to the ground. But *I* never wasted anything: no matter what it was, I could always make a profit of it.

I was the only child, so I used to be the shepherd. I used to go round the sheep on the hill, and I always took a mouth-organ with me. I'd go round playing it to get 'em together, and by the time I'd got back to the house I'd have all the sheep following: that was when we wanted to get 'em all together for shearing, or washing.

And that's another thing they don't do now, washing sheep. But *we* always washed our sheep before we sheared 'em. There was always a brook around, and we'd what we called 'stank'* it – dam it up and make a pool in the stream. Then we'd make a bit of a pen around the stank with stakes, and get the sheep in there. One man'd go in the pool, with his clothes on, to make sure they was washed properly: he'd keep rubbing like if you was bathing a person!

RON MILLS: You'd do that a week or a fortnight before you sheared – it would help the wool to rise. But, of course, clean wool wouldn't *weigh* as much: and that's why they don't do it now. If you washed it, you'd get a penny or two more for a clean fleece: but you was losing weight, because you was washing the grease out, so you'd probably lose more than you'd earnt. But then, where you'd gain a bit *again* was with the combs and cutters of your shearing machine. When they're not washed, th' old bits of sand and muck off the hill are in the fleece, and they'd get into the cutters and take off your edge: perhaps you'd only do a dozen sheep then, whereas if they'd been washed you may have done twenty without sharpening. So it worked out about the same in th' end, whether you washed them or not!

MRS MILLS: And when you'd finished washing, perhaps a neighbour would bring *their* sheep, and do theirs the same. People were very neighbourly then. Some of the neighbours would always come when you was shearing: we'd have, say, a couple o' hundred to shear, and a few neighbours would come and help, and it would only be perhaps a couple o' days' work then. And then when they'd be shearing, they'd come after you to send a man to help them, in place of the man they'd sent to help we.

I always used to help with the shearing, and I'd make up the wool, too. You'd spread it all out, like if it was on this table: you'd turn this side in and

Rolling a fleece of wool. The fleece is spread on the board on its clipped side with the neck end furthest away, then rolled up and tied with some of the neck wool.

that side in, and roll it up. And when you'd got to the end, you'd pull some of the neck wool out and tie it round, and make a big knot.

Then that would be sent off to Newtown, and it was bought by a man as was having it every year. He was a man that sold beer, and when they came back from selling they'd always have a barrel of beer – say eighteen gallon or so. I think it was a case of 'I buy off you, you buy off me'.

Back now to Maggie Joe, to hear about

THE WISE SHEEP

Of course, sheep were the main thing. We generally had about 180–200 breeding ewes, apart from the lambs and the hogs – that's a one-year-old ewe, not breeding yet. They was all Swaledales, nothing else. Breeding ewes went to the tup [ram] end of November, and we kept tup going 'til Christmas. We let him go a week clear, unmarked, and then we'd mark him – you know, with dye on his chest, so's we'd know which ewes had been with him, and roughly the order they'd lamb in: we put ruddle [red] on for second week, and then blue on for third. Then they used to call ewes 'ruddy-arsed 'uns' and 'blue-arsed 'uns'!

So we'd start lambing about 6th of April, never before that: we wouldn't be like these down-country farms, weather wasn't fit for early lambing. I always helped, and I always helped after I was married, because I was more a sheep-farmer nor [than] me husband. He was brought up here in Askrigg, and he was very good with cows, but they'd only have a few better-bred sheep. He could go and shepherd 'em on moor, but when lambing time came, he stood back for Maggie!

Hogs wouldn't go to tup. We always used to send wir hogs away in November, for winter. They went to same place for forty years, and that was down to Hurst, below Reeth – that was quite a bit down dale from us, and not so hard: the farmer there took 'em in, gave 'em hay, and looked after 'em for us, and we paid him. That helped hogs a lot: they grew a lot better down there, and they did better for the change. We used to bring 'em back at end of May, and then they'd get onto wir moor here. Older sheep would be on moor most of year. We never kept 'em on older than four-shear [four years old], and then we sold 'em at Hawes here: down-country fellows would take 'em, that was rearing half-breed lambs, and they'd put 'em to a down-country tup for a year or two.

It wasn't just ours, the moor: it was what they call common. So much was ours, and so much was the next fella's, and the sheep all knew their own part. Wir moor went to that tarn up there, and then came Summer Lodge's moor. They call it Summer Lodge Tarn now, but *we* called it Hill Top Tarn, because it was ours: it was right on our boundary. Of course, the boundary wasn't fenced – it didn't need to be, because the sheep all knew their own part, and they'd stick to it. They were 'heughed'* to it, we said. You see, when your sheep's heughed, and you turn them out onto moor with their lambs, they heugh their own lambs there: the sheep stay there, so the lambs learn to stay there, and only odd ones go astray. They're not as silly as people think, aren't sheep.

And I'll tell you another thing, a remarkable thing. When you saw your sheep draw down off the moor, it was going to come snow. *They* knew when it was coming snow, and they were always right – they knew better than you did: they'd hang down to the moor gate, and Father would let 'em onto inland fields round the farm. Mind you, me father would go right round moor, to make sure they'd all come down: and if there was any overblown with snow, you'd maybe have to stick a pole into drift, to see if you could feel for 'em. But nearly all older sheep would come down, because they'd felt the snow coming. And just as well, because shepherding on moor tops in snow, it wasn't fit. Better to lose your sheep than lose your man!

The danger of 'losing your man' was a very real one, as Kit Calvert has good cause to remember:

I'll never forget, one wintry day, I had to collect a flock of sheep from Simon Stone Moor. I well remember the boss fetching me up from Coleby Hall onto that moor, and I had to fetch the sheep from a big slack* [shallow valley] over towards Muker – they'd got right down in there. So I had 'em to collect up, and take back down to Coleby Hall. And it was a wild day of snow, and if ever I was near done it was that night. Because I set off with a big army greatcoat on, and on the way there I had the wind behind me, and I got that hot I loosed me coat. But on the way back I had the wind against me, and all the front of me coat froze stiff wi' snow and ice. And when I tried to get buttons fast, I *couldn't* get 'em in. So I got me knife out, and I cut bigger holes, and in t'end I got 'em fastened, and I went on. I seemed all right at first: but when t'ice inside me coat melted, the wind kept blowing it open again, because the buttonholes was too big. And the more I tried to fasten it, the more it blew open, 'til eventually I had to face back down to Coleby Hall with a bitter wind blowing snow straight at me. Then I got that feeling into me that I was exhausted, and that I wanted to just lay down. And if I'd lied down, I'd have been a dunner: because I'd have laid into a quiet place and just frozen to death. But anyway, I struggled on and got through, but I was exhausted and starved [frozen] stiff. No one knows what it's like on them tops, if they haven't been shepherding up there.

HILL FARM FAMILY

Maggie Joe recalls that it was not only on moor tops that extreme cold made itself felt:

Oh, it could be bitter cold in winter-time, even inside your house: you see, we'd just have a coal or peat fire, there was no central heating, and not many stoves. I'll tell you how cold it could get. We had no inside lavatory, of course, so we had a 'jerry' each, all on us: well, in cold snowy weather, I've seen all those jerries frozen over – so she's been a bit cold i' that bedroom, hasn't she! But we always had plenty of blankets on, and we cuddled up.

And we always had good beds. Now me mother was *most* particular on a *good bed*, a very good bed: never nothing raggy on wir beds, but good blankets, good sheets and a feather mattress, what we called a feather bed. They were home-made, you know, from our own goose feathers, because we used to do a lot o' geese for Christmas. After you'd plucked your geese, Mother used to roast all feathers in the oven, and then we had to clean 'em all. That was a job, them blooming feathers! We used to do it in the outhouse, and the small feathers just had their ends cut off: but the big ones, you had to pull 'em off pens [quills] this way, and then that way, to just get the feathery parts off. They were lovely beds, but, oh, they took *ages* to stuff.

But then, you see, that's all you had to do in that day. I mean, we went to a dance once a year, and a concert maybe once a year: Muker Fair and Gunnerside Fair, and that was it. And me mother was very strict about *them*. We had three miles to walk back after a dance, and she used to time us! She knew how long we *should* be, so we couldn't stop off on wir way for half-an-hour! So you had to amuse yourself in the evening. When we were children, we used to love Saturday bath night, because we didn't have to go to bed so early. We were only bathed on the Saturday: you weren't splashing in water all t'time, as you are today. Of course, there was no bathroom. Water was boiled in the side-boiler, and we had a big settle; us four children used to sit on there in a row, and Mother used to fetch this tin bath and bath us all in the same water. She started with the youngest first, and it was pretty clear then, but it was getting a bit thick when it got to me!

Because, of course, there was no running water: you hadn't a tap to turn on. All that water was to cart from our pasture. We had a spring of lovely water there: it sparkled when it came out o' limestone, and it was as clear as a bell. But it was hard water: you had to put an awful lot o' soap on to get a lather with it, it was that hard. It all was to carry to the house in buckets, or sometimes me father would take his back-can,* what he fetched his milk in, and carry that filled up, so's we hadn't to go for any more. Then it was all to heat in side-boiler. That was why Mother would always wash herself in the afternoon: she couldn't wash in the morning, because there was no hot water in a morning. You got up and got dressed and downstairs, and then you lit your fire, and that had to heat boiler before there was any hot water.

Very few coals we burnt then, except for a bit of coal to get fire lit. We burnt peat: it's lovely to burn, is peat, because there's no cinders with it, just ash. We always went peating in June. We went up to what they called the 'peat pots' by Satron Moor, and the men dug the peat out in square blocks, barrowed it out, and then cut it into slices: and us kiddies spread 'em out to dry on a flat piece of moor. We used to take the little Shetland pony, and we'd put a little peat-sledge to it, and that would sledge the peats for us: after they'd dried for a week, you turned 'em over to dry t'other side for a week, and then they were ready for leading in to the farm. We used to get forty-four or forty-five cartloads of peat in every year, for the winter, and we'd fill all the loft with peat.

So you didn't waste hot water, no! And on bath night, when we'd all had wir baths, all wir underwear went into bath-water to steep, and then 'twas carted away and left in that water steeping 'til Monday. You never washed anything on a Sunday, you know. Sundays *was* Sundays, and we couldn't even bring wir games out, on a Sunday.

Winter evenings, of course, we'd mostly be knitting. We used to knit with four needles, and what we called a sheath – there's some hanging up there. You put a belt round you, and then you put your sheath in your belt, and you put three needles in the hole at top of sheath, and use the fourth one to knit with. I always use straight steel needles, and so did Mother, and she rattled away and rattled away, right round the three needles in your stocking. There was crooked needles too, but Mother never used 'em, because she was rather a stoutish person, and she couldn't reach crooked needles when she'd got her sheath in her belt.

You only used to knit stockings and gloves wi' a sheath – you didn't knit jumpers and that. And we didn't knit to sell, just for wirselves: that was enough, because there were four of us, and Mother and Father, and we always had a servant girl and a servant boy, and Mother would always knit for them, too. She had one o' them old-fashioned tin boxes, and she'd keep two pairs of stockings for each of us in there: that was so nothing could get to them, because in a wood drawer what they called worms [moths?] could get

Margaret Guy, later Maggie Joe Chapman (rear right), with her brothers and sisters, c. 1910. Her brother Dickie, who survived T. B., stands beside her.

into them, but in tin nothing could. And if we wanted a pair out to wear, then she *must* knit another pair to go in tin box in its place: she always kept two pair each of new stockings in that box. They *were* stockings, you know, not socks: they came right up above knee, and then we wore garters on them, and then wir bloomers came down and over wir knees, them days. You didn't have little short pants! Wir bloomers had a strap at knee and a button on, to fasten. You'd look at people now, if they went about wi' *them* on! And stockings was always black, there were never no coloureds: they were made o' 'blackings', thick black wool, four-ply.

There was another thing we used to knit. You've seen these, what d'you call 'em – 'leg-warmers', about now: well, we had something like that. The men wore them when snow was on, *over* their trousers; they were made o' thick white wool, very thick, and not washed, so it had all the oil on; and they came right up over the thigh, like a wader, and they were held up wi' straps over the shoulder. They used to call them 'lofrums'* – I don't know what *that* means. And they wore these lofrums over their trousers, and they went out into snow with them, because there wasn't any waterproofs then: there wasn't such a thing as a waterproof, and I remember the first waterproofs coming onto market. But snow wouldn't soak through these lofrums, and they were very warm.

And all women wore white aprons, you know: clean white aprons. When me mother got washed in afternoon, she didn't change her dress, but she always put a clean white apron on. Then me granny and all the old ladies, they always had a bonnet on their head, made of black cotton: they was always black cotton, never coloured. I had an old dresser: it belonged to my great-grandmother, and it's always been handed down to the Margarets in the family: there's always a Margaret in our family, and my daughter Margaret has it now. Well, in the top cupboard of that dresser is a hook my great-grandmother kept her bonnet on, and on the top shelf there's a burnt hole: because she'd always put her old clay pipe on that dresser, and heat from that pipe had burnt a hole right through. Oh yes, they all smoked clay pipes, the old women of Muker: my great-grandmother did, and my granny did – but me mother never did, it'd gone out of fashion by her time.

And then, a lot of people used to wear clogs: there was a proper clogger in every village. We used to get ours from Gunnerside, from old Batty's, they called him: and he'd repair wir clogs as well. If they wanted new woods [soles] on, Mother used to send us off to Gunnerside with wir clogs on, and he did 'em while we were there. He'd keep us all day, but he was a wonderful fella, because he'd talk away to us, and of course, he always got all t'news of Hill Top off us – and he always gave us a meal. Oh aye, *he* used to give us a meal. But when horses was to shoe, we had to take them to the Gunnerside smith – he was a Calvert. Now he used to keep us all day, too, but he nivver gave us anything: he'd shut up shop for *his* dinner, but he never gave us anything at all.

So our clogs came from old Batty, and our knickers and that we had from Gill the grocer, that used to come once a month from Askrigg. He used to go round all the farms. He came at Monday, with his bag on his back, full of vests and knickers and underwear, and he took his orders then for his groceries – a stone of sugar and all that sort o' thing: and then his cart came at Wednesday, wi' t'stuff on. He used to come for orders with a blooming old push-bike, that wasn't hardly fit to ride. And I always remember, we had one cow that was short o' minerals of some sort – *now*, they would give her something for it, but of course we didn't know what trouble was. Well, she would eat *anything*. If she saw wir clothes-line out wi' clothes on, she'd come galloping down t'pasture brawling [bellowing], and if you weren't quick she'd eat bottoms off the shirts – you had to watch her. And this day Gill came wi' his old bike, and he left it outside gate: and when he'd got back, t'old cow had eaten his front tyre! 'I hope she's stuck up with it!', he says.

But she was a good cow. Our cows were all good healthy cows, because we replaced wir own, and we never kept old ones. Some people milked old 'uns as long as they had a bit o' milk in their bags, old rubbishy cows. A lot of them had T.B. too, because there was no T.T. [tuberculin tested] milk then: they knew nothing about that. So of course a lot of young people died with T.B. [p.205]. Me mother's first young man did; and me eldest brother Dick, *he* contracted T.B. Well, me mother made such a set* – they nearly all died with it, you see. They'd just built a sanatorium over at Aysgarth, but Mother wouldn't have Dick go there. So she cleared everything out of a bedroom, *everything* out; she stripped the walls of paper, and she whitewashed 'em with lime, as a disinfectant; and she took out carpet, and she scrubbed floor with disinfectant every day. Then she took window right out, frame and all, and bed was put in t'middle of room, so's the air could circulate round.

Me father and us other three lived at this end of house, and she went and lived wi' Dick at that end. She lived *with* him, and she lived *for* him, and she got him better, and he lived to be an old man: but ever after that he was, like, the odd man out, because I suppose Mother spoilt him a bit.

Yes, they died like white mice of T.B., and a lot died with pneumonia too, because there wasn't a cure for it then. If you got pneumonia, you died. I remember us burying a school pal that died wi' it, at thirteen year old: all our class had to be bearers, and we had to wear white dresses. We had to carry her a good mile before we came to the road, before we could get her on the hearse. They gave us a drink before we set off, and we carried her to the hearse in relays, because she lived at Moor Close, about a mile from Thwaite, and there was only a very rough track from there to the road.

Of course, they used to always make a big thing of funerals then – much more than they did of weddings. They always had a big meal, and they always had wine or whisky, or something like that. But you didn't go to a funeral unless you were all in mourning, and you didn't go unless you were what they called 'bid'. When anybody had died, there'd be a young man come round to bid you to the funeral – it was always a lad of maybe fourteen or fifteen, that belonged to the joiner who'd made the coffin: it wasn't a woman that would bid you, and it wasn't one of the family, it was always the joiner's lad. But Mother didn't go to a lot of funerals: Father went, because men went to funerals far more often than women, them days.

*   *   *

5

ALL IS SAFELY GATHERED IN

Come, ye thankful people, come
Raise the song of Harvest Home
All is safely gathered in
Ere the winter storms begin

Hymns Ancient and Modern

HAYTIME

*E*very farm which keeps animals – which is to say, until a few decades ago, every farm – must have hay for fodder: so haytime is still a busy and an anxious period of the agricultural year. But within the memory of the men and women I spoke to, it was a great deal busier and more anxious yet. Busier, because before the advent of modern haymaking machinery, the greater part of the process – strewing, turning, gathering, carting and ricking – had to be done by hand, with every available man, woman and child working at full stretch. And more anxious, because the necessarily greater period then needed 'to save the hay' – significant phrase – exposed it for longer to the peril of rainfall which, at worst, could rot the precious crop where it lay.

And if all this was true on the arable farms of the lowlands, it was doubly so in the uplands of the north and west, where climate and altitude forbade the growing of much, if any, corn. For there, farms were entirely dependent on their livestock – and thus upon their hay – and the weather was even more unreliable than English weather usually is. One such area is Wensleydale, a thousand feet up in the Pennines and near the North Yorkshire boundary with Cumbria: and it is from there that the greater part of my account of haytime comes. The tellers are two men we have already met at 'the hirings': Kit Calvert, MBE, of Hawes (the quarryman's son who rose from farm labourer to saviour and chairman of the Wensleydale creameries, producers of the famous local cheese) and Bob Metcalfe, well known in his home village of Askrigg as captain of the bell-ringers.

KC: Hay was the farmer's bank balance. If the season had been bad, and t'hay was bad, the farming was going to be bad over the winter. But if t'hay

Labourer with 'hook and crook' at Mordiford, near Hereford, c. 1930. The home-made wooden 'crook' (right) was used to gather together enough corn to make a sheaf, and this was then cut with one blow of the heavy, broad-bladed 'fagging hook'.

was good, you could reckon your cows'd get through the winter wi'out any cake or artificial food.

When I was a lad, we always mowed our hay with a little one-horse machine – they called it a 'clipper': and then, when I was growing up, a number of wealthier farmers got a two-horse machine, which had a horse on each side of a main pole: and that had a bigger cut.

BM: Your single-horse machine could cut the hay a yard wide, and your double could cut four foot six. Most of 'em was single-horse machines, and the trouble with them was, you couldn't mow uphill. There was no single-horse machine made that would mow uphill: if you tried, you did your horse in for t'rest o' t'day – you knocked stuffing out on 'em. So if you'd a field with a hill in it – and most of 'em had, round here – you had to go up empty: and if it was a long way up, well, you just took it in plaits, a bit at a time.

If you'd a good wall round your field, you could maybe mow right up to it with the machine: but with the majority of fields, you had to go round the edges with a scythe. They used to call that 'piking it' – that was just trimming round t'wall side with a scythe: they don't trouble to do it now, and by! the fields do look a mess.

And when it was all mowed down, some people used to go and shake it out wi' pitch-forks: but we used to go wi' rakes, wooden rakes. We'd throw hay grass a bit this way and a bit that way, so's sun could get at it: you'd got to get it clean off t'ground, not just knock t'top off. How long it would take to dry would depend on t'weather, and it would depend on what the herbage was. If it was the kind o' grass that had lots o' straws in, it would dry quickly. But if it was broad-leaved grass – if it was what we called 'yerby' ['herby'], it wanted a day longer. Wi' that kind, you could go out at tea-time and look at it, and you'd think it was nearly hay: but next morning, after t'dew-fall, it was green as grass again.

KC: The whole cycle, in good weather, was to mow it, leave it overnight, and straw [spread] it next day wi' rakes; then, at the beginning of the third day, you'd turn it by hand again in the morning, and then leave it 'til after dinner; then you'd make it into what we called windrows,* and in t'late afternoon, if it was ready, two men and a lad on a pony came round to load it onto t'sled.

Loading that sled was a skilled business. First chap gets an armful o' hay, and he loads it into one corner o' the sled, diagonally, and then t'other chap loads a heap in th' other corner. Then t'sled slips on a couple o' yards, and they'd put a third armful on t'third corner, and so on. You had to load it corner to corner, wi' twelve armfuls overlapping: and when you'd done that you put two more on top, and put t'tail rope over all to bind it together. So you'd fourteen armfuls on a sled, or if it was a strong horse they'd maybe put eighteen on, or even twenty-one. But however many there were, they all had to be loaded overlapping, all the way up: and if they didn't do it right, it was loose, and it'd maybe tumble off if t'old horse jogged a bit. And then there was a real cussing and swearing!

But if weather was bad – if you saw a shower coming in at top o' t'dale – you maybe wouldn't have time to load it properly: so you'd get it up in heaps as fast as you could, to save it all getting wet. We used to call those heaps 'pikes'.* Sometimes you got half o' t'field piked before rain came, and sometimes you'd get it all gathered up – then you were really satisfied. And if that happened, you just loaded it onto t'sled with a fork, a day or two later.

BM: If you were making pikes, you had to keep your middle up: you had to make hay up into pyramids, like, so the water would run off. And sometimes, if it was coming windy as well as rain, you'd make pikes a bit bigger. When you'd done that, you'd pull a lump o' hay out o' the bottom and fasten it round t'other chap's rake-teeth: then he'd walk backwards and twiddle rake round and round, while you kept pulling hay out. You made a hay 'rope' like that, you see: and you took that rope right over t'pike and pushed it under t'other side, to hold pike down – that held it all from blowing away.

KC: And when you'd sledded off most o' t'hay, you'd go over t'field with what we called a 'knag-rake'.* It were called a 'knag' rake, but it wasn't pulled by a nag, it was really a man's rake. The head was about four to six feet long, with iron teeth: you pulled it along behind you, and then about every forty yards you made a row with t'hay you'd collected. Then you went on 'til the field was all cleaned up, and you'd got every bit o' hay that'd been lost. If loaders'd been clumsy, and there'd been lots of armfuls dropped off t'sled, you used to storm and swear: because you'd have to keep dropping your rake and picking up these armfuls. 'Blooming owd Johnny', you'd say, 'he can't load a sled.' So you'd make maybe one sled-load o' what you'd got, and that was t'last scraping up. Because you needed every scrap of hay you could get, in them days.

Leading and storing the hay

With the hay safely gathered in, it is now time to say something about how it was transported and stored. On lowland farms, it would be carried on four-wheeled waggons ('haywains') or two-wheeled carts – in both cases often fitted with 'shelvings' or 'hay-ladders' to increase the carrying area – or on local cart variants like the north-eastern 'long-carts' or the Welsh-border 'gambos'* (p.197). But in those upland areas where slopes were so steep that a conventional wheeled vehicle would be in imminent danger of overturning or running away, the only practicable hay carrier was some variety of sledge – too low on the ground to turn over, and guaranteed to stay put if parked at right angles to the slope.

Empty 'hay-bogie' or 'pike-bogie' in Co. Durham, c. 1930. This distinctively north-eastern wheeled sledge would be drawn up to 'pikes' of hay like those in the background, and tipped backwards to form a ramp. Next, a rope or chain, attached to the roller at the front of the vehicle, was passed round behind the pike and this was then hauled into the bogie by turning the handle of the roller.

Some upland regions, however, got the best of both worlds by evolving various kinds of wheeled sledges, combining a low centre of gravity with greater ease of movement, particularly along roads. One such was the ingenious Welsh-border 'wheelcar'; and another was the north-eastern English and Scottish 'pike-bogie', which also did away with the laborious loading process described above. Here it is, remembered by Cissie Elliott of Ovingham:

In the summer, we used to have hay-bogies going up and down the road, when the farmers were haymaking. First we'd collect the hay into 'windrows', then we'd split the windrows into little piles, called 'kyles';* and then the little kyles were carried to make big pikes. And after that the pikes were drawn onto the hay-bogie, and led to the farm to be stacked in the sheds.

Now a hay-bogie was a flat cart with two little wheels, very low on the ground. They used to tip it backwards, put a chain around the pike, and wind it onto the bogie all in one go: there was a roller at the front of the bogie, you see, and the chain that went round the pike wrapped round it, and you turned the handle on the roller to wind the pike onto the bogie. Many and many a pike I've wound onto a bogie – and hard work it was, for a young girl.

But in Wensleydale, as we have heard, they generally stuck to the sledge pure and simple, probably because they rarely needed to carry their hay very far. In most parts of Britain, it would have to be carted to within striking distance of the farmstead or cattle sheds – often some way from the hayfield – and there made into outdoor stacks. These were usually large and rectangular in the sunny south and east, but in wetter regions they tended to be small and round, the better to allow half-made hay to continue drying out: in either case, they would be thatched to keep off the rain. (Nowadays, of course, stacks are composed of hay mechanically packed into rectangular bales or, on the most modern farms, into huge 'swiss rolls'.) In Wensleydale, however, the 'field barn' system enabled hay to be both stored and eaten within a few hundred yards of the place it was made.

KC: We used to lead our hay with a sled: it was very, very exceptional we carted it wi' carts, because we didn't need to. We only needed to lead it to the field barn: and if you look round the country here, there's little square

---

Yorkshire Dales hay sledge at Crow Trees Farm, near Muker in Swaledale and about a mile from Maggie Joe Chapman's 'Hill Top'. Principally used during summer haymaking, sledges also proved invaluable in wintry conditions like these.

barns in every field, all but. There's not above two fields, but there's a barn in 'em: if you had a farm with about forty acres of meadow ground, you could easily have five or six barns on it.

Your home farm would have about four cows: you'd have four cows in the home barn that was built as part of your house. That was to bring 'em in to calve, or if they're sick, or anything like that: and there'd be a calf-house in the corner of it, to keep a young calf or two in. But the main milking cattle was out in the field barns, all t'way round: and you used to go with a back-can* for your milk, and milk 'em in these out-barns, and then you had to carry the six or eight gallons you got back to the farm.

One reason you had cows in these out-barns was so's you didn't have so far to lead the hay, and another was to help with manuring. Because these barns was set in such a way that the liquid manure from 'em could be guttered across to manure the fields round about: they were set high enough up for a large amount of the area to be fertilized by the liquid manure running out by itself. And the bits it couldn't reach, you'd muck that with the hard and thick manure from t'barn.

We used to call these barns 'laithes',* and a laith carries a 'shippon'* and a 'mew':* the shippon was at one end, and that was where the cows lay, and t'mew was at t'other, and that's where you put your hay. And in nine cases out o' ten, there's a loft above the shippon, and that's 'the balks'.* Any hay which wasn't quite dry, you put it on the balks, so air could get to it: but if it was well dried, you put it in the mew.

BM: You used to take your sled up to t'barn, pull up, loose your rope, and tip sled clean over onto its edge, and it tipped all t'hay off. Then you'd fork it all up into the mew, through what they called the forking hole. There'd be one outside forking in and another inside taking it and treading it down. Because you *must* keep your mew level – you must keep walking round wall-sides and keeping it down. Of course, a lot of those buildings was dry-stone walled, so that made them a bit airy: and some on 'em had square holes in, right through, to keep the air circulating.

KC: The shippons in these little barns were generally made for four cows – two in each 'standing', tethered so they could stand up or lie down. And in front of where the shippon was, there was generally a wooden partition [BOB METCALFE: We called that a 'skell-boose'.*] low enough for the cow to put his head over. So that before t'winter came, when the cows were in the barn a lot of the time, you had to cut the hay back from that partition, so the cows couldn't reach over and get it – and they might hurt themselves trying. You'd cut it with a hay-spade, and fork it back up onto the mew, because the mew had settled down a bit by then. Then you had a gangway, the mew on one side and cows on t'other.

* * *

Irishmen

Another distinctive feature of haytime in Wensleydale was the presence of large numbers of Irish seasonal labourers, almost the last remnants of the itinerant Irish 'harvest-gangs' which had penetrated to virtually every part of England during the nineteenth century. Where local labour was plentiful, they were at times resented – or even assaulted – by native farm men. But in the sparsely populated dales, where the hay could never have been got in without them, they were welcomed – especially by Maggie Joe Chapman:

Haytime hirings was always second week in July. There used to be five or six hundred Irish come to Hawes, first Tuesday in July, and it was a marvellous sight to see them all standing round by Black Bull – we often went, as kiddies, just to see them. They used to stand round in marketplace, and all t'farmers from Wensleydale and Swaledale used to go there and hire 'em for the haymaking: because there was no machinery then, and all hay was to get in by hand – there was lots hadn't even a horse-drawn mowing machine. And they stopped coming as soon as ever machinery came in, tractors and all that sort of thing: because after that people could haytime on their own. There was maybe one or two came after Second War, but only for a few years.

These Irishmen would come over, and they'd start off doing a month's haytime over in Lancashire. Then they were with us for a month; and after they left us they went down Northallerton and York way, and did a month's corn harvesting; and then they went into Lincolnshire for the potatoes; and then they went back home at about the end of September. They all had their places to go to in England, you know, and they made as much money in the four months they was here as would keep them all winter – they couldn't manage without it. They was nearly all farmers themselves, in Ireland, but their women could manage while they was away, because they only had small farms.

Now we had same man came to us for twenty years – Hoystin, they called him: he came to market, but he didn't put hisself up for hire, because he knew he was coming to Hill Top. We had two Irishmen every year, but we always had Hoystin as one of them. We looked forward to him coming, and he had the run of the place when he came. Mother wouldn't have him put out in the loft, like some did with their Irishmen: no, he had a room in the house, and he was part of our family. But we had to have beer: the Irish wouldn't come without that, oh no! So we had three barrels of beer in the cellar, just for haytime, because Father wasn't really a beer drinker. I well remember us kiddies tossing them half-gallon bottles of beer to our Irishmen.

They were a wonderful bunch, the Irish, very decent people. They always went to Catholic church, down at Leyburn – they always made a point of that, Sundays. But of course they talked different from us, you know, so it was a job to tell what some of them said, and there were people that couldn't get on with them. Now we used to have a deaf and dumb lad at Hill Top: he was born at Muker, and his mother hadn't a father for him – you know what I mean. Folks couldn't make a lot of him, but we always used to have 'deaf and dumb Tommy' at haytime: his mother used to ask if he could come, and we'd pay him four pound ten shillings a month and his food. Well, *he* never liked these Irish. And he used to have to go into mew – into the part of the cow-byre where hay was stored – and he'd keep treading down the hay as the Irishmen forked it in to him. Well, one day we were haymaking, and we couldn't find Hoystin, so me father shouted for him, 'Where are you?' And the shout came back, 'My God to me, I'm here in the mew. I'm treading for the dummy. I've lost him, he must be here under the hay!' But he was a cute [cunning] one, was the dummy: he was up in the corner, keeping out o' sight, and laughing his head off. 'Cause he didn't like the Irish, and he thought he'd be master of 'em.

And I remember, when I was in me teenses, I fancied some silk stockings, and you couldn't get 'em, because Fourteen War was on. Now Hoystin said they could get 'em in Ireland, but the law wouldn't let 'em bring 'em into England. We didn't know what he was at, but one day here comes a newspaper for him from Ireland, and when he opened it out, there were my silk stockings! He was a marvellous fella, was Hoystin.

We used to pay him ten pound for the month: and if he finished before month was up, we'd let him go on down-country, if he wanted. But he came back to us next year, every year for twenty years, and t'last time he was over, he brought his eldest son with him. They were a grand lot, the Irishmen.

In at least one case, however, the shadow of 'the Troubles' followed them to England, as the remarkable story here recounted by Kit Calvert shows. 'Sixty year ago' would place it during the brutal Irish Civil War of 1922–23, and the 'marked man' must have been either a lone Free Stater surrounded by Republicans, or vice-versa.

I well remember one night, when my old boss at Coleby Hall had hired one, and told him wheer to come to. He had to sleep in shed above stable: it was kept purely for that, it never had any hay in, and there was a good bed in't and a bit o' carpet. Well this Irishman arrived about eight o'clock, with his bit of bag with him, and boss gave him supper, and after we sat and smoked and chatted about a bit. We had a real grand talk. Then boss said, 'Well now, Pat, we'll show you your bed, and you can go when you like': and he went to kitchen door to go out.

'Sure, master, you're not going to put me out of the house?'

'Yes,' he says, 'I haven't room in t'house for you. But it's a nice clean comfortable place, all tidy for you: you'll be comfortable as in t'house.'

'Sure and master, I cannot stay out overnight, for the sake o' me life.'

'What's the matter?'

'I'm not of the same persuasion as most of the men that are in the market, and they know all about it. I'm a marked man.'

'You'll be all right.'

'No, I can't. Here, I'll give you my money back, and I'll pay for my supper.'

'Nay, you'll not pay for your supper. But what are you going to do? You'll still not have a bed.'

'I'll keep awake, then. I'll be walking, and I'll know if anyone's near. But I'll not go to sleep outside this house.'

And he went, he wouldn't stop, and where he went I don't know. That was sixty year ago, and it's just the same today.

HARVEST

With haytime over, the Wensleydale stock farmers could congratulate themselves that 'all is safely gathered in'. But on the arable farms of the lowlands, there was often scarcely time to draw breath between haymaking and the second, greater, campaign of the agricultural year – the harvesting of the corn.

Nowadays, one-man operated combine-harvesters (as their name implies) carry out all the processes of harvesting in a single operation, converting standing corn to grain and straw so rapidly that 'harvest' on an average-sized farm can be completed in a few days. Well within living memory, however, it could call for over a month of unremitting dawn-to-dusk labour from every man on the farm, and frequently from women, children, and Irish or other temporary hands as well. First, the corn had to be cut, and tied in sheaves – often by women, using 'bonds' made by the children; next, these had to be piled in stooks for further ripening (because fully ripened corn, as instantly processed by today's combines, would have scattered and wasted its grain if subjected to the rough handling of yesterday's harvest methods), and then carted and stacked. And even after 'harvest home', the corn had still to be threshed to separate grain from chaff and straw – a business so lengthy that it was generally left for the slacker winter months.

By 1914, corn cutting by some form of horse-drawn mechanical reaper was fast becoming the norm: but cutting with divers kinds of hand tools lingered on well into the present century, particularly on small farms in out-of-the-way areas. The oldest method of all – going back, indeed, to the dawn of civilization – was reaping in its strict sense. The reaper passed the curved blade of his sickle around a few stalks of standing corn, grasped them near the ears, and cut through the stalks: he then tucked the cut corn under his arm, cut another handful, and went on doing so until he had enough to tie into a sheaf. A more advanced variation on this was cutting 'by hook and crook', which Ron Mills of Velindre near Hay-on-Wye saw in action only a few years before the Second World War.

Back in those days, they used to use a 'hook and crook' for cutting the corn: I've seen 'em at it. You'd get an old piece of stick, like a walking-stick, with a crook on it, and you'd put it round the corn, and bring the sickle – what we called a hook – around and cut it off, and that'd be what they called a 'shiff'. You'd leave that there, and maybe go on and cut a acre: and then after, you'd have to go back round again and tie it up by hand. Some places they might have someone to do that for you, if there was plenty labour, like: but I've often seen the same man do it all. I've seen two boys in a field about eight acres, cutting with this hook and crook: I'd be about twenty then, so it'd be about 1937 or '38.

With a scythe, you see, you wouldn't get the heads all the same way round: but you'd have the heads all the same way with a hook.

This 'hook' – sometimes called a 'bagging' or 'swopping' hook – was a heavy sickle with a broad, strongly curved blade, which could cut a whole sheaf at a time – an obvious improvement over reaping proper. But a still quicker way of hand-cutting, and one far more generally used within living memory, was to mow the corn with scythes. The problem of getting the ears 'all the same way round' could be overcome by fitting the scythes with 'cradles', which Alf Friend of Preston-by-Wingham remembers by the Kentish name of 'creets'.*

When I was a boy, I remember they used to cut corn with a scythe, and a creet on it: that was a wooden framework made out o' willow wood, that used to be fitted to the scythe shaft and the scythe blade. So that as you cut, that would follow round, and that creet would carry the corn with it: and as you drew the scythe back, the cut corn left it, and was standing against next row of the standing corn. And a man would come behind, shuffling on his knees, and gather it up: and he'd put it round, and gather it up in a bond. He didn't use a string, he'd make a bond out of the corn to tie it up with, in sheaves. That was my job when I was a boy – making bonds: I'd take a handful of wheat like that, tap it on the top to knock it down level, split it, put it across, double it back, and there's your bond! And if I dared lay this bond down an eighth-of-an-inch out of where this fella wanted to put his sheaf, I used to hear about it!

They reckoned to do 'bout an acre of corn a day with the scythe: but when the reapers and binders came in, they could do seven or eight acres a day.

Bill Partridge, born in 1900, remembers working with some of the earliest corn-cutting 'engines' used at Lindsey in Suffolk.

A 'clipper', 'rack-engine' or 'put-off reaper' at work near Polstead, Suffolk, c. 1905. An early type of mechanical reaper, this adaptation of a hay mower cut the corn near ground-level causing it to fall onto the comb-like 'rack'. The man on the machine kept the rack raised by foot-pedal until enough had been cut for a sheaf, then he lowered it and pushed off the corn with his angled rake. The men following behind then tied it into sheaves (right).

They used to mow all the corn with scythes, you know, when my father was a young bloke: there wan't no machines at all. And when *I* was a young man, there wan't no self-binders round here: I can remember them a-coming out, I can. They hed what they called a 'clipper' when I first went on the farm. That was 'zactly like a grass-mower, but they used to put a ladder on it to cut corn – a wooden rack-thing so the cut corn just laid on it. You worked it with your foot: when you were cutting, and you wanted it up, you kept your foot on a lever. And when you had enow (enough) on the ladder to make a shook [sheaf], you'd take your foot off, and that ladder would come down, and the corn slide off. There used to be one drive the horse, and one set in the seat to work the rack. Then there was a gang o' people came on behind, tying that corn in shooks with a bond.

These 'clippers', alias 'foot-engines' or 'put-off reapers', were already old-fashioned in Mr Partridge's youth, and by then only used on smaller farms. Their chief disadvantage, as he says, was that they could only move at the pace of the sheaf-tiers.

But when you hed a clipper, you couldn't git round no more until one row was all shooked-up, because that laid in the way o' the engine. So they brought in what they called a 'sailer' [sail-reaper], and that shifted it out the way, so you could keep gooin'. That had three–four sails, like an old windmill: they used to go round as you were cutting, and that shoved the shook off by itself, but that still didn't tie it up. So after the 'sailer', the self-binder came in, and that cut it *and* tied it up in shooks, and pushed them out behind. I've tied a lot up meself behind a clipper and sailer, but a self-binder tied 'em up itself.

But enthusiasm for the new machines was by no means universal:

You didn't use a clipper or sailer to cut barley. When I was a young lad, that was *still* mowed wi' scythes. There was nine or ten men on most farms, and they'd mow the barley: they had enow on the farm to do it, they didn't hev no hired men about here, Irish or any o' them. They all went together,

Harvest gang at Red House Farm, Witnesham, near Ipswich, Suffolk, on August 21st, 1905. They are mowing barley, which could not be cut by the early mechanical reapers. Their scythes are fitted with curved 'bails' to help the cut corn fall more tidily for gathering and in their right hands they hold the 'strickles' used for sharpening.

and mowed in a long line, and then they'd cart it loose [unsheaved]. And them old men, they loved it! When the first binder came about here, they didn't like that: them old men, they dew* [? complained] like the devil when that first come on the farm. They'd rather mow it, that's the truth. They were so used to it, it was nothing only play to 'em.

They also realized, no doubt, that their livelihood was in danger. For the 'self-binder' was, of course, by far the most efficient of the horse-drawn 'engines'. Introduced from the United States in the mid-nineteenth century, it survived (often converted to tractor haulage) until the coming of the combine in the 1950s. Here it is in action, recalled by Bill Denby of Heslington, near York.

First of all, you mowed a track right round the field edge with a scythe, so's you wouldn't trample any corn when you brought the binder in. Round here, we generally had three or four horses to a binder: if you had three, they'd go three abreast, and you'd drive 'em yourself, from the machine; but if you had four, they went two and two, and you had a driver sat on one of the back horses. If you only had three, though, you had to keep resting 'em or changing 'em over, or they'd soon get tired out.

It was a very tiring job for the horses, because machines was all ground-drive, in horse days – there wan't no power-drive. All the moving parts – the sails, the knives, and the canvas – was driven by chains from the ground-wheel, and of course the horses had to pull that along: it had spade-loops on, so it wouldn't skid, but it *did* use to skid, and if there'd been a lot of wet it didn't use to drive too well.

As you went along, the sails pushed the corn back onto the cutting knives: then, when it was cut, it fell onto this canvas, which was moving sideways towards the packers and the butter-boards, and they shook and packed it into a sheaf. End of canvas used to ride on some loose boards, hinged at one end: and when it had got a certain weight of corn on, it used to sway down and trip the knotter, and the needle and string would come round and tie it into a sheaf. The sheaves didn't come out the back, they came out o' t'side – and then there was a space for your horses to walk down again when you went next round.

Even with this comparatively advanced method of cutting, however, there was a very necessary delay before the corn could be carted to the stack.

But you couldn't lead those sheaves straight to the stack, oh no. With a combine, you cut the corn pretty ripe, because it's thrashed straight away: but with a binder we had to cut it when it *wasn't* quite ripe, else the grain would have scattered when you was handling it, and you'd have lost a lot. So we had to cut it and then let it weather in the fields. If you had plenty o' men, you could stook the sheaves straight away. But we often used to let 'em lie: then one side'd get dry first, and later on you'd turn 'em over to get t'other side dried. Then, when you came to stook 'em, the straw wouldn't be so soft, and you could lead 'em sooner. Because if you'd led 'em when they *hadn't* dried out, they'd heat up in stack and get warm with internal combustion, and then you'd have a stack afire. It had to be weathered first, you see, and we used to reckon to leave oats three Sundays out, and wheat a week or a fortnight, according whether there was any rubbish in.

You see, in them days there was no sprays to do away wi' the rubbish – to get rid of the weeds that grew in among the corn. You used to get all sorts: thistles, of course, and dog-daisies – that's mayweed,* but we used to call it 'Stinking Nanny' – and ketlocks [charlock*] as we used to call 'em in West Riding, but round here they call 'em 'brazzocks'. All the weeds and greenstuff was tied up in wi' the corn, and you couldn't do owt about it, except the men handling the sheaves could cut the thistles out, it they had time. So if you had lots of rubbish with it, that would take longer to dry.

'Leading' the corn – or 'carting' it as they say in the south – had to be done with great care, if the inconvenience and disgrace of 'pigging' was to be avoided.

You really needed three waggons to lead it to stack – or two waggons and a cart, whatever you had: you'd have one being loadened in field, one unloading at stack, and t'other coming or going. At our place the foreman and the horseman used to do stacking, and labouring fellas used to go back and forth wi' the teams: they'd either loaden their own waggons, or there'd be a stand-loadener in the field all the time, just to stand forking – that was generally my dad.

Now you had to be very careful the way you loadened the waggons, else they'd shake off when you went through a gate, or over a bit o' rough road or anything o' that. But we didn't say load had slid off, we said waggon had 'pigged'! When we used to be leading corn off Kimberlow Hill, we often used to have 'em pig: because, wi' waggon being stood uneven, you think you've loadened it straight, but when it come on level ground, it was bent – and then it would pig!

Stacking – performed by the senior employees on the Denby farm – was also a job for 'clever men', as Bill Partridge remembers from his Suffolk youth:

After we'd cut it with a clipper or sailer, we used to stook it in shooks, and thet used to stand out about a fortnight or three weeks to ripen up. The corn wan't hard when we cut it them days, you see, not like it is today with a combine. Then we went with the waggon and horses to cart it. There used to be four on us afield, two a-loading on the waggon and two a-pitching: and four at home building the stack; and one to drive the waggon home and bring it back afield. There wasn't no elevators, you got to put it all up by hand. Proper stackers were clever men, some o' they: they could put up a stack looked lovely. There was round stacks, square stacks – same shape as a house – and some what we called 'boat-fashion', where they used to draw both ends in, like a boat. There used to be twenty or thirty stacks in the stackyards, and you hed to hev a thatcher come and thatch 'em all.

In 'the olden days', the hard work of harvesting ended in universal celebrations. These might focus on the leading in of the last waggon of corn, surrounded by harvesters proudly singing songs like the Berkshire:

> *Well ploughed, Well zawed*
> *Well ripped, Well mawed*
> *Narra load overdrawed*
> *Whoop, whoop, whoop, Harvest Home*

or on the cutting of the last sheaf – as around Bishop's Castle in south-west Shropshire, where I talked to two young corn-dolly makers.

There used to be an old custom round Bishop's Castle called the 'gonder's neck'. A long time ago, the farmhands at harvest time would throw their sickles at the last standing stalks of corn, and that was called the 'gonder's neck' – the gander's neck. And whoever cut the corn down – 'cut the gonder's neck' – made the corn dolly out of it: that was considered very lucky, and the dolly was kept on the farm 'til next year, to ensure good luck.

That's all died out long ago, but in some respects we still do it. I live on a farm, and they always leave me some corn in the middle of the field after they've combined – so I always use that corn to make next year's dollies, and we keep them in the farmhouse or use them for harvest festivals.

And in every case farmers were expected to obey Thomas Tusser's Elizabethan dictum:

> *In harvest-time, harvest-folk, servants and all*
> *Should make, all together, good cheer in the hall*
> *Once ended thy harvest, let none be beguiled*
> *Please such as did help thee, man, woman and child.*

Even before the First World War, however, such jolly and bibulous 'harvest suppers' had in many areas been discontinued, commuted for a half-crown or so extra payment to the 'harvest folk', or transmogrified into a tamer and more sober 'harvest festival' in church or chapel. But in Suffolk, Bill Partridge and his mates still had their 'horkey': *

Then, after the harvest, farmer'd give 'em a 'harvest horkey', we used to call it about here: some call it a 'harvest supper'. Perhaps they'd have a pig to kill, and there'd be plenty of meat, and plenty o' home-brewed beer – you weren't short o' drink very often! That was lovely, home-brewed beer: that was as good as food, that was. That's how them old men worked so hard. They'd drink that home brewed, and they'd goo out, and the work they'd do 'ud kill a man today: chaps today couldn't keep nowhere with 'em. Tough as old nails, they was.

THRESHING

The harvest is home, but it still has to be threshed – to separate corn from straw; and winnowed – to remove the husks from the corn grains. Threshing, traditionally, was done by laying the sheaves on a hard floor of wood or beaten earth and thumping them mightily with a flail. Known graphically in East Anglia as 'a stick-and-a-half' and along the Welsh border as 'two sticks', this implement consisted of a wooden 'handstaff' topped by a swivel, to which a 'beater' of some hard and heavy wood was attached by a band of a pliable material like leather, pigskin or willow. Grasping the staff in both hands, the thresher swung the beater round above his hand and brought it down on the corn ears, thus chopping and beating them from the stalks: I have tried it, and can confirm that

Threshing with flails at Great Oakley in north-eastern Essex, c. 1895. This method of separating grain from straw, used since Biblical times, was already being widely superseded by the threshing machine when this picture was taken, but it continued on some small and remote farms until very recent years.

inexperienced flailers were in acute danger of knocking themselves out cold; but practised operators could measure their blows to within a fraction of an inch. Once threshed, the corn was winnowed by being thrown up into the air from shovels, or shaken from a sieve held over a sack: the wind would then blow away the chaff, while the grains fell to the ground. This was usually done between the back and front doors of the barn, purposely built opposite each other to induce a through-draught, and in calm weather 'wind' had to be produced by some such expedient as the waving of sacks.

The hand-processing of even a single stack was thus a lengthy and labour-intensive business, while that of an entire crop could necessitate daily work throughout the winter months. It is scarcely surprising, then, that threshing and winnowing machines (initially driven by hand, horse or water power) were among the first 'engines' to appear on the farm, where they preceded even the earliest mechanical corn-cutters. On large-scale arable farms, then, the flail-threshing of corn was already a thing of the past by the beginning of this century: but it still persisted on some smaller and more remote holdings, where the crop was light – like those of the Welsh border hills, here remembered by Ron Mills.

At my mother's place, up at Llaethdy, they used to thrash the corn with these 'two sticks' – 'Dick and Mary', they used to call 'em; 'Come on, we'll have to get out Dick and Mary.' And they still used to do it up here at Pen Cwm, not so many years ago. The woman used to do it. There was an old man and his wife, see, and after they'd cut the oats with a hook and crook and got 'em in the building, he used to tell his wife, 'You can do it a lot better than me. You be a lot stronger' – it was nothing only saving his own bones, see!

The most generally remembered method of threshing, however, was to call in 'the contractor', with his mechanical 'threshing-box' or 'drum' and its attendant paraphernalia, all powered by a mighty traction-engine and presided over by:

The engine-man

Will Flinton, born in 1900 the son of a Nottinghamshire shepherd, moved to Burgh-on-Bain in the Lincolnshire Wolds during his early teens, and has lived there ever since, marrying the daughter of a local miller. For nearly forty years he has been sexton of the parish church, and 'All the people nearly what lived in this village when I was a boy, I've buried 'em all in the churchyard. It makes you wonder, how fast time goes.'

Most of his professional life, however, has been spent 'in steam' – a demanding, skilled and at times risky calling, as the following account shows.

When I was a boy, all the steam-thrashing round here was done by these here 'portable' engines. I remember carrying water for 'em. They used to have a trough by the side of 'em, and they'd say, 'Keep that trough full, boy', and you'd be carrying water out of an old beck or a pond. You used to have one o' them yoks [yokes], wi' two chains hanging down, and hooks on the end to carry your two buckets – a shilling a day, they paid then.

These portable-engines were made just about the same as a traction-engine, but of course they had no road-gearing, and they had to be pulled wi' horses. At that time o' day, these here farmers used to have to fetch all the tackle from the contractor: they needed two horses for the straw-elevator, two for the chaff-cutter, four for the drum, and four for the engine. So they needed all their horses, and sometimes they'd to borrow some more from a neighbour. Because a portable-engine was a good weight, you know: it was full o' water, of course. They used to take two bolts out, and lay the chimney down across the top of the engine: then they'd couple her up to four horses, and away she went.

I should say *traction*-engines really came in round here, in a big way, in about 1914 or '15. But the farmers couldn't afford to have their own – not even the biggest farmers, at that time o' day. So when they wanted to do their thrashing, they'd hire one from one of these contractors. There was

*Steam threshing in full swing at Branston, near Lincoln, in 1917. In the centre two labourers are
taking sheaves of corn from the part-threshed stack to the 'band-cutting man' on top of the threshing
machine. Having cut the fastening, he feeds the loose corn onto the 'drum', which separates grain
from chaff and straw. The grain pours into sacks at the nearer end of the machine; the chaff comes
out at the side, where it is gathered by the sun-bonneted woman and the boy; and the straw,
emerging from the far end, is lifted via the elevator to the straw stack (left).*

Wardendales that used to come from Sleaford, and Macdonald's o' Louth,
and there was my boss, Mr Crisp of Ludford. He had four whole sets of
tackle – four engines, four thrashing-drums, four elevators and four chaff-
cutters – and he used to thrash all this here area. It would be in the late
twenties, I started wi' him. He wanted a man to go and help a driver
through a season, so I thought I'd try it. I started by going out wi' a trained
man, and I stopped wi' him and got used to everything, while I got so I
could do it wi' mysen' [on my own] – I could take one out on me own, and
be responsible for it.

We used to go round all these farms at this time o' the year, in September,
and thrash all the corn what had been harvested. We'd start as soon as ever
the harvest was fit, and goo right through 'til next May, right through the
winter. You set off wi' the engine, pulling the drum, the elevator, and the
chaff-cutter, all coupled up one behind the other. The engines was Clayton's
and Shuttleworth's, of Lincoln, and they'd be painted a pretty green,
perhaps, wi' brass bands round the boiler: and the sets'd be painted in the
firm's colours that had made 'em – Clayton's or Foster's, so they'd either be
pink or red.

You'd usually keep wi' the same engine all the season, and two of you
would go with it – me and a mate o' mine. We'd goo to a farm and set
between two stacks, and next morn we should set off to thrash 'em. There'd

be so many men on the stack, putting the sheaves down onto the drum: and there'd be a man stacking the straw at yon end o' the drum, and another carrying corn at this end. They'd all be farm chaps, but one of us always used to actually feed the sheaves into the drum: he had what we call a 'band-cutting knife' in his hand, and he used to cut the band [string], round the sheaf and shed it all into the thrashing-box. One of us'd do that, and the other would drive the engine, and we'd change over every two hours.

Now, say this particular farmer had only two stacks he wanted to do. Well, when your second stack was out – about five o'clock at night it would be, in the winter-time – you'd couple all the set up and start off, and you'd goo up these hills and down these dales to some other farm, and set down there to begin at seven o'clock the next morning. I suppose you could go five to seven miles an hour – no faster: so it could take two or three hours to get there. But there wasn't much traffic on the road, only horses and carts, and some o' them would have a job on when th' engine came by, specially at night! Then you'd goo off home on your old bicycle, and come back again in the morning: because there was no cars about then, and it was very seldom you saw a motor-bike, except perhaps a little old belt-driven Douglas.

Steam skills

Now whichever farmer you were thrashing for, he'd have to provide the coal and water. Mostly we used to use Welsh hard coals, and in an ordinary day's thrashing you'd use about five hundredweight: you could do a hard day's work on that. It was a shilling a hundredweight, that time o' day: the farmer'd have to fetch it from the station wi' his waggon. And when I'd got finished, I'd fill my tender up wi' his coal and water, and that would take us along some way over these here Wolds. Because your tender would hold a quarter of a ton o' coal, and you'd have a water-tank there too: and if she was a compound engine, she'd have a water-tank under her belly as well, so she'd carry enough water to work all day. And then, when I got where I was going, I'd start wi' *his* coal, and I'd fill her up again.

Then, on top o' that, we used to charge forty-five shillings a day, for however many days you'd thrashed: that was if you paid cash, but if you put it in your book – on credit – it would be fifty shillings a day. And there was two men – me and my mate – to pay out of that, and there was all the tackle to keep in first-class condition. The main driving-belt on the engine was sixty-five feet long, and we reckoned we could keep that replaced for about a pound a year. And then you'd all the oil to get, cylinder oil and lubricating oil for all the bearings: and all the little belts on the thrashing-box and the elevator, they all had to come out o' that same money.

So my wages could be thirty shillings a week, when an ordinary farm man had seven and sixpence. But when it was a wet day and we couldn't thrash,

Will Flinton with the 7 HP Fowler compound steam-roller, which he drove in the summer intervals between steam-threshing. Lincolnshire, 1934.

we were only getting half a crown a day: so if you had three wet days in a week, you wouldn't be taking home anything like thirty shillings. And in the summer we often had nothing to do at all: that was the worst part of it. It was very seldom anybody would want an engine in the summer, unless you might get a couple o' days driving a steam-saw or anything o' that. So in the summer I sometimes used to drive steam road-rollers for a firm in Caistor – he had forty or fifty of 'em, contracted out to tarmac these roads and suchlike for County Council. And me wife used to come wi' me, living in a caravan towed behind the roller, and our boy used to go to the school wherever we was. That used to be nice in the summer, and we made some good friends, too, while we were steam-rolling.

And what money we did make, we certainly earnt it, I can tell you. On a Monday morning, I used to have to be gone from here before five in the morning, because I had to go to wherever the engine was and light her up: you'd to get steam up for seven o'clock, and you wanted a good hour-and-a-half to get pressure up. Then sometimes I didn't come home while ten or after at night, if I'd been flitting [moving farms] and there'd been a bad yard, a bad setting.

Because your thrashing-drum had to be set exactly level, and you'd spirit-levels for this way on and that way on: then you'd to set the engine, and if she was dropping a bit at front end, we'd have to put pieces of wood under front wheels until she was right. And it could be a very difficult job, you know. You'd go in somebody's yard, and it'd be all clean and tidy, but in other people's yards, you could easy get the engine stuck fast.

Once, me and the master's son got stuck fast in a yard down at Donington, near the river Bain, and the engine sunk while the flywheel was touching the ground. The yard just gave way under her, and the more we tried to get her out, the more she ground hersen' further in. We'd big spuds [spikes] we used to put on the wheels: there was a clamp round the wheel, and these spuds would dig in underneath. We'd all them on, and we put railway sleepers underneath, so she could get a grip: but she just shoved the sleepers back in the sand, as fast as you could put 'em in. So in the end we had to have another engine come from Ludford and cable-haul her out. It was the only way.

And, of course, driving the engine was a skilled job. You'd to keep your fire level – spread the coal about, and don't let it pile up, or you'll get no draught through it. You want it so it's moving on the fire-bars wi' the beat o' the engine: you want it lifting with the roar of the exhaust. Then, when we'd done thrashing for the day, and we was going on at the same place the next morning, we used to bank the fire down at night. You'd shut the dampers down, and put the damper on the chimney-top with a heavy weight on to stop it blowing away wi' the wind, and leave it like that while morning. And when you went to it in the morning you'd hear the water singing – she was just coming to the boil! Then you'd pull the damper up, and fire was roaring away again: in an hour she was well ready. I shouldn't think there's many men today could drive you a steam-engine: you dorsn't leave him with it, because he'd blow his head off!

... and steam risks

Because, of course, an engine could burst her boiler. There was one did it at Benniworth near here, in 1913. I was only a boy then, but I remember it well, and so does my wife. There was a terrific bang, a *terrific* bang, and we could hear it here at Burgh, two or three miles away. It blew all to pieces, and killed the men, and it threw pieces of iron I don't know how far.

She blew up because she got short o' water. You see, a steam-engine has a long firebox, and in the top o' that box there's a big plug, as far round as that there clock-face, and it's threaded, and screwed into the top o' that firebox. Well, that's the plug of the water-tank, the tank from which the water's pumped into the boiler.

And in the centre o' that plug, there's a hole bored right through, top to bottom. So before you put that plug in, you put it on a piece of iron, and put some sand on the iron. Then you get your saucepan, boil up a piece of lead

The Benniworth Disaster, August 1st, 1913. The remains of the traction-engine which exploded and killed its driver at Benniworth, near Louth, Lincolnshire, due to the removal of a safety plug.

piping, and team [pour] lead into the hole, while it's full: and you let it stop and set. Now then, that there plug's all right. It's got a lead core, and the fire won't melt the lead out, just so long as there's enough water in the tank to keep it covered. It's a safety plug.

So, supposing that engine was going downhill, and there wasn't much water in the tank. Your water naturally runs to the bottom end o' the tank and then it goes off this plug. And that'll stop you blowing up for want of water. Because if you've lead in this plug, your lead'll melt out as soon as water's off it, and when you're on the level, and water comes back, it'll pour through the hole and put out the fire.

Now, here's where the question comes. Because at that time o' day you could get a full plug from the engineers: a full plug, sealed, wi' no hole bored through. So some o' these 'clever chaps' would wait while the engine was cold, and they'd take out the safety-plug and put one o' these full plugs in instead. They was always busy, you see, and on these Wolds their engines was sometimes this way up and sometimes th' other. They didn't want their fires putting out, and if they had a full plug in, it could save them time. It was a terrible risk, of course: and if the inspector had found out, you'd have got locked up. Because if you ran low on water, that plug would get red-hot, but fire would keep going. And then you was in trouble, because she'd blow up. That was what happened over there at Benniworth.

['GEORGE': I was leading water for that same machine, the week before it blew up. Now I was damn lucky, wan't I? I was at Campaign at the time, and I was leading water for that very same engine. And the foreman came to me and said, 'By gor, we was lucky.' 'Why?' 'That there engine's burst, and killed a fella.' I remember it well, it was 1913.]

So that was a risk, and so was another trick *we* used to do, if we were stuck fast. Well now then: the steam-gauge on an engine was set at a red mark, a safety mark. And you could have a great roaring fire, and she'd be making pounds and pounds of steam, but she wouldn't hold any more. Because when that needle got to the red mark, she'd blow the extra steam off at the cylinder, and it would just go roaring into th' air. But if you wanted extra power, and you said to yourself, 'I'll *make* you sit down', you could go get a clinker shovel or a scraper off the side of your engine, and you could hang it on the rod above the valves. That would keep the valves pressed a bit, and put a few more pounds of steam in: and it would shove that needle past the danger mark, and you could get that bit more power to pull you out o' the hole. But it was a terrible risk, and as soon as ever you'd got out, you got that shovel off just as soon as you could. By, she used to roar then, but she'd soon get back to safety level.

Well, after a while the farmers did start to get their own engines, or oil-engines, or tractors, and Mr Crisp faded out. But I stuck with steam, and I went to a farmer, Mr Sleights of Kelstern Grange. He had two sets of his own, all Clayton's o' Lincoln, built for him a' purpose. And his driver died, so I got the situation, and I was there for thirty-some years. Mr Sleights sold his engine just after the war, though, in about 1946: she went down to the south of England, to go in these here traction-engine rallies, and she won't have stopped working yet, I should think.

So I was in steam most o' my life, and the boy was brought up wi' steam: when he grew up, he went as fireman on the railway, and now he's a boilerman. We've always been in steam, me and Henry. It's fine stuff to work among, if you can be trusted with it: but you've got to be careful with it, else you'll soon blow your hat off!

While the 'drum' greatly reduced the time needed for thrashing, quite large numbers of men – often casual labour, glad of any winter work – were still needed to feed the monster with corn from the stack, and to carry away and store the grain, straw and chaff it produced. Nor did the substitution of tractor for steam-engine as thrashing-box motive power, well under way by the 1940s, change this situation greatly. The real revolution, in Bill Denby's opinion, was the coming of the combine.

A tractor could drive a drum just the same as a steam-engine, you see, and you didn't have to get up in t'middle of night to stoke the fire up. Fella used to come in about seven o'clock, and just tip a drum of paraffin into the tractor engine, and that's all it wanted, to start. And of course, they wouldn't need a man on tractor all t'time, like they did on a steam-engine. But they still wanted all t'farm men to fork sheaves down to drum, and carry all t'sacks o' grain, and build straw stacks and that. Them jobs went when combines came in, because they didn't need to thrash separately at all – the combine did everything.

Thus the story of the mechanization of harvest – which some of the people I talked with have seen from beginning to end, from 'hook and crook' to combine – is also the story of the 'flight from the land'. First, sickle- and scythe-men are replaced by the early horse-reapers; and the thrashing-drum supersedes the flail, reducing the number of labourers employed during winter. Then 'self-binders' appear, the sheaf-tiers and bond-makers leave the harvest field, and 'harvest homes' decline or cease. Next, tractors drive out the horses and their waggoners – and with them, incidentally, most of the blacksmiths, wheelwrights and harness-makers. And finally the combine makes its entrance, so out go the engine-men, stackers and sack-carriers of 'threshing day'. Bill Denby has seen men leave the land.

I think that's the biggest change I've seen on the farm in my time – employment. From a lot of men doing small jobs, it's gone to a few men working big: where everything used to be done by hand, it's all done by machine now. That's the biggest change: you don't see the men in the field any more.

HOP-PICKING

They set out as jovial as could be
To Maidstone it was their intent
To meet with their jolly companions
To go a-hop-picking in Kent.

The 'jolly companions' continued to go hop-picking long after this Victorian ballad was composed, for hop harvesting remained unmechanized until very recent years. I myself well remember (largely because I fell into a pond) the day I went visiting hop-pickers' camps with my father, and even the largest hop-farms did not go over entirely to machinery until the 1960s. Before then, vast numbers of pickers were needed, many of them on an annual 'working holiday' from the East End of London: for the hops had to be gathered at just the right time – September – and then gathered very quickly indeed.

Hops, Reformation, Bays and Beer
Came into England all in one year

says the old rhyme, though hops have been used for flavouring and preserving English ale – which thus became 'beer' – since at least the fifteenth century. But it was not until 'Reformation' times, the reign of Henry VIII, that they began to be grown on a large scale in England – and particularly in Kent, which with neighbouring parts of Surrey and Sussex remains their chief stronghold. For those who have never seen a 'hop-garden', it had better be explained that the plants grow from parallel rows of 'hills', twining their bines upwards round strings supported by a network of poles and wires. Long before the pickers arrive, all this had to be carefully prepared by local men like Will Forman, the Ash-by-Sandwich waggoner, and his stilt-walking brother-in-law.

The hop poles 'ad to be done by hand: they all 'ad to be shaved, to take the bark off. We used to git larch poles from Betteshanger, and to do that we used to get the hutch of the waggons off – that's the body of the waggons, cause we didn't want those: we used to take the waggons to the cart-lodge, and swing the hutch off on roops [ropes] from the beams. That made the waggon into like a timber-tug, just the axles and the framework: and you'd got what they call a gin-pole in the middle of the waggon, so you can put the wheels further back, when you're poling, to make the waggon longer. You put your poles on that and chain 'em down, so they wouldn't jar off.

Then you 'ad to string 'em. There used to be a bloke walking along on stilts, walking along and fastening the strings to the top wires – that's all done from a tractor now, of course, and the bloke stands in a 'crow's nest' you can move up and down. And another bloke used to walk along be'ind, he used to tie the strings to the breast wire, the middle wire, and then tie 'em to the bottom wire.

It's the early part o' the spring when they start growing, like: they're asleep all the winter-time. They reckon a hop grows six inches in a night – a hop grows in the night, it don't grow in the daytime: if you're in a hop-garden the early part o' next year, you tie a little bit o' string on that hop, and then goo the next day – I bet I ent far out. And when them hops grew up, and we was working with the 'orses between 'em, we used to 'ave a bit o' netting over our face – else them hop-bines they catch on your face and tear you raw, because they're very rough, you see. And if you didn't 'ave a bit o' 'orse-net over your face, you'd 'ave a job to wash your face else. Oh, I've 'ad some scratches.

And when they'd got to growing, they'd come along with stilts and twist the hop-heads round the strings. They'd make no trouble of it at all. My missus's brother Dick, he was a rare one for hop-garden work on stilts, over to Brook: and he bet 'em one or two pints o' beer that he could walk from the hop-garden to the pub on them stilts, and back again. 'E did, too! No, they didn't have no pole to walk with. They'd 'ave a ladder at the end o' the alley, to walk up onto the stilts: and you'd got like a shoe on the upright stilt, and you'd 'ave a strap to go round your waist. You'd put your feet in these cases – these shoes – and strap 'em in, and the case is attached to a wedge on the pole. So you'd put your feet in, and away you'd goo. You'd got that top wire to 'elp you along, 'cause out in the hop-gardens, if it's wet, you'd sink in a bit: a good many times they'd have an extra piece round the bottom of the stilt, to stop 'em gooing too far into the ground. I don't 'spect you'd git anybody to walk on stilts now!

Another job us horse chaps had was collecting up the pickers, come September. They was all women pickers, from out the town: when I was at Brook, we used to 'ave all pickers from Deal. There used to be a public-'ouse, the Jolly Sailor: we'd go there with two–three horse-waggons. Three waggons it generally was; one waggon would have the people and the others'd have all the baskets and stores, and tackle and clobber. And we'd bring 'em out to live in these hopper-huts. They lived there then for five or six weeks hop-picking, and the kiddies used to have the 'olidays then, so they could goo hopping. Then there was what we called 'didikoies'* – they came from all over the place, and there used to be a lot about at one time, with their caravans. They weren't 'zactly gypsies, they was didikoies: but they was nice people, I got on very well with 'em.

Pickers'd pull the hop-bines down theirselves, and they'd sit on an old stool or box – a box was best, 'cause it didn't sink into the ground. They'd pick into bushel baskets – you 'ad to find your own bushel baskets – and then they'd shoot 'em into a bigger basket at the end of the alley: that was a five-bushel basket, what they called a 'tally'.* And you'd 'ave a man come round every so often with his book, to tally how many bushels they'd picked: and two more blokes which shook the hops into the green-bag. Two tallies to a green-bag, so that was ten bushel.

Picking into bushel baskets, the traditional method, survived into the present century only here in East Kent – where, incidentally, the best hops are grown. More generally, the hops were picked into large 'bins', made from sacking supported on a framework of poles and placed at the end of the hop-alleys. From these they were measured out in baskets into sacks called, not 'green-bags', but 'pokes'. This is the system remembered by Daisy Record, who was brought up in the midst of the great West Kent hop-fields, at Hunton near Yalding:

The first job I remember doin' was 'elping Mum with 'op-training – putting the 'ops on the strings after they first kick off. You gotta put your bines up the string so you don't break 'em, and git 'em up straight, that was the main thing. And when you twiddled 'em round the string, you mun't turn 'em the same way as the bean, you 'ave to turn 'em the same way as the sun goos: the bean turns th' opposite. They used to do them piece-work. Then that wouldn't be long 'fore they was ready to pick: 'cause they grow quick, specially when the nights are warm.

Then when 'op-picking come, we'd git crackin' to scratch 'em off, and git some money: they was six a shillin' then – you 'ad to pick six bushel 'fore you got one shillin'. You 'ad to be right out in the 'op-garden by seven o'clock, when that whistle went: the measurer blew that, the measure man.

And 'e used to do the weighin' up in the basket. Soon as you git out there, you'd pull some bines down and git scratchin': you'd sit on the bin and pick away and pick away. 'Bout quarter to ten, 'e'd be round with the first measure: ten bushels in a measure. Then you'd git on pickin' to fill up for the next – half past eleven, then half past two, then four o'clock. We used to 'ave a break 'bout twelve o'clock. Mum used to cook runner beans and 'ave them in a saucer with potater, and then put a bit o' butter in another dish: then you mashed all that in together – 'cause you couldn't cart the gravy. Some used to 'ave cold bacon, but I didn't like that. Then we used to ha' two bottles o' lemonade and a bottle o' water.

But 'home-dwelling' pickers like Daisy were nothing like numerous enough to cope with the hop harvest, by far the greatest part of which was gathered (particularly in West Kent, nearest the capital) by immigrant Londoners. These were already coming hopping in droves by the 1750s, when Christopher Smart wrote, in his poem 'The Hop Garden':

> *See! from the great metropolis they rush,*
> *Th'industrious vulgar ...*

In September 1908 their number was estimated at near 75,000, mostly from the East End; and in 1945 almost 30,000 came by 'Hoppers' Special' train alone. Their presence was viewed with deep suspicion and disapproval by some Kentish residents (including my grandmother), with delight by most publicans, and with the greatest interest by young Daisy:

An' the Londoners'd come down for hopping – miles of 'em! Oh, an' we git on well with them! They lived in the 'opper-'uts, they 'ad all the 'opper-'uts all fumigated out for them, and they'd git them their wood. Before 'op-picking, they'd goo and get them loads and loads of brish [brushwood] on the waggons: and they used to 'ave two bundles of brish a day, and Sundays they 'ad six bundles. That'd be for cooking their dinner, frying an' that. They 'ad little places built in bricks, to put the frypans on: if it was nice weather, so you'd light a fire outside, that'd be all right. But if it was raining, they 'ad to 'ave these fire-places – if it was wet and cold first thing in the morning. An' we used to goo down and see what they was doin'. They used to make a meat-puddin', and put it in a pea-bag: and they 'ad a fish-kettle, and they 'ad the puddin' tied up in there, and there was cabbages, and peas, and potaters: then they might 'ave another little saucepan for a plain suet-puddin', or a spotted dick.

Them Londoners, they used to 'ave to 'ave the sub [advance] every night. The measure man an' his bookie used to come round and arsk 'em what they wanted – a pound, two pound – an' they 'ad it there and then, an' it was ticked orf on their card. Then they might goo and 'ave a drink – specially Saturday nights. Oh, they'd goo anywhere. Bloomin' great sticks,

Hopping in the Whitbread's Brewery hop-gardens at Beltring, near Tonbridge in west Kent, c. 1950. Most of the hop-bines have been cut down for picking into the sacking 'bins' (foreground) at the end of each 'alley': after measuring, they will be packed into 'pokes' like those carried by the men in the distance, and taken to the oast-house for drying. Women and children are prominent among the pickers, most of whom will be East End Londoners.

they used to 'ave, whoppin' great sticks. 'Cause we didn't 'ave no street-lights, like they was used to, and they was frightened, I 'spect. And they used to sing, like, 'cause they was afraid o' the dark.

Once picked, I was told by the company in the Volunteer at Ash, the hops have to be dried almost at once:

There's a time limit for drying: you've got to be quick. The minute they start going brown, they're useless, and you can't sell 'em. When you pick 'em, they've got to be green, and they've got to be straight to oast, and dried and pressed – so you need your men on there full-time, maybe five or six men working round the clock.

These oast-houses, familiar to all travellers through Kent, are round (or occasionally square) brick buildings containing several furnaces: their steeply conical roofs are topped by a white-painted wooden cowl, which turns with the wind to ensure the maximum up-draught. Above the furnaces, inside the roof space, is the drying-floor of laths: and next to that, somewhat away from the furnace, is the solidly floored area where the dried hops are 'pocketed'. Will Forman describes the process:

When them green-bags got to the oast, they'd be took up to the top on a wheel. A bloke stands up the top, and a bloke on the waggon: he'd put the chain on 'em, two at a time, and they're pulled up. Then they go on the kilns to dry: they're all shot out onto slats, with a black netting over so the hops can't drop through. There's a fire underneath in the kiln, that's done with coal: it was a special kind o' coal, it was a shiny-looking coal that come from away by train, and it's terrible hard to break.

Them hops'd be drying quite a time: if you load on at nights, they'd come off at about six o'clock in the morning. And you used to have to plough through 'em, to get 'em all moving and turn 'em over: you'd put your feet together and plough 'em. Then they're pushed off there with a big wooden scoop, and shoved out on that floor: 'arter you done that you put your pocket on – that hangs down through the floor, on a ring to keep the top open. You push your hops into the pocket, then you press 'em down into it tight. You do it with a press – it's a proper press, all done with cogs – so's you'd get as many hops in there as you could.

The 'head dryer' had to be a most skilful and responsible man, for it was he who regulated the whole farm's picking to his drying rate, and who judged exactly when the drying hops needed to be turned. He also had to make do with very little sleep, since during the five weeks or so of hopping he was on duty twenty-four hours a day, six days a week. Among his assistants were Alf Friend and Filmer Measday, of Preston-by-Wingham.

AF: I used to go with the dryer, hop-picking season. I used to go up and sleep with him. I used to have a bed on a couple of hurdles slung up, with a couple of pokes over it, and go to sleep. And two o'clock in the morning, you 'ad to get up and turn the hops. You 'ad a great big shovel, very light, made of some foreign wood: and you 'ad to take your boots off, you daresn't go in the hops with your boots on.

FM: It was a very, very skilled job to get the fire just right. They burnt anthracite or Welsh coal: and they 'ad barrels full of brimstone, to put on the fire and make it burn clear. The old boys said that was to put strength in the beer: sticks, like candles, the brimstone was.

AF: Then, at about six o'clock in the mornin', they were nicely dried and ready. And we 'ad to clear that lot out onto the floor. Then you 'ad to work them into a round press: they 'ad a long hop-pocket hanging through the floor underneath – about eight feet long, they were. And they hung on a ring, to keep the tops open. You'd shovel the hops in, and push them down with a hand press: they was a round bore that went inside the pocket, and fitted snug. You'd press that down – in with a few more hops – and round would go the press again, until it was filled and solid.

You had to fold the tops over, and get some strong string, and oversew that with a needle. They had a certain way of tying it up, that pocket. You'd make an ear on the top first, and you'd sew and oversew along to the other side, and make another ear, then tie the string round the ear to finish off.

There'd be three or four hundredweight of hops in a pocket, and they'd already be overprinted with the farmer's name, and every one would be numbered. And after they'd been standing a couple of weeks or so on the bottom floor of the oast, all packed away like glasses, there'd be a man come along from the brewery one day – by appointment, I presume. And he would get a knife out, and he'd cut a flap, like, out of the middle of the pocket, so that he could lift it up: then he'd got a special tool, that he'd put in there and take out a square sample, and label it with the number of that pocket an' all. Then that would be neatly sewn back again, and he'd perhaps do three or four pockets like that. His samples would be tested at the brewery, and those hops'd be sold on that result.

According to an East Kent lorry-driver (whose name, may he forgive me, I failed to record) a certain degree of secrecy was customary when transporting the hops to the brewery: 'because you didn't want your neighbours to know how much money you'd made'. But there was nothing secret, as the company at the Volunteer informed me with great glee, about:

The biggest thing that happened on the last day of hop-picking, that was to shove the bailiff [farm foreman] in a basket! You used to get the bailiff, pick him up, and stuff 'im in a basket, head-first. The bailiff knew 'e was gonna git stuffed in a basket, full stop: and he knew that by the end of that evening, he was gonna be so drunk he couldn't stand on 'is feet. He'd be dragged back home on a hop-pocket!

He was dragged, no doubt, from one of the end-of-hopping celebrations remembered by Alf Friend:

After the hops were gone, they'd clear the upper floor of the oast, and 'ave a party in there, and they called that their 'harvest supper'. There'd be one fella, 'e could rattle a tambourine, and another fella with a set o' bones in his hand, and another with an accordion or a mouth-organ, or a drum: there'd always be four or five to entertain you for an evening. And o' course there'd be a big barrel o' beer stuck up in the corner, for everybody to help theirselves to; and another corner there'd be some cider. And if they were still drying, they always used to chuck big spuds onto the fire, baked spuds. They was grand do's, the 'harvest suppers'.

Servants' togetherness: Lizzie Grange (right) with the cook (left) and parlourmaid, outside 'Madam's' holiday home at Seahouses, Northumberland, c. 1925.

6

IN SERVICE

The rich man in his castle
The poor man at his gate
He made them high or lowly
And ordered their estate

'All things bright and beautiful'

THE ONLY THING GIRLS COULD DO

Whenever I asked a working-class countrywoman over sixty what she did when she left school, I learnt to expect the answer, 'Oh, I went into service, of course.' For during the first decades of this century, one in every three of all British women between the ages of fifteen and twenty were employed as domestic servants: and, at nearly one-and-a-half million strong, the predominantly female 'household army' outnumbered any other occupational group in the land. In most rural areas, indeed, service was virtually the only occupation open to women. As consolation, it could be regarded as an indispensable training for marital housekeeping: whereas 'field labour' (much less in demand with the coming of the new machinery) was merely 'rough', while factory work, where any existed, was regarded with utter horror – says Mrs Libby Low (b. 1900), a smallholder's daughter from near Knighton on the Welsh border:

Going into service was the only thing girls could do. There was only one factory in Knighton, and people wouldn't talk to you if you worked *there*. Well, it was so *low* to come down to that. You see, most of the men were farmers about here, and I suppose they wouldn't let their girls go to the factory. Service, they didn't mind that, though there was less money, because I think the factory paid more. They did have girls working there, but I didn't know any of them. But they said round here it wasn't good enough work for us.

HERDEN APRONS

Some country girls followed the old tradition of starting service in a 'petty place', 'obliging' a neighbour or relation: then, having supposedly been introduced gently to working life, they proceeded via the local hiring fair to a post in some farmhouse not too far away from home. So began the career – which she ended as head of Lord Rennell's dairy at the Rodd, near Kington in Herefordshire – of Mrs Edith Watkins (b. 1900), daughter of the shepherd of Cwmgilla, near Knighton.

I wasn't very old when I went to service, because I left school and went to an aunt when I was thirteen and a half. You could come out of school for 'half time' then, when you were thirteen: and I used to go to school for a couple of days, and go to my auntie for the rest of the week, like. I used to help her out: they'd got a smallholding by Clunton [Shropshire]. But I didn't like her, she was a real old slave-driver! We used to carry wood for baking – we used to go up in the wood: and she used to say, 'Fill up that apron!'

We used to have an apron made of sacks: they used to be washed and boiled. You wasn't smart unless you'd got a nice apron made of flour-sacks: they'd be white when you boiled them, because the flour was white and the sacks were white – beautiful. The old people used to call them 'herden* aprons' – 'herden' means 'made out of sacking': and you were thought to be very smart and very industrious if you wore a nice clean herden apron.

And Aunt used to make me fill up this apron with wood, and carry as much as I could: it was heavy work! Then we'd have to carry water from a little well, in buckets: I had what they called a milking tin, white enamel, and I used that to carry water – and I often used to carry two. But when my aunt used to carry two buckets, she had a square frame about the size of this table – and with that you wouldn't hardly know you were carrying a bucket of water. You were *in* this frame, you'd step in the square: and you'd have two buckets, one on either side. And your bucket handles came up on the outside of the square: and the weight's on the square then. You'd be surprised. You don't hang the buckets onto the square, you just hold the handles: and you come along quite comfortable.

But I didn't stay with my aunt long: I ran away! She took me up to Knighton one market day, and she took me to my home – we were at Cwmgilla then. And I said to my mother, 'I don't want to go back.' 'Oh, but you must.' And I said, 'No, I haven't left school.' And they were having tea, and my mother said, 'We'd better get tea now, it'll be time to go back on the train': 'Oh yes,' my auntie said, 'We mustn't miss the train, or we shan't get home: because there's nothing after that.' So as soon as I saw them sat down comfortable to tea, I was missing! And I went to Cwmgilla Farm, and found my dad. And I said, 'I don't want to go back, I don't want to go back with Auntie tonight.' 'Well', he said, 'there's no need to, if you don't want to.' I said, 'I don't. She's too hard. She makes me work.' 'Well', he said, 'that won't hurt you.' So I said 'Well, I'm not going back': and I left him then, and I thought – they can't find me, because Auntie won't have time to come and look for me. And she had to go, to catch the train. So I didn't go home 'til I met me dad, and I went home with him. And I said to my mother: 'I didn't want to go back, Mum, I wanted to stop. I couldn't do with Auntie, she's awful hard. She's got no children, and she doesn't know how to treat children!'

So then I went back to school, and finished my schooling: and you was out of school then at fourteen. So my birthday was in March, and Knighton May Fair was on the 17th and 18th of May, so I went there and hired into service. People'd know you, and they'd say, 'Are you looking for a job?' And I said, 'Yes.' But it was Mr B—— of C——, and I didn't like them much, so I said, 'I don't know as I'm in a hurry just yet' – and I just put them off. Then I met some people from Beguildy – Daykins their name was: and Mrs Daykins was from the Bowens of Hidmore, and I liked her. And she said, 'Are you looking for a job?' 'Yes.' 'Have you left school?' 'Yes.' 'How much are you asking?' 'I don't really know,' I said, 'What would you pay me?' 'I'll give you five pounds a year.' And I said I wanted a holiday before I came – we generally had a week's holiday when we hired. 'Well', she said, 'I'll come and collect you after that. And to make sure you'll come to me, I'll give you two shillings.' That was earnest-money, they called it: and then she came and collected me later, in a horse and trap, and away we went.

It was right up at Bettws-y-Crwyn, a little farm called Cwm House: and there I stayed for several years. She gave me five pound for that year, and you were only supposed to spend, if you were very good, half a crown out of that five pound for the year! You were very, very good if you could live on half a crown for the year: but, no, *I* didn't. I had to get a little bit more, because I wanted a pair of nice, *best* boots: little boots with buttons on the side. And of course they provided all your food – we had very good food. And she was very good about getting my clothes, too. We used to go to Newtown, to Price-Jones's, the Royal Welsh Warehouse: and she used – you'll laugh when you hear this – to get beautiful red flannel. And she used to wear red flannel petticoats. And she said, 'I think you must have a red flannel petticoat: it's so cold I think I'd better get enough to make you two.' So I had two. We didn't have any kind of uniform: just a skirt, and a blouse, and red flannel petticoats, thick black stockings, and boots. And a coat to go out, like. And, of course, these herden aprons – they were very warm. You were good working people if you had herden aprons.

I did everything: because there was just me, and she didn't have any family. We used to bake, and kill a pig, and I used to do the milking. I used to like that – you get so attached to the cows. I had a little stool to sit on, and often I'd get a bucket of milk from the cow. We only had two cows for the house, and the butter. Just a bucketful would do us, like. There was no cream separators in those days, and in some places there was just big milk pans, and you had to skim off the cream with a skimmer. But at the Cwm House they had leads: big square things, on four wooden legs. All the base of the pan was made of lead, pure lead: and then you had a lovely brass stopper to put in the hole in the middle of this. Then you let out all the milk, and you had to be so careful to mind it didn't let the cream out as well: the milk would go down into a bucket underneath, and you'd have lovely thick cream left. That was the latest thing, then, these leads.

Then we'd make butter. Only just enough for the farmhouse, though. We'd put the cream in one of those end-over-end tumbler churns: I used to be churning and churning, and all of a sudden the cream'd go 'flop, flop': you knew then as it had 'broke', as they called it. Then you just turned about half-a-dozen times, and you'd hear it go 'plonk, plonk': then you'd know it was gathered in one big lump. You poured the buttermilk off to go for the pigs, and put the lump of butter in a butter mitt, a big round thing – you had to scald that first – and patted it with butter prints [butter hands] until you got all the buttermilk out. And then you got salt, and worked it well in with these hand prints ; and then made it up nice into little half-pounds, and put it in the dairy to keep cool, because you'd nothing like refrigerators then. And that was your butter.

And when I was there at Cwm House, I remember how we used to look forward to Knighton May Fair. That was a great thing. But before we could go, we had to do all the winter washing – all the winter bedclothes and blankets, all those things had to be washed and aired and put away. And the trap had to be washed and the harness had to be cleaned and polished, and the pony was brushed. And then we could go to the fair!

I stayed there several years – 'til I was seventeen I think. I then thought I'd like a change. 'Whatever for?', they said, and they wasn't willing for me to go. So at last, I ran away: I just ran away from there. At that time Dad and Mother had got a by-tack [a sublet farmhouse] at Gwerneirin ['plum tree meadow'] on the Newtown Road, not very far away it wasn't. He was living in the house, and working for the farmer that lived elsewhere, at Black Hall in Llanfair Waterdine. Usually I used to go on a Sunday to Black Mountain Chapel – you've heard talk of that little place? – with Mr and Mrs Daykin: they were Baptists, and he was deacon at Black Mountain Chapel. They thought a lot of him: he'd got plenty of money. But this one Sunday, I said I wouldn't come, I'd go to my parents – and I ran away. And I said to Dad, 'I mustn't go back.' So he borrowed a pony and trap, and he went over to Cwm House, and he fetched my box – the box I kept my clothes and bits of belongings in. And that was that.

So I went, and I hired again. And I came then to Prices of Pilleth, and I got a little bit more money there – I think it was ten pounds a year.

By the beginning of this century, nevertheless, the old system of 'hiring-on' was used only by those maids who preferred to choose employers they knew (at least by reputation) and to remain in a community where any ill-treatment would either quickly come to the ears of their parents, or could be remedied by a short 'run' home. But for those who regarded hiring fairs as 'slave-markets', who had seen quite enough of milking and butter-making at home, or who hoped to improve on the generally low wages paid to farmhouse maids (which is to say the majority of country girls) the beginning of service meant a first journey into the great unknown. Another Knighton girl, Mrs Libby Low, remembers her own departure from home:

My sisters went to service away, and two of them went to Birmingham. And I didn't go into service round here, either. A friend of mine worked at Aylesbury College, that's how I went there. It seemed like a long way away to me, because I'd never been on the train so far before, and I had to make three changes. I was only fourteen or fifteen, but, no, I wasn't frightened. I went as a dining-room maid at the college, and I had to set the tables, and serve the boys with their teas: then we each had our different job after, to wash plates and things. We had to wear uniform – blue dresses in the morning, and black in the afternoon, with caps and aprons – and we only had little tiny rooms, only boxes really, with two of us in each one.

SHEETS AND FRYPANS

Much the greatest demand for maids, however, came from the rising middle-classes of the large towns, for whom the keeping of a servant (regarded as absolutely indispensable in 1906 where a family's annual income was three hundred pounds or more) was a symbol of emergence from the 'great unwashed', and the addition of extra domestics the index of progress up the social scale. Nor could this insatiable appetite be coped with by the towns themselves: for town girls, far from sharing their country cousins' aversion to factory work, increasingly preferred it as better paid and less 'lowering' than service. So the vast majority of town maids were, like Daisy Record of Harrietsham in Kent, country bred.

I've bin Kent all me life. Dad used to say, 'e come from Kent, and 'e's still gonna stop in Kent. But people 'ave asked me so many, many, *many* times: they said, 'Daise, you 'ave different ideas you do, and now and agin you gotta 'ave a word different.' But I says, I bin Kent all me life: my mum and my dad was Kent, an' I never bin nowhere else.

I was born nineteen-hundred-four, at Hunton near Yalding – 'ave yew bin out Yalding way? That's not round 'ere – I should think it's about twenty-three mile away. Dad was always on the farm: 'e was all-round man, did everything – hop dressin', stringin', diggin', plantin' trees, whatever was on the farm, 'e did. 'Course, that was a hop-farm, that was all 'ops round there – not like round 'ere. We all 'ad to go 'op-picking – oh, 'an I loved it: I cried me eyes out when we came up 'ere, 'cause there wasn't no 'ops.

But now I like bein' up 'ere at Harris'ham, up the hill. 'Cause down Yalding way it floods so, it's flat. It was shocking. We couldn't goo to school many and many a day, couldn't git out. And Dad used to ha' to stop up all night, to see it din't come indoors. We lived in a big farm 'ouse then, big ol' Bishops it was: awkward ol' house, with ol' beams. It was a tremendous big 'ouse; with an ol'-fashioned pump outside. I'll never forgit Bishops. There was nine of us livin' there, with Mum and Dad.

Well, I was jist left school, an' I was jist fourteen. So I came home, and Dad used to say to me, 'Well, young lady, you're not gittin' your feet under *my* table: you git your feet under somebody else's table.' 'Cause there was nine of us, and the money wan't much. So I says, 'All right, we'll git a job.' So I wrote to me sister, that was the oldest one: that was at Sydenham [South London], right up the top o' Sydenham Hill, and it was lovely up there. An' I asked if they'd got a job up there, and she said somebody wanted a kitchenmaid. So I says, 'That'll be jist right, that will,' and away I went.

I 'ad to goo only daily. So I 'ad to sleep with me sister at night, and then goo up there in the mornin': they wanted me earlies, I 'ad to git up there 'alf past five, 'cause they wanted to be called by six. I 'ad to make the tea, and cut some bread an' butters and take 'em all round – there was ever so many of them there, a big family. Then I 'ad to do the baths; oh dear, oh dear, they *wouldn't* git up.

There was the cook, the parlourmaid, the 'ousemaid, and I was the kitchenmaid. I used to wear a blue print frock and white apron every day, and the collars, an' a little peaked 'at: and in the afternoon you 'ad to change. You'd ha' a little coffee-apron and a black dress, for answering doors and servin' tea: now and agin I 'ad to 'elp the parlourmaid with the silver, when she was busy with people. And there was a cook, too: I'll tell you about 'er in a minute. She used to goo up and see what was wanted for meals, and I used to ha' to 'elp 'er with everything in the cooking line, specially the veg'ables. *And* I 'ad to clean the shoes, 'cause they 'adn't got a gardener.

So the first thing was, I cleaned the shoes: and ooh lumme, there was quite a bushel! Now this very particular mornin', I forgot to clean in 'ere, in the instep: I forgot to do it. And the cook come along, and 'it me on the 'ead with the frypan! She said, 'The master won't like that, and you got to learn to do things properly.' I said, 'All right, I know how to clean shoes, I done me mum and dad's.'

So I went up to the missus, and I says, 'The cook 'as 'it me on the 'ead with the frypan!' And she says, 'Whatever for, Daisy?' And I says, ''Cause I never cleaned the instep for the master.' So she says, 'Wait a minute, an' I'll come down wid you.' And she came down, and she made a proper shemozzle to the old cook.

Now this cook was a biggish person, and nice when she was all right. But she was full o' whisky, *full* o' whisky: when she was out o' drink, she was all right; but when she was full o' whisky, she was terrible. Now the mistress didn't know anything about it, 'til this very day she come down. 'Cause she was full o' whisky, and she 'ad a little cubby-hole, where she used to git 'erself in when she was in a mess. And the missus went *in* there. Oh, honest to God! there was piles and piles o' whisky bottles, and gin bottles. So she said, git a bag, Daisy, and rake all them out: we had three or four sacks of empty bottles out o' there. So she had to goo, and they got another cook.

I stayed up there six years, and then I went over to Penge. And I slept in there, so I didn't have to git up so early: an' I had to rake it out best way I could. But I din' like always being in London, 'cause all me mates was down 'ome. So I served me notice out, an' I went 'ome, and went as a kitchenmaid to Wickens at Yalding – that was a farm'ouse.

But it come that I left *there* in a 'urry. Because the mistress's sister blamed me for nicking some sheets: well, my godfathers, I'd never nick nothing! I'd been out that day, an' when I come in the mistress says, 'Daisy, I've 'ad a bad report of you: my sister says you nicked some sheets.' An' I says, 'Well, that's news to me. They're not up in my bedroom, an' I ain't never took 'em 'ome. My mum's got plenty o' things like that, she don't want 'em!' Then I goes flyin' into the dinin' room, an' there *she* is, the sister. 'Excuse me,' I says, 'what did you say, that I've been nickin' sheets? You better come out 'ere, and let's 'ave a sort out. I don't like this, 'cause I don't reckon never to nick nothing. It ain't *you* hid 'em up, and blamed me, is it? Tomorrow mornin', when I git up, I'm goin' to go all in your room, an' 'unt 'til I find 'em – 'cause I think it was *you* put 'em away!'

So arter I done me jobs next mornin', I gits th' ole steps: an' up on top o' the wardrobe I see this big parcel – and there *was* the sheets. The old bitch 'ad 'id 'em up on top o' the wardrobe, all covered in paper. There was three pair in there, an' she'd been busy 'iding 'em up. So I took 'em down there and threw 'em at 'er, an' I left there and then. I din't stay there.

An' arter *that*, I came on the farm: I'd 'ad enough of service, what with the sheets and what with the frypans! So I said, I'm gooin' on the farm now, and that's what I did. [See p.37.]

BAD-MEAT PLACES

Daisy's experience of ill-treatment at the hands of a fellow-servant was by no means unusual. Yet indubitably the least enviable – as well as by far the largest – class of maids were those employed as the only domestic in a small urban household. Known politely as a 'general servant' or more truthfully as a 'maid-of-all-work', she had at best to carry out her demanding round of tasks without companionship. At worst, she fully justified her nickname of 'the slavey': for she was all too often grossly underfed and underpaid even by the standards of the day, and frequently the petty spite of her mistress added to her sufferings. Open-handed, friendly, and even indulgent employers of general servants did, of course, exist in large numbers: but, it appears, they were least likely to be found among families who had themselves only just emerged from the 'servant classes'.

It was with such as these that Mrs Lizzie Grange had to contend when she first went into service. Born the daughter of a miner in 1906, she now lives surrounded by relations and descendants at Prudhoe in Northumberland – where I found her busy raising funds for that peculiarly north-eastern phenomenon, a kazoo-playing 'juvenile jazz band'. But she hadn't been speaking more than a few moments before it became clear that she was not 'pure Tyneside'. For though she and her parents were born in England, she has inherited good measure of the Irish accent, Irish eloquence (and, she says, 'Irish temper') of the grandparents who came over in the famine years of the 1840s. She must have needed all her good humour and overflowing high spirits, however, to survive her years as maid-of-all-work in 'bad-meat places'.

I was fourteen-and-a-half when I left school. And I was a week at home when I went to service, and I went down to Wylam: there was no buses then, and we had to walk up through the clarty [muddy] fields. And I was in with an old lady, an old maid she was: and I was half-*starved*. It was in the paper, the job: and after that I would never have a place out of the newspaper. Because with this old maid, we used to get two potaters – one each: and if 'twas a big one it was one cut in two, and that was your dinner: and a wee bit carrot, one carrot between two of us, and that's the God's honest truth. I was ill through it, to tell you the honest truth. You might think I'm exaggerating, but 'tis the truth, my God to me. She'd have one-and-sixpenceworth of meat, I'm tellin' you, lasted us the whole week: she'd stew it, cut a bit off for a bit stew. Then she'd make a broth on the Sunday, and on the Monday we'd have a wee bit cold. Then she'd make a bit of a tatie-pot on Tuesday: and on a Wednesday we minced a bit up of it, and on a Thursday I had a bit cold meat: and on a Friday she finished it off. Because on Friday I never ate meat then, being a Catholic. Me and her shared this one-and-sixpenceworth of meat.

Was she that poor? No, she was rich! She had a three-bedroomed house, with a sitting room and a kitchen, and a back kitchen. And Mr Tulip came round there with a basket, selling buns. And of course she'd have two buns, one would be for her one day, and one for her the next: and I would sit on the table-end with me bread and marmalade, which I didn't like – that was at tea-time. Then at supper-time you had a bit cheese. And when I first went, me supper was set for me: and of course, leaving a houseful of bairns at home, I was full o' tears. So she had cheese, and bread, and coffee, for me supper: and of course, at home we had margarine or butter with our bread – though we didn't get much butter, because they couldn't afford it: the only one that got the butter was me father! But she had no butter or margarine on the table. So I says to her, 'Oh, Miss Robson, have yer any margarine or butter?' 'Oh, yes.' And she brings me out the margarine, but she takes the cheese away! And she says to me, 'Don't you like cheese?' I says, 'Yes, mum, but at home we have cheese *and* margarine.' 'Oh, *far* too extravagant, that's how you pit people never have any money.'

And this day I was getting fed up. Now every afternoon, she had herself a half a glass of whisky and she went and lay down. And this was how I got me own back. I thought, I'm not putting the marmalade out today. So I put the jam out, and I started me tea before she got in. 'Oh, Lizzie', she says, '*you* don't have strawberry jam.' 'Well!' I says, 'I happen to be having it the dee [today], because I'm sick to death of marmalade: I *don't* like marmalade. You get a teacake for yourself, but you never think about me wanting to be fed, and doing all your work' 'Oh', says she, 'I didn't know you liked cakes.' So after that I got a bit teacake, and strawberry jam.

Because I used to get me dinner on a Sunday before I come home to me mother's – I used to get half-a-day off on a Sunday – but I used to sit down there again at half past two, and eat as much as me father and mother, and three–four lasses. And she'd say, 'Lord, I thought you'd had your dinner.' And I used to say 'I have.' 'What have yer had?' Then she used to say, 'Good heavens, one tatie between two of yez!'

And when I had to leave there 'cause I was ill, me mother went mad aboot me not telling 'em aboot being starved. So I said, 'Well you know Ma, me da always said that if ever we left our jobs he would put us into the workhouse.' That's what we were frightened of. So me mother said, 'He'll never say *that* again.'

So I left that after twelve months – I'd only been getting five shillings a week – and then I went to another place at Wylam. And it was a good-meat place, like, you had good food there. But her and I fell out – it had got too much, because I had all the washing to do meself. I was only sixteen, you know. So I put me notice in, and went on to another place, at Wylam again.

And that was just as bad as the first! They were corn merchants, that had just brought themselves up from nothing: people that knew them said that when they first went to Wylam, all they had was what they could put on a flat-cart. And there, *it* was a bad-meat place. You just got one tatie each, even the men: and a tomato was cut up between me and the mistress, and a tomato between the two sons. It made you very weak, in fact I came up in boils! And everything was under lock and key, even to your black lead that you did your fireplace with: and even your Monkey soap and grey rubbin' stone. Monkey soap was for washing paint, the doors and that: of course then I had me hair long, and I had hairgrips. I used to take me duster, and the hairgrip, and rub this Monkey soap in all the crevices – I hadn't to have a bit dirt. They had these fancy panelled doors, and you had to go into every one with a hairpin. Grey rubbin' stone was for doing the steps – three great big steps, every day: and that rubbin' stone used to get wore down. And if you went before that rubbin' stone was finished, she said to you, 'And *what* have you been doin' with the rubbin' stone, Lizzie? That should have lasted you 'til tomorrow.' Mind, if I was as cheeky then as I am now, I should've said, 'I've been eating it, to fill me up!'

And we used to 'post' the washing [wash clothes in a dolly-tub, pounding them with a 'post stick']. And without a word of a lie, I used to have to stand and post, and count out loud, and I used to have to post to two hundred, so she could hear me. And I used to start and count, and of course sometimes I got meself wandered away: and it was, 'Lizzie, I can't hear you counting.' So I'd come in with, 'a hundred and sixty-four, a hundred and sixty-five, a hundred and sixty-six'.

You were up at quarter to six, and you had to black lead that fireplace every morning, you had to scrub all the tables down, and you had boots to clean, and you had to do your steps – and that's before you got a bite across your lips. They were hard days!

After that, I went to a farm up Allendale way: and I think that was my best place of all. It was very different from the others, different altogether. I was milking cows, and I did the housework. And when the hay was on, the boss used to come in and say, 'Come on out, leave the work, and get to the hayfield.' I liked it up there, and the food was good – up there it was all home-bred: we used to get a dinner every day, and bacon and eggs too for breakfast. And I got ten shilling a week: because it was heavier work on a farm than in a private house. I was there three years, 'til me mother come up on a visit. And she said, 'You're not stopping *there*, for 'tis a lonely place.' We were right the way out in the wilds, and me mother thought 'twas terrible, me being up there: because we had three mile to walk to the village, so she made me come away. But that was my best place.

BIG-HOUSE TWEENY

Though most modern fictionalizations of life 'below stairs' are set in large multi-servant households, such establishments were in fact becoming relatively uncommon by the time Mrs Grange entered one in the mid-1920s. Gallowhill Hall was unusual in employing so many laundrymaids – by now the prerogative of the very wealthy – and in its resident monkey: but it seems otherwise to have been a fairly typical example, complete with tyrannical Nanny and rigid divisions between 'upper' and 'lower' servants – it was a popular maxim that 'there's more class distinction below than above stairs'. As a 'tweeny', Lizzie was near the bottom of the scale – though not so low, apparently, as the maids who ate their spinach in the kitchen.

After that I went to a big house, called Gallowhill Hall, near Morpeth. That would be in about the middle 1920s. I was there as a 'tweeny', a between-maid: we used to do all the back-ends, the passages and that, and look after all the servants, in the servants' hall. There was two of us: and an 'odd man', and he used to do all the high places for us. And if they needed you in the kitchen, if they was a maid short, you went in there: and if there was a housemaid short, you went there – you was at everybody's beck and call, that was what a between-maid was.

They had a big staff there, about twenty. There was four housemaids; two lady's-maids; there was a butler; there was a parlourmaid which was the butler's wife; there was the footman; and there was three laundrymaids, two kitchenmaids and the cook; and there was the housekeeper. The house-keeper was the top, and then the butler. All the staff came to eat in the servants' hall, but the butler and the parlourmaid and the housekeeper used to go into the housekeeper's sitting room – oh, and the lady's-maids would go with them. But the footman, and the housemaids, and the odd man and the gardeners would be with me in the staffroom, and the kitchenmaids had their meals in the kitchen. Then they had a groom, and four men looking after the dogs: because, he, the master, was head of the Morpeth Hunt. And they had these big horrible dogs: if you left the doors open, they'd come in and snarl their teeth at you – I used to be terrified, and I'd say, 'Bob, come and get these dogs oot!'

I enjoyed it there, mind. But the only thing was, we got rabbits to eat, as many blinking rabbits as they could find! I like rabbits, but we got too many: we got a one nearly every day, one at dinner and one again at night. You got two dinners a day, you know, and we were well fed. But there was spinach too, and nobody would eat *that*. The spinach used to come into the servants' dining room, and it went back into the kitchen again: then back it would come at night-time, and back to the kitchen.

And once a month, the mistress would allow dances, in the servants' hall. The staff was all there. That was the only way they could keep a maid, because it was lonely, right out in the wilds: I've seen kitchenmaids come one day and go the next.

Monkey business

Another servant there was there – and she'd been there longest of all – was old Nanny. See me, she'd brought all the family up, and though they was all grown when I was there, they kept her on. And she had this great big nursery, and Ivy the nursemaid to look after her: and you'll never guess who *she* had to look after in that nursery – a monkey, and a dog called Precious, a Pekinese!

Eh, we used to laugh at Ivy, the nursemaid. Because when old Nanny went away, she'd leave all orders: 'Now Ivy, you'll go into the kichen, and you'll get poor Nigger' – that was the monkey – 'two bananas and an apple, every day: and don't forget to feed him!' And Ivy would say, 'Right.' But it was Ivy who had the apples and the bananas! She used to sit in the kitchen and eat them, and get some carrots for the monkey. I said, 'You'll get found out one day': but she said, 'Why the hell not, the damned things!'

Because that monkey was a blinking nuisance. When me and the housemaid was having tea it would be running away, along the great big long passage and up the stairs, and we'd always have to run after it. And another time, when we was having breakfast, who snuck down the staffroom but that monkey: the footman went mad. 'If old Nanny thinks I'm going to sit and have my breakfast with *that* damned thing there, she's got something else coming!' So he took and he pushed it into the passage. And along comes Nanny. '*I* would like to know who put poor Nigger out in the passage.' Well, none of us dare open our mouth, 'til the footman says, '*I* put Nigger in the passage.' 'Poor Nigger, he'll be cold.' 'Look', he says, 'Madam likes her meals clean and comfortable. We're servants, but we're as particular as what Madam is: so if you want Nigger to have any comfort, take her around to old Madam.' And there was such a row! And at times, with the way Nanny used to talk, we'd say, 'Old Nanny's turning like the monkey!'

Madam was very fond of monkeys. They once went away – I think it was to Bermuda – and they came back with six monkeys. They had a cage for them, but they'd getten out. There was ructions at Seahouses about it! They'd getten on top of the telephone wires, and the electric was all cut off!

Madam

They'd often be going away, because they was rich people. The master was a coal owner, and Madam was an American. And she was a bad little thing. Sometimes she was very, very nice, but they reckoned, when she's nice, you can look out for trouble. I always remember, the housemaid was doing the front room, and she said to the odd man, 'Ooh, Madam's lovely today.' So he said, 'Margaret, you're in for your notice!' 'Don't talk such rot, Bob!'

Next day Margaret broke a little wee ornament. She'd dusted it, and she caught it with her duster. She got a minute's notice. They could do that then: she had to pack up there and then.

And sometimes they used to come down to the staffroom and say, 'Madam's on the warpath!' Well, you know these great big high places and shelves, that you needed steps to get to. If she was on the warpath, on a *Sunda'* she'd get the odd man to get the steps, and she'd get right up the very top, to the picture rail, and she'd take a white hankie and run it around. And if it wasn't right, they'd have to start and clean – on a *Sunda'*!

One thing she'd insist on: when we were coming back to Morpeth from our days off, we used to have to change into our uniforms to go on the train. Because, they reckoned, the mistress wouldn't like anyone to think that we were the daughters. One of the housemaids said, 'You know what's the matter, because we're better looking than what the daughters is!' And they *weren't* good looking, they were anything but good looking.

Madam had ructions with one of the daughters. The mistress had been to Bermuda, and the daughter, Miss E—— had getten on with a young man – she'd been meeting him for about twelve months. And Miss E—— was going to marry him, and it was all planned. And one night, the lady's-maid and the housemaid and I had been to a dance, and we were walking back about midnight, and we saw Miss E——'s light was on, and the Madam's light was on. So the lady's-maid said, 'Oh, dear, whatever's happened.' We didn't know nothing 'til next morning, when the lady's-maid came down and said, 'Miss E——'s run away!' Madam had went in that night, and told her she couldn't go and marry this man. So she took off. And Madam wouldn't allow her to use the car, or allow the chauffeur to take her, or anything – she had to walk to the station, and take what she could carry. But she still said she was going to be married!

So Madam sent the Master to stop the wedding: and he went up to where the wedding was. And what did he do? He gave her away! So she *was* married, whatever Madam said.

Oh yes, we had some good times in service, and we had some bad times too. But mind, I preferred service before factories. I think, meself, that in service you learn more. Because, if you notice, these that doesn't go into service, they don't seem to know how to cook or clean – or anything, hardly. They were hard enough days then, but I don't regret it: and I think I've learnt something from it.

THE GARDENER

So far we have heard from 'indoor servants' – among whom, at the turn of the century, women outnumbered men by more than twenty to one. Now it is time to move outside, to the almost exclusively male world of the gardeners, grooms, and keepers – sometimes regarded as grubby inferiors by their domestic colleagues, though many of them were craftsmen in their own right. The most numerous of these 'outdoor servants' were the garden staff, ranging from the single gardener-cum-odd job man of the small household to the all-powerful commander of twenty underlings on a great estate: not until the 1914–18 war, however, did female gardeners appear in any numbers.

Among them was one of the nicest old ladies I've ever met: Hannah Clark of Clyro, near Hay-on-Wye, a Welsh border village made famous by the diarist Francis Kilvert, curate there in the 1860s.

My name is Hannah Clark, with a 'haitch' at the end of the Hannah and no 'e' on the 'Clark' – my father was most particular about that! He was head gardener at Clyro Court, and our cottage was in the gardens: and that's where I was born, in 1893. We were a family of ten children: I'm the youngest of ten, and I'm the only one left now. It was a nice big cottage, three big bedrooms and a big landing where there could be beds: and there was a lot of downstairs to it, a big living room and what we used to call the back kitchen where the water was, and where the washing was done in a big old copper. We had proper tap water, a proper cold-water tap, I suppose because it had to be in the greenhouses. But we had no sanitation, of course – as far away from the house as it could be, *that* was, right up the end of the garden.

And, of course, some of the children had gone off to work before us younger ones arrived. My own brother was 'prenticed to a wheelwright, he learnt the trade of wheelwright; and the one went on the line, and came to be a guard; and the youngest one was very fond of horses, so he worked in the stables at Clyro Court. He worked in stables as long as people kept horses and carriages, and then he turned over to be a chauffeur. The girls, well: domestic service was the only thing that was for them. They all got married but three old maids – we three last ones.

Dad was born at Brilley: and Mam was a Hay girl – she was a Parry, and she used to tell us her father was a nailer, he had a little factory in Hay and made nails. And he made all the nails for Clyro Court: he employed a couple of men, I believe. My father's father, he was the cowman at Cabalfa Court. And when Mam and Dad were first married, Dad lived out here at Oakfield; he was gardener there: but when I was born he was head gardener at Clyro. The Baskervilles owned it then.

And that's how I came to be a gardener. At the time of the [1914–18] war, I couldn't go from home, because my mother was a good bit of an invalid by then – my mother couldn't be left a lot. So I couldn't join the forces, I had exemption. Now I think there were five gardeners by that time, but they gradually had to go into the army: and we were left with my father, and one old man, and myself! We had big gardens, big walled gardens: and it's three-quarters of a mile from the Court to the gardens, the kitchen gardens where we lived. There's a place close up against the gardens that used to be the old Clyro Court – it's now Cae-Mawr: the present Court was built about a hundred and fifty years ago, I imagine, but they never moved the kitchen gardens, they carried on with the same kitchen gardens.

I didn't used to start 'til ten in the morning, because I had to do the indoor work first: as I said, Mother was a good bit of an invalid. But she was a wonderful cook, she'd cook anything that came along. It wasn't everything electric then! No, she used to cook on an open fire: we didn't have a range, but we had a baking oven by the side of the fire. Dad always had to stoke that, and put it ready – you don't use anything in them but wood, do you? So we had the home-made bread, and we kept a couple of pigs, and we had a few chickens – I'm sure we never went short of anything. And there were always rabbits, which were very cheap. My brothers used to tell me they'd go out with the young gentleman who lived at Cae-Mawr – they'd go out rabbiting with him on Saturdays: and they could either have a brace of rabbits, or a shilling. Mam usually let them have the shilling, but sometimes she'd say, 'You'd better bring the rabbits today' – and that nearly broke their hearts, of course.

But I worked every day of the week in the garden. In the summertime there was always work to be done on Sundays. My first job was washing pots and picking the fruit, but gradually it got so that I did everything. I got very interested in the vineries. We tried to carry on the vineries and the lawns, and all that sort of thing: some of the less important things had to go. My father was a marvellous fruit-grower – his grapes and peaches and all were a picture. There were lots of greenhouses, of course, and there were three big vineries with different kinds of grapes in, that came all at different times. What few people realize is that every single bunch of grapes had to be thinned out – I used to love it, though. Then there were peaches, and nectarines, and apricots, all on the old brick walls: and plums, and pears, and apples, and all the small fruits.

My father's princely wage as head gardener was one pound two shillings a week, and the cottage, and our firing: now that put up against the farm labourer's about twelve shillings was quite affluent, wasn't it? But you couldn't manage on it now, good gracious no! He was a great country man, he knew all the old home remedies. We used to have all sorts of different concoctions. When us children had terrible colds, Father had a great idea of cutting up a swede in rings, putting it on a plate, and sprinkling brown sugar on it – and quite a lot of liquid came from it. The brown sugar would gradually melt, you know, and you drank what came off – you had it in spoonfuls. I don't know as it did any good, but it was lovely and sweet, I remember that! And we had poultices, too. I was very chesty, and they used to save the old fat out of the goose and rub it on, with a piece of brown paper put over it. I suppose the idea was to keep the grease off your clothes – and it kept the heat in.

And apart from my garden work, when there was anything wrong in the nursery, I had to give up my garden work and go and help with the children – take them out and do their rooms. They had pretty well all the top floor of the house, and they had a head nurse and two under-ones; and a governess too, of course. But when anything went wrong, *I* got called in. Oh, it used to annoy my father terribly, taking me from the garden when he wanted me.

I don't remember how many staff there were in the Baskerville days. But later on the Court was let, and then a Greek gentleman had it, a Mr Mavroyanni: his wife was an Englishwoman, she was a daughter of Sir John Aird, who had a lot to do with building the Nile Dam. The

Mavroyannis, I suppose they had about twenty-four servants, indoor and outdoor: because they had a big family, six little girls. But there wasn't a housekeeper – Mrs Mavroyanni was her own housekeeper, sort of. They had a staff of three in the kitchen, and three men in the pantry – well, a man and two young fellows – they laid all the meals and did the washing up. Then there were a lot of clothes to see to – a lot of the gentlemen's clothes, and a lot of riding things to get ready. Oh yes, they used to entertain a lot. When the otter-hounds used to come round our part of the river, they used to put the men up. I've know the house be absolutely full. Oh, wasn't it all a long time ago!

We had to give up the cottage when my father retired. That would be 1925. I took over the Clyro village shop, though I didn't like it at all, after being out of doors. But we had to do something to make a living. I never had time to think of marriage! I was too busy, and I couldn't be spared, in any case. I often laugh about it, because I had two proposals after Mother and Father died: but the one was from an old man of eighty-four, and the other was a man who'd been left a widower with three little children. So I didn't think I'd be bettering myself!

THE GENTLEMAN'S GROOM

After gardeners, grooms and coachmen were the next most frequently-kept outdoor servants. Even quite modest households needed a man to care for the trap or riding horses which were the only means of private transport before the cheap motor-car boom of the 1920s: while 'setting up a carriage', with its smartly liveried driver and attendant groom, was a common synonym for arrival in 'high society'. But the aristocrats among horse servants were those employed by gentlemen whose passion was the hunt, the turf, or both; and who possessed the very considerable means necessary to maintain a breeding stable for hunters and racehorses. These flourished around Malton in Yorkshire – 'the Newmarket of the North', set in a famous hunting country – where Alfred Tinsley, son of a travelling head-groom and nephew of a racing trainer, was 'born to horse work' in 1905.

When I first went into gentleman's service, in 1922, we'd start at six in the morning: six in the morning 'til six at night were easy days in stables, and it was more or less a seven-day-a-week job. First you'd muck out the horses, and then take out and exercise those that had to go out, all before breakfast: after breakfast you'd dress your horses over – we did two horses apiece – and set them right for the day. Then you'd take the second lot out that had to go for exercise in the morning, and there was always plenty of jobs for the afternoon. Because, apart from the hunters, we used to breed horses as well. There was an average of six of us in the stableyard (the head man was stud groom, he was in charge absolutely) and we had upwards of fifty-five horses of one kind and another, all belonging to Major B——: there were brood-mares, foals, young horses and so on, and they were all to see to.

The best job of the lot was breaking young horses to hounds – getting them ready for the gentry to ride out hunting. First you'd break them in to be able to ride them: that took about six weeks. You started in February or March time by getting the bridle on them, and then you took them out for a couple of days with that and just a lunge rein* on, to lunge them round. Then you gradually got them introduced to what we used to call a roller, which was a piece that went round the stomach, and was fastened to the bit: that was to get them used to a girth, and get them used to being handled by the mouth – we called it 'mouthing them'. Because a horse is no good at all, of course, unless you'd got control of its mouth.

After that we'd get the saddle on them, and within six weeks we were riding them about. And when we'd got them used to us, and they were going nicely on the roads, we'd give them up altogether for the summer – let them run out to grass: you'd got to give them a break in the summer from all that continual work, because they were only three-year-olds, only just coming to their full growth. Then, at the back-end of the summer, we'd get them in and start all over again, but in a very modified form – you weren't very long before you were on their back again, because they were used to you and remembered what they'd been taught.

When we'd got them right again, we used to ride them about until they were fit to start a bit of hunting, and then we'd take them to a meet of the Sinnington Hunt, or the Middleton, or the Middleton East – we'd take them all by road, because there were no horse-boxes in those days. It used to be a really tiring job with some of them: they used to get that worked up when they first heard hounds, they used to get real upset – the first couple of times, they'd let you know you were on their backs! We had quite a job to get them settled down, to forget their skittishness and get into some graft.

We had to begin by gently taking them on behind, and then gradually get them worked into the field – into the rest of the horses that were hunting. And it used to take a couple of years before they were really fit for the gentry to ride: well, they'd maybe be fit for the younger gentry by then, but not for the older ones, because they still had this bit of skittishness about them.

And when they were really fit to hunt, we'd take them to the meet and ride them for quite a while, until they were steadied down: then the gentleman would take them. Because at that time each gentleman would have two horses in the day: he had a 'second horseman' – that was one of us grooms – who rode the first horse as easy as he could ride it from point to point, while the gentleman was having a good morning's hunting on his other horse. Then he'd change over: I used to take his horse, and he'd take mine, so he'd have a fresher one. We used to take six or eight horses hunting three times a week; we needed those just for Major B——'s family. There was him, and the Honourable Mrs B—— – she was a Rothschild – and Miss Peggy and Jack and William, and they were all very keen.

You'd start off back-end of August time, with the cub-hunting. At that time of the year I'd be leaving home at half past three in the morning, to get to, say, Stittenham at half past five: they don't do that now! The cub-hunting was all to get the horses and hounds into condition, and to get the foxes stirred up. They used to stand round the covert, and try to keep the foxes in until the hounds'd given them a good warming up. Then, when the time for proper hunting came round, the fox would get up and get away as soon as the hounds went into covert – which he wouldn't do if he hadn't been hunted at all. Because if he hadn't been hunted, he'd keep dodging back into covert – but when he'd been stirred up a bit by the early cub-hunting, he'd make a run for it. *That* was the whole idea, of course: and that was why they'd stop the fox's earths, when they could. They didn't really go to *kill* in those days. If they killed a fox, they killed a fox: but if they got a *good run*, that was what they wanted. A good run'd be anywhere from twenty minutes to two hours: if hounds were running over a twelve-mile stretch, it'd be about a two hours' run, depending on the country and the scent – if they got a good scent, it took you all your time to keep up with them.

But the fox was a cunning old devil: he'd double back on his tracks and branch out somewhere else. Well, naturally hounds'll go straight through, and when they got to the end of the track, they lost scent, and he'd probably be miles away! And very often they'd change foxes: some hounds would go on one fox, and some on another. They didn't use to like that, didn't the huntsmen.

And the Sinnington Hunt in those days was a hunt that took a bit of following! Small fields and big hedges, and lots of ditches as well. But when you got to the Middleton East, they were on the Wolds, and it was mainly grassland: big fields, and hedges you could nearly gallop through, if you liked. Major Foster was the huntsman of the Sinnington then, and he was one of the finest gentleman-huntsmen you could meet – it was grand to hear him play his horn. Of course, us grooms had to get to know all the three hunts' country. Because if I'd had a day's hunting, and the boss wasn't out, I'd to go and see him at night when I got back, and he'd have to know just exactly where we'd been. And Major B—— was one of those gentlemen that used to put his hand in his pocket to keep the farmers sweet – to make sure they didn't do anything to interfere with the hunting. If he got to hear that there was some barbed wire in a fence, he'd get to know who the farmer was, and make his way to go and see them, and arrange things.

Of course, a lot of the wealthier farmers came out with the hunt. They went in a black or a dark-grey hunting jacket, Bedford-cord breeches, hunting boots, and a bowler hat. But the gentry used to wear stiff hats – top hats – and their scarlets: they had to pay a royalty to wear scarlets, I think. And us grooms would be got up very smart, too, like a farmer. I'll tell you the clothes I used to get per annum. I used to get a stable suit, to be tidying up the stableyard in – breeches, leggings and all. And then I used to get a new hunting outfit every year: bowler hat, half-a-dozen hunting ties, dark jacket, lighter breeches, and plain hunting boots. All provided free by the boss!

The boss would have to see you were well turned out, of course, to keep his own credit up. Because a gentleman's grooms had to be well kept, or people would talk – and they did talk, too! That was one thing you always had to be careful of, when you were out amongst gentry – you hadn't to talk about one to the other! There were a lot of gentry round here hunted their grooms: there was old Lord Grimthorpe at Easthorpe – he was huntsman to the Middleton – and then there were the Dawnays, from Old Maltongate.

That was why breaking horses to hounds was such a wonderful job, towards the latter end of it: because you were hunting with the best of the gentry. In fact, my boss had to pay two hundred pounds a year to the hunt, just for me to be able to hunt with them! And the wages were good, too, for the 1920s. When I got riding young horses, and the average wage was thirty-five bob a week, I was getting three quid a week, which was a big wage – and I was living rent and rates free, in a house on the estate. It was as different as chalk and cheese from, say, a farm boy's wages. And we were considered just that little bit better than a farm chap. I don't know why, because we were only human, like anybody else, but the farm man didn't think he was good enough to associate with the gentlemen's grooms. Of course, we were much better clothed. As I say, I used to get two suits provided every year, so you could afford a good suit to walk out in – which a farm chap couldn't. I always had a blue suit, a bowler hat, and a stick. I always carried a walking stick. You could afford to get good clothes of your own, when you were so well equipped for your job: because that cloth the stable- and hunting-suits were made of was thick, good-quality stuff. You just couldn't wear it out. Your last year's hunting suit would go for second-best, and so on: and you might have three or four suits going at once. *And* you wanted them, if you hunted three or four days a week: you wanted plenty of changes, in case you got wet or mucked up. You'd got to look specially smart if you went to a strange country. One time we went down with the Major to the Quorn Hunt, in the Midlands: they were a very posh lot. We took four horses down on the train, and two of us grooms. And another time we went for Christmas to the Rothschilds, at Tring: that was a good fortnight's working holiday.

We'd never have much to do with the hunt staff, though, because they were mightier than us! They were a grand lot, but in the field they were the select of the workmen, like, and they'd not want to have much to do with us.

We didn't mix much with them

And another lot of people we were supposed to look up to were the household staff. They had a lot of domestic staff at Swinton Grange. There was the butler, the housekeeper, the footman, the hall-boy, ladies'-maids, parlourmaids, kitchenmaids, laundrymaids – the lot: in fact, they used to have about thirty in the house at one time, apart from us grooms and the outside staff. We didn't mix much with them, and if you *did* mix with them, you hadn't to be seen by the gentry, 'cause they didn't believe in it in those days. When you went up to the house for a meal, such as Christmas time or any special occasion, *then* you could mix in. And sometimes the grooms and household staff'd get up a party to go to a village dance. We'd walk over there – it was about two miles – and we'd dance 'til two in the morning. We'd have a violin and a piano – well, we'd be lucky if we had both – and when two o'clock came round, we'd go round with the hat for the orchestra to stay on another hour. I've very often walked home and just changed into my working clothes, and never been to bed – but you used to get over it! I'll tell you why I finished dancing, and the wife as well – it was when the Charleston came in! And I thought, 'What a bloody fool I look doing this.' So I said to wife, 'If that's dancing, I'm not going any more.' And I didn't.

But when grooms and domestic staff went to a dance, we'd go in a party, and stick in a party: you were allowed to do that, but you hadn't to take a girl out on her own, not if she was from the house. The girl I married was our head groom's brother's daughter, but she worked on another estate. Because for any of the grooms or gardeners to be courting a girl out of the house, it just wasn't on with the gentry. The household staff, to the gentry, were something separate: they were better thought of. I don't know why; but that's how it was in the gentry's service.

Most employers, indeed, considered it their right – and duty – to supervise the private as well as the working life of their servants. And one Cumbrian estate – where the next, anonymous, speaker succeeded his father as head gamekeeper – operated both a dog patrol and an 'intelligence service' for this purpose.

Oh yes, the keepers did mix with the household staff: but we never got too intimate with any of the maids, you know. We were never allowed to get too intimate. It eased off a bit during my time, but before the First World War, and for a good bit after, it was *not* allowed at all. I don't know whether the gentry were frightened there might be a bit of scandal attached to it, or what: but they felt responsible for all the maids in the house – they protected them, you see.

It was part of my father's job as head keeper to find out what was going on outside. And before the First War – I was just a boy, but I remember it – he used to go out at night patrolling. Because no chaps that were courting the girls had to go anywhere near the house: they could go up the path so far, but they hadn't to go through the gates and into the woods.

I've heard a tale since then, from two chaps who lived in the village – they're both dead now – and they were both courting girls up at the manor. Now they used to go in by a roundabout way: and these girls used to go upstairs, and they'd throw the lads some cake and stuff out of the window. But they were always on the watch, because they knew my father'd be patrolling around. One night, they said, they were in front of the manor, on the lawn, and these girls had thrown these here cakes down. Then one of them says, 'Hey, there's a dog about. The keeper's about.' And the other says, 'I'll tell thee what, I'll offer it a bit o' cake, and when it grabs for it, you hit it wi' your cap, and we'll be off.' And they did that, they were over the fence and down to the wood: they'd never forget it, they said, because they both rolled into a big bed of nettles. But they got away.

Oh no, chaps weren't allowed anywhere near the house. But they always had a big staff dance at Christmas. The tradesmen were always invited, the butchers and bakers where they dealt with: somebody from that shop would be invited, and some of the tenant farmers and their wives. And any of the maids that had boys outside, off the estate, then they could invite them. But of course my father would have to screen them: he'd have to get to know about them. Because Miss – who helped run his Lordship's household – would discuss it with Father. '*This* boy, now . . .', she'd say. And if the chaps were really hard drinkers, that got out of control, or if they were shady characters, he'd say no: and if he did say no, that was it. But those were very, very few: and if they were all right, they were allowed to come.

And of course, they all had to parade before his Lordship: they had to go up and parade, and my father used to introduce them. His Lordship would wish them a happy evening, and then they'd go down and have a right good feed in the servants' hall. For the dance, the dining room was always cleared out. The outside chaps'd come in about four o'clock and lift the carpet, and get a good fire on: and the girls'd wash the floor, and put a bit of polish on. There was always a bit of an orchestra came: a piano, a violin, and perhaps some drums, or a piano-accordion. So after supper, the young ones'd come up, but some of the older ones would go to the housekeeper's room.

The housekeeper's room was where all the senior servants usually used to have their tea and their supper – that would be the head housemaid, the lady's-maid, the butler and the cook – and the others had to wait on them. But for their breakfast, they all dined together in the servants' hall, with the butler at the head of the table: then, at lunch, the cook'd be at the head and the butler at the bottom.

That was on ordinary days, but at the Christmas do the housekeeper's room would be kept for the older folk to play cards or dominoes, while the dance was going on for the young ones.

And of course, the young ones would be inclined to sneak off, if they could: and I was responsible for stopping 'em. They'd make the excuse that they were going down to the servants' hall for a drink – lemonade, or tea or coffee, because they wouldn't let them have beer – but I knew where they were at, they'd be sitting on some stairs. And my father'd say, 'Go fetch 'em', and off I'd go: they called me all sorts. 'Bloody boy', they'd say. It was a rotten job: but Father was the boss man.

Then, about half past twelve or one o'clock, it'd knock off: and we'd all go downstairs for a drink then – it'd be port, usually – and mince pies and cake.

Such paternalism was one of the principal reasons why, even before 1914, service was beginning to be considered less desirable than virtually any job 'where your evenings and weekends are your own'. And after the First World War – with thousands of 'servant class' girls reluctant to lose the freedom they had discovered as bus conductresses, 'canteen ladies' or munitions workers – the servant shortage became so acute that a government commission was set up to investigate. Long hours, it found, discouraged would-be maids: but much more resented were the wearing of uniform – especially caps; the deferential attitude required; and the general loss of social status now associated with service.

In 1931, all the same, there were still over a million privately employed domestics in England and Wales: and it was not until after the great social changes of the 1940s and 1950s that servants virtually disappeared from the scene. For though the spread of smaller, more convenient houses and of appliances like washing-machines also played their part, what finally killed off 'service' (as Alfred Tinsley reflects) was the ultimate refusal to 'bow and scrape'.

I've spent my life with the gentry, and that's why I don't speak broad Yorkshire: you'd get your broadness rubbed off. But, to tell you the truth, I think working men were a bit put on in those days: and I'll tell you, I didn't like all that nonsense. I went into gentleman's service just as the bowing and scraping was being done away with – but it was still hard. Mrs B—— was a Rothschild, and she'd been brought up to servants bowing and scraping: I don't think they realized that a working man could be anything more than they thought he should be. All those times were just finishing, but when I first went into stables the older servants used to – well, I won't say they grovelled, but they stuck to the old traditions.

The big change came very quickly: I think it was the First World War that started it, and it was changing a lot between the wars. Then, after the Second War, the gentry had to start looking after themselves, almost. My boss, the present Colonel B——, was brought up with servants, and wasn't allowed to do a thing for himself: if there was anything to be done, the servants did it, no matter what. And now he maybe just has someone to help out in the mornings. It must have hurt the gentry, the change: it must have been terrible for them.

7

THE VILLAGE

WE WERE THEIR PEOPLE:
LIFE IN THE ESTATE VILLAGE

The power and influence of the landowning gentry did not, of course, cease at their imposing park gates: it extended, often scarcely diluted, into the great estates which could stretch for miles into the countryside beyond them. And it was felt particularly in the 'estate villages', whose every inhabitant – from the retired gardener in his one-roomed cottage to the richest farmer – was a tenant, if not also an employee, of 'the manor'. One such community, Hannah Clark recalls, was Clyro in Radnorshire:

Most people in Clyro then worked for the Baskervilles, or rented from them: the ones directly in the village mostly worked at Clyro Court, and the majority of the houses were rented at half a crown a week – but there was no water in them, it had to come from the pump. And they had rent-dinners then, of course, twice a year at the Baskerville Arms. There were two evenings each time: all the gentry and the farmers went to the first, and the second evening the cottagers went. I can remember two ladies in the village talking about going down to the Arms to peel the swedes and potatoes ready for the dinners. I think the gentry and the cottagers all had about the same dinner. It was usually roast beef, and these swedes and potatoes, and something in the way of a sweet – and some drinks I suppose, because I'm sure they were very jolly affairs. That's when they'd pay their rents: there was an office set up opposite, and they went in there to pay their rents, and then they went over and had their dinners. But it was all done away with. They appointed an agent instead, who had a regular office in Clyro, and they took to go there to pay the rent – but they had to pay the cottagers back half a crown, I believe, instead of their dinners!

And of course the vicars and their wives were very helpful in country places in those days. Not that I remember Mr Kilvert, of course, he was before my time. All our childhood it was an old Mr McFarlane, and he had a daughter at home to help him, because it was a big parish. And she was splendid with all us children: she used to be getting up little amusements for us – what they called 'penny readings', and the lantern slides. And then I was in Clyro church choir sixty-one years, from the time I was nine until I was seventy! But there's no choir now, nor no regular organist. Everyone went to church then, and we had a choir of about forty a lot of the time – it'd be full, the church, especially on a Sunday evening. Of course, people's staff in those days *had* to go to church, whether they wanted to or not – so it wasn't all voluntary, was it?

On many estates, it was not only the manor servants who had to go to church. Anglican squires (the great majority) could and frequently did expect all *their tenants to attend the parish church every Sunday, as Mrs Flinton of Burgh-on-Bain, Lincolnshire remembers. And if – as was by no means uncommon – they possessed the right to choose its vicar, they could also ensure that its services accorded with their own 'High', 'Low', or 'Broad Church' leanings. Roman Catholic squires likewise gathered Roman Catholic tenants about them: and landlords of both factions tended to frown on Methodists and other Nonconformists, as suspect of harbouring dangerously radical and egalitarian notions.*

When Dad came to be tenant o' this mill, he had to be a churchman, and he had to attend church with his family. We had to go twice a day on a Sunday: Mother used to always take us in the morning, and Dad used to go at night. And when we went to church the first morning, there was Sir John himself to meet us. 'Oh, Smithson', he says, '*this* is supposed to be your seat, but I can't get you all in it! I'll tell you what you'll have to do, Smithson, you'll have to have *two* seats – your family's too large for the one.'

And we sat in those same seats every Sunday, because all the farmers had a certain set seat. All the gentry would come to church too, and of course all their maids and servants had to go. Yon side o' the church was full wi' maids, in their uniforms and bonnets: and up in the Communion – in the chancel – was full o' the gentry, and there was all us tenants in the body o' the church: Russells, Walters, Smithsons, Browns and all the rest.

Some squires, moreover, required a great deal more than rent, deference, and religious conformity; as Bill Denby discovered when he came to Heslington, near York, in 1930.

There was a big difference between being a farmer here at Heslington and being a farmer where we came from. We'd been on another estate, that belonged to de Yarburgh who lived at Campsall, not far off Doncaster: but he didn't interfere at all, and there everybody did more or less as they liked. But if you lived on Heslington estate, you had to behave yourself – it was a known thing. You were supposed to go to church on Sunday, and you hadn't to cut ivy off your house, because his Lordship liked to see it: there was ivy on all houses in Heslington at one time. And all t'houses was painted same colour; the doors'd all be red, or they had 'em all green another time, and windows had to be white. Estate used to buy paint, and tenants'd do painting.

Then you hadn't to chop branches off trees, and you'd to leave a good big wide hedge-bottom, for game purposes: and hadn't to have your horsemen at work in fields, if it interfered with the drives of the birds. Nor you musn't shoot hares, except one day a year, when they had the farmer's shoot: that was at February time, the last of the hare-shooting, when the Hall had had their pick of the hares. Dinner used to come down from Heslington Hall that day, in containers: it was always hot rabbit and dumplings.

And the estate organized the 'ploughing day' when a new tenant came. You just had that the one year you came, and the idea was to get your new land ploughed: the tenant would come about April time, and all t'farmers would help to get 'im well ploughed up and give 'im a good start. The head gamekeeper used to organize that: he'd say, 'We've a new tenant coming, and we'd like to give him a ploughing day.' Then he'd go round and reckon up how many ploughs there'd be, and how much ground they'd cover: some farmers'd have to send one pair of horses, and others'd send two pairs or three, depending on what they'd got. So there were about thirty-six teams the day they 'ploughed us in', and they pretty near ploughed us up all our hundred and thirty-odd acres of arable. And everybody that went got beer and pork pies!: Dad paid for those, but it was gamekeeper that got farmers to come, and he did it for his Lordship. Ploughing days was a known thing on the Heslington estate.

That gamekeeper was a powerful man: anything he said was law. When we came, there was thirty applicants for the farm we wanted. Well, this old gamekeeper, and me father, and the head woodman, they went down to bottom pub and all got drunk! And me dad was the one that got farm. But you hadn't to think about poaching, oh no. Because if you was caught for poaching, or anything of that, his Lordship's estate agent was on the Bench of Magistrates: and, well, you was convicted before ever you attended court.

Another thing us farmers had to do – it was on your tenancy agreement – was to lead coal for Heslington Hall. They used to burn a hundred and fifty ton a year there, and it came into Foss Islands siding at York, maybe seventy [railway] waggons at once. And each farmer had to cart it with one or two or four carts, depending on how big a place he had: we used to supply two horses, two carts, and two men. The railway used to fill the carts, and we had to bring it to village: and every time you brought a cart to village, there was a half a gallon of beer and a cheese sandwich for you – the butler used to see to that. Then, when you finished at night, you got a shilling each: but that was only an acknowledgment like, because you'd no choice about doing it. It was in your agreement, though they didn't have to do it on the other estates round here: but Heslington was always a bit old-fashioned.

'Old-fashioned' indeed – for this last requirement was a remarkable survival of a compulsory 'labour service', such as the serfs of medieval Heslington had to perform. 'All the bondmen of Heslington', it was ordered in 1295, 'shall cart the lord's hay from Fulford to York or Heslington at the lord's request, and on the day when they cart it the lord shall give them each one meal a day. And they shall cart the lord's firewood wherever it is bought.'

On the other side of the coin, there is no doubt that most estate villages were better built, better maintained and better serviced than their squireless neighbours; or that their poorer inhabitants – so long as they behaved themselves – enjoyed far more 'social security' than they could hope for in the outside world. The best squires, indeed, cared deeply and generously for 'their people' and – as Mrs Flinton testifies – were genuinely respected in return.

Then, at Christmas, Sir John and Lady Fox used to give us children a lovely school treat. We used to go down to Girsby Manor, and they had a great big table, *laden* with presents: and we had to walk right round it three times, before we could choose. Three times, she said, so that we'd know what was on and what we thought we should like. And they were lovely presents, really good presents. I know when I took my little boy, and he'd just got to run, he got a lovely chicken on wheels. But when *I* was little, I very rarely got [there], because I nearly always had asthma: so the butler picked my present, and he always picked me a doll – I had fifteen dolls once, and they were the loveliest dolls. And then one year, her lady's-maid set to and made all us girls 'red riding hoods' to go to school in, in winter. My word, wasn't they warm! They had a hood all gathered, and they were made in the best thick cloth.

And when the eldest boy of a tenant came twenty-one, they always gave a do for him, down at the manor. We had one for our boy, and there was a dance in one room, and whist in another, and a lovely spread.

Oh, they were very, very good, were Girsby Manor. Burgh's been going down ever since they left. We thought a lot of Sir John and Lady Fox, and they did of us: we were *their* people. We didn't need no sick club to look after us, not with having Sir John.

Duke's cottages

Many 'estate folk' also took pride in 'their' squire's position and exploits in the world at large, and villagers whose manor house held a knight or a peer had a tendency to lord it over those forced to make do with a mere 'Mister'. Nor was the reflected glory much diminished if – as on the vast acreages owned by great landowning families like the Dukes of Norfolk or Westminster or the Earls of Derby – it had to be shared among the inhabitants of half a county. Perhaps the proudest of all, indeed, were the hereditary *tenants of the Percies, successively Lords of Alnwick and Earls and Dukes of Northumberland – where they ruled almost as monarchs from the fourteenth century until well within the memory of our next speakers, the Elliott sisters.*

Born respectively in 1898 and 1904, Mrs Mary Watson and Miss Cissie Elliott have lived all their long lives at Ovingham, not ten miles from the centre of Newcastle. But their accent, with its Northumbrian rolled 'r's, is as distinct from Newcastle 'Geordie' as chalk from cheese. For Ovingham stands on the north bank of the Tyne, and looks northward again to the rural Northumberland of fell farms and market towns, rather than southward to the industrial county of pits and steel works. And though their father worked as a miner at Prudhoe across the river, the Elliotts were first and foremost 'Duke's tenants', whose smallholding was a constant reminder of their 'fore-elders'' share in the glory of the Percies.

MARY: We were born in this village. The generations'll have been here three hundred, nearly four hundred years, all told. They came here as the Scotch raiders, sheep stealers and heaven knows what – in caravans: that was the story. And the last man that was hung on Elsdon Fell for sheep stealing was an Elliott – and then it was denied, that it wasn't him.

Father worked at Low Prudhoe, just beside the station there. There was like a drift mine, that they walk in: not a deep mine, you know. He was a deputy 'owerman', they called him: a foreman, an overman. I think he would have been a hewer [face-worker] when he was young, but when he got older he was an owerman: then he would look after safety, pit-props and such. But Mother's family were farming: there's a farm up here called Mount Hooley, and Mother was born there. And they went from there to a place near South Shields, and Grandfather was managing the Blue-coat or the Ragged-coat farm school. And he had an accident, he slipped off the top of the stack and was killed.

CISSIE: And my grandmother couldn't carry on, so she went to be housekeeper to Paddy Freeman – where that hospital stands. He was a great man in Newcastle – owned an awful lot o' land: and he left the land for the Freeman hospital.

MARY: We had cows, and pigs, and a few hens: that more or less fed us. That was quite common for people who were Duke of Northumberland's tenants. They had a cottage and land given to them, when they fought for the north of the Humber – for the Percies. Well then, these people who were volunteers were promised a cottage and land – they were like soldiers, you know, and they got him his dukedom. That's the tradition, that the eldest son would get the cottage: it would fall in the family. And we had a cottage and four acres. Because my father was a Duke's tenant, and my grandfather, and him before, the fore-elder; and so on back a few centuries. And my sister-in-law, my brother that died's wife, she still lives in the Duke's cottage.

CISSIE: My grandfather paid three pounds a year, and when he died my father – being the eldest son – got the cottage, and he paid thirteen pounds a year – he paid that up to 1933, and that was the land *and* the cottage. We used to pay it once in six months, when the bailiff came to the Adam and Eve pub by the station. And they had rent-dinners, for the men – Grandfather would be there! It was a wally [fine, pleasant, excellent] day, that.

MARY: They were there all day, mind! The bar was open, it was never shut: and it was all paid for.

CISSIE: They got a rollicking good meal, roast beef and everything that went with it. But they had to pay the rent first, or they'd spend the money! Then they had the dinner. I've gone many a time to pay the rent, but in those days they got either cigarettes or tobacco, instead of the dinner. Because the dinners ended in the First World War: it was the war that stopped them.

MARY: I can remember the men coming tottering over the bridge from the dinner: and they had to walk to Horsley. There were a lot of Duke's cottages there. It was a great day. And it was a great day when the Duke used to ride the boundaries, because he used to call in at the pub and gave them all a drink. He had a boundary here of his property, and it was known that he could ride from Alnwick Castle to Prudhoe Castle on his own land. He used to ride the boundary once in two or three years, and the tenants used to join on, walking with him. Oh, Father would be there. They were hard men, you know, they were tough: they didn't mind if they'd had nine or ten pints of beer – it was no bother, no bother at all.

CISSIE: Did anybody ever tell you about the Farmers' Folly at Alnwick? Well, that was when one of the Dukes had lowered the rents of the farms: so they put up a monument to him, in Alnwick. And he thought, if they had that much money they could afford that, he could put up the rent again – and he did! So they called it the Farmers' Folly. It's still there, by the Lion Bridge. You know the story of the Lion Bridge? Well, the King huffed the Lord, you know: so the Lord came home and turned the lions round – turned their tails to London!

TWO VILLAGES:
OVINGHAM AND RUDSTON

Leaving the squires and the lords behind, let us now hear about villages as villages – and as livelier, more self-sufficient places than they are now, recall the Elliotts.

MARY: They made everything in the village. My father didn't use to go out of the village for anything. I used to cry to get button boots with bright toes, like other girls: you could get them at the store at Prudhoe – but they wouldn't last. We had to get all our shoes and boots from the village cobbler, old Tom Forster. And he used to make clogs in the winter. He used to have an upstairs room in his cottage with candles, just candles: my brother and I used to go together, the one next to me, and he used to measure our feet. The tops were pure good leather, that he'd treated himself. And when the boots were too small, the tops were parted from the side, the wooden soles put on, and the leather studded round: then we used to go to the blacksmith to get irons put on. There was no such things as wellington boots.

CISSIE: Everybody had clogs for the winter: you'd hear them coming with their clogs on.

MARY: They were lovely and warm: the wood sole was warmer than the leather sole, in the snow. And the leather was waterproof, absolutely waterproof.

CISSIE: And we had skates, and they were screwed onto the wooden clogs. They were permanently on the clog, then. And we used to go skating, and then there was a boy drowned: and we had been forbidden to go skating – but we went: and Father saw us do it. And he came down and ordered us home, and the skates were taken off the clogs and put on a red-hot fire, and twisted. He said, 'You'll never be drowned by skating with those.'

MARY: The blacksmith used to put the irons on the sledge, too, and make our hoops. We had iron hoops – what we used to call a 'gird'* – and a hook, and we used to run along with it.

CISSIE: And then my brothers used to go with my father, to get their Sunday suits made. They had a best suit, and an everyday suit.

MARY: Our dresses, our auntie used to make a lot for us. I remember going to Aunt Maggie's, at West Wylam. We always had a Sunday outfit, and a play outfit, and an outfit for school. And then when school outfits got old, the next year they became the ones for night-time: and the Sunday ones went for school, and you got new ones for Sunday.

CISSIE: We always got new things for Easter: everybody had to have new clothes for Easter – all the village children turned out in new clothes for Easter Sunday.

MARY: As long as you had something new on, you were 'in'.

CISSIE: There was a legend about that. There used to be a joke about it: they'd say that a bird would do its business on you if you hadn't new clothes on at Easter. The birds would make a mess on your clothes!

MARY: They used to make a great thing of weddings and funerals: funerals were most reverent. I can remember the first time I saw a dead person. There was an old lady lived at the shop at the end of the village here, and she was a bit eccentric. And her eldest daughter died – Bella, she was twenty-one. My brother and I, we were cooking potatoes and peelings to make the pigs' food, in the wash-house: and she came, and she said to Matt and I, 'Would you like to see Bella?' Well, we didn't know what to say. You hadn't to be rude: you daren't for your life, else you'd have got more than you bargained for. So we said yes.

So she took us upstairs, and here was this dead girl in the bed. And it was all beautiful white sheets, covering her up to here: and her hair was beautifully done, and there was big bows of lilac-coloured ribbon on all the posts, the big brass posts with the knobs on. And we were *terrified*, we didn't know how quick to get down the stairs and away. And when we told my mother, she thought that was a terrible thing, to take two kids to see a corpse.

CISSIE: They went in for a lot of mourning then. They wore deep mourning for twelve months, and then they went into what they call half-mourning for six months – which was grey. And then you were allowed to wear your ordinary clothes after that. Children, too: I can remember Nancy Holt wore a white dress and a black sash, when her mother died.

MARY: And a boy would probably wear a black band, and a black tie. And they had long processions at funerals, with everybody walking. There was the village hearse, you know, that stayed at the cemetery, in the hearse house: and the farmers in the village lent the horses – you didn't pay for the horses.

CISSIE: When my father died, my brother had to go to the cemetery and get the stretching-board, which was the board they laid the body out on, until it was coffined. The joiner made the coffins – Jimmy Thompson made the coffins for everybody in the village, and they were three pounds. And the night before the funeral, two friends of the family – not necessarily relatives – used to go all round the village, and knock at the doors, and tell them they were bid to the funeral. They were called the 'bidders': they'd say, 'Will you come and be a bidder?' And they'd stand at the church door as the coffin was coming out, and say, 'Mrs Elliott would like you to come back to the house', or whatever. Then they'd all have a ham tea – *always* boiled ham: and the best china was got out. Everybody in the village sent someone: because everybody knew everybody.

MARY: And the undertakers hadn't to bring men to carry the coffin, like they do now. It used to be local lads in the village: I can remember my father going many times – they would *never* say no, because they had to oblige their neighbour.

CISSIE: They'd wear white sashes for a child, purple or mauve for a young girl and black for an adult: and there'd be the same coloured ribbons on the horse's mane and tail. Then two or three of the underbearers would walk on either side of the hearse, and two men would walk in front, if it was a man; or two women in the front, if the dead person was a woman. That was to indicate the sex of the person that had died. [Compare the similar but rather less elaborate funeral customs of rural Swaledale, p. 113.]

'They had long processions at funerals, with everybody walking . . . and two or three of the underbearers would walk on either side of the hearse.' A funeral in north-eastern England, c. 1914.

MARY: And children being born was the same thing. The neighbours used to help out. I can remember my sister being born, my sister here. I was just six, but I can remember standing at the end of the bed and looking up, and my mother held the baby up. And my brother and I looked together, and we'd had a brother before that, and we were a bit fed up. So when we went into the back, he said, 'Let's drownd 'er': he was sick of having to look after younger children. We had to take little Jack out, you see. I remember once going up the Dene, and we crossed the burn, and Jack fell in. Well, we got him out, and he didn't have trousers on – they didn't wear trousers 'til they went to school, they wore dresses, like girls: so he had a red dress on, and all the way home Jack was trailing red. So we sent him in, but we daren't go in ourselves.

CISSIE: They didn't wear trousers 'til they were five, and they went to school. And they used to say, 'You're going to be breeched' – you were going to get your breeches on. It was marvellous when a lad got his breeches on, 'cause he was going to be a man then: they fastened at the knee with a button. He wouldn't go into long trousers until he was fifteen.

MARY: And a wedding was a big affair. That was the day of days. The kids used to be thrilled to bits: they used to tie the church gates together, and the bridegroom was *obliged* to throw pennies to get out. They'd fasten the gates when the couple went into the church.

CISSIE: Two children held the rope, one at each end, and they couldn't open the gates. They'd say, 'Howay canny man, hoy yer ha'penny out' – 'hoy' means throw, throw your halfpenny out. Then everybody threw money, and they left loose o' the rope, and the couple could get out. It was unlucky if you didn't do it: you'd be unlucky. They still do it, I think. [They do.]

MARY: Then there was the big annual cricket match, when the county used to come here to play. The cricket teas were marvellous. The house that's standing down at the bottom there, the lady there used to put out trestle tables all loaded with home-made stuff, I remember this fine. Because the home team had to provide tea for the visitors: and after they were all finished, we could get our tea – we used to love that.

CISSIE: And once a year the Northumberland Fusiliers would come on a Sunday night, with a band, in this field here. That was a real night out, the whole village would be assembled in the field, listening to the band.

MARY: Then sometimes people would go to Hexham – that was always our market town, not Newcastle – to see the Hexham hirings, when the farm men were hired. That was in May and November.

CISSIE: The farmers would come from away, right up in Cumberland and up in 'the Shires',* used to come into Hexham. 'Is tha for hire?' they'd say: 'How awd is tha?', and 'What can tha dee: can tha milk?' Because everybody had to be able to milk.

MARY: There was no writing, you know: they'd just hand them half a crown, or a shilling, and shake hands, and you were hired.

And there's one other thing I can just very faintly remember – King Edward VII's coronation. I can remember my brother in the pram. And there was a big day here: racing, and a tea, and a band. And I have a faint recollection of going along with my mother: I can just see her, in a long skirt, and a hat like a straw boater. It's funny, isn't it, how these things stick in your head!

The Elliotts' obvious pride in their community is – or perhaps I should say was – echoed by villagers all over England. And however ordinary and insignificant a place may seem to the passing stranger, its older inhabitants can always point out some special feature – the tallest church-spire or the deepest pond, a secret passage or a famous resident – which makes it unique in the shire, if not the entire country: and, at any rate, infinitely superior to the next village.

Rudston, in the bleakest part of the notoriously bleak East Yorkshire Wolds, is almost unfairly well endowed with such landmarks: the foremost being the towering prehistoric monolith – truly 'the tallest in Britain' – from which it takes its name. Over the centuries, a folklorist's delight of colourful explanations have been produced for its presence in the hilltop churchyard, and my informant Arthur Wade (b. 1900) confesses to concocting a few of his own for the benefit of gullible visitors. But when, in more serious mood, he declares that it was 'a worshipping stone, the headquarters of the religion of Baal they used to have in these parts', he is perhaps not far from the truth. Certainly, Rudston is surrounded by enough ancient burial mounds, trackways, dykes and processional ways to keep both archeologists and 'ley-hunters' speculating for years, and there can be little doubt that the area had some special religious significance for prehistoric man. Or that the early Christians, unable to remove the mighty stone, sought to neutralize its power both by topping it with a crucifix or 'rood' (hence 'rood-stane', Rudston) and by building their church within a few yards of it.

RUDSTON FEASTS AND FIGHTS

Rudston is celebrated, too, as the birth and burial place of the novelist Winifred Holtby, best known as the author of South Riding. *But, at least among older Wolds people, it is perhaps chiefly famous for the village festivities remembered here by Mr Wade. These centred round 'the Ancient Shepherds', some of whose splendid regalia can still be seen in the Bosville Arms. Despite its claims to hoary antiquity, this was in fact simply the local branch of a nationwide Friendly Society, set up in the eighteenth century to provide much needed sickness-benefits for contributors. Over a hundred other branches once existed in Yorkshire alone, but Rudston's was exceptionally flourishing and long-lived, and it remained the focus of village life until well after 'Lloyd George came in' with the first National Insurance scheme in 1913.*

The 'wedding races' held at Rudston and neighbouring villages are harder to explain, but I can't help wondering whether they were a reminder of the time when the bride was symbolically (or actually) carried off by the groom and his band of local young men. And would it be too mischievous to suggest that the red silk handkerchief (the prize for the single men's race) had its origins in the bloody cloth once brandished by the triumphant groom?

One o' the big days in Rudston was the 'Waggon Day'. They used to take decorated horses and waggons, and tak' t'women and children to Bridlington for t'day: some other villages only did that kind of thing for the Sunday-school treat, but in Rudston it was for the whole village – anybody that wanted to go. They always had it when I was a young lad, but how long it'd been on before my time, I couldn't tell you. Farmers used to send in waggons, and horse lads had to decorate their teams. That was about Midsummer, and we used to set off about nine in the morning from the top o' the hill here, just agin' our gates, and off we used to go to Bridlington. One time o' day – it'd be one year before the First War – there used to be eleven waggons go. There was two waggons from Low Caythorpe; and High Caythorpe's waggon; and there was one from Littlethorpe; one from Dickey – that's Rudston Grange; one from Spring Dale; one from Mr Richardson's,

Horses decorated by Arthur Wade's sister, on Rudston's last Waggon Day, East Yorkshire, 1919.

and I believe there was two from Holtby's – that's Winifred Holtby's people, you know.

But it got less and less, because there wasn't so many big families. Then they knocked it off altogether during t'war, and though they started it up again in 1919, they only had it that one year, and that was t'finish of it. So this here photo's the last Waggon Day we had. We had nine waggons that year, and I took the last team, so I had 'em to decorate: they were all done up wi' their brasses and decorated wi' sweet peas – my sister made all them sweet peas. And that mare there, she's going wild! Because they'd put us where they were just building t'boathouse, and she didn't like all the hammering – it was a daft place to put us!

The wedding race

And d'you know what they used to do here for a wedding? When anybody got married, they'd have a race that evening, at about six o'clock. No matter what evening it was – winter or summer – nor no matter who was being married, they'd have a race down the street, and the bride would hold one end o' finishing tape, and groom the other. The race'd perhaps finish where the wedding party was on, and all wedding party would come out and watch – there'd be a fair crowd of 'em. And there was prizes – a silk handkerchief for the single men, and a pound o' tobacco for marrieds: and the winners would have to go in for the evening, into the wedding party.

I have a red silk handkerchief somewhere, that I won at a wedding race. I'd been off footballing all afternoon, and we'd just come home: I'd jumped out o' the old carrier waggon, and I'd just set off for home, when I ran into me cousin, and he says, 'Races is on, they're running from t'pump to Blue Ball pub.' So I says, 'Tek 'old o' my jacket', and off I went. And I nearly crippled the bridegroom! Because it was pitch black, and my old pal had a big 'cetylene lamp on his bicycle: and just as we were running towards the tape, he turned the blooming thing on me. He thought he was showing me the way, but instead o' that, he blinded me. Well, the bridegroom was holding one end o' tape, and I ran slap into him!

But it wasn't just at Rudston they had these wedding races, you know: they had them all over the Wolds. But they died out, it's all died out now. [SAM ROBSON: We had same kind o' wedding races at Bempton, too: me dad won several of those red silk handkerchiefs, but I never took part meself, because they'd more or less died out by t'time I'd growed up. I only really remember one, when they raced down what we called 'Mucky Lane'.

But I remember another thing they had at weddings here, for us kids. It was allus horse and carriage then, you know, for bride and groom. And they used to cut a bit o' wedding cake, and throw it ower top o' this carriage to crash into road, and all t'kids would run for a bit. And another stunt was to warm up some coppers, and throw them over, and all t'kids would scramble for 'em: and sometimes they were that warm, they had to drop 'em!]

The Ancient Shepherds

But the really big day in Rudston was the Club Feast. Because we had an old club here, the Ancient Shepherds: I wouldn't like to think o' when it started, because it's a very old club. Me father was a member, and all me brothers was, and I joined in 1905, when I was five year old: we was all members, we had to be. But there was no women in it, just the men and the boys – though there was a few that didn't go in for it, and the gentry wasn't in it, it was mostly working men. No, it didn't have any connection wi' religion, or wi' temperance – if you saw 'em on Club Feast night, you'd soon know that!

This Ancient Shepherds was a club, a sick club, same as 'the Buffs' (Buffaloes) or 'the Foresters' that my wife's dad was in, round Doncaster district. You paid so much a week into it – juveniles didn't pay as much as adults, of course – and then you could have a free doctor. Our doctor was Dr West, from Kilham, and he was the first fella round here that ever got a motor-car – it bloody frightened my hosses to death! And the Shepherds'd pay you if you was ill and couldn't work – I used to get ten bob a week when

I had me operation – but you wouldn't get anything in them days unless you was a member. It was a kind of insurance, you know.

It all finished, as near as I can tell you, in t'mid-thirties. Of course it all packed up in t'First War, and t'Feast stopped an' all. It went on again after, but it was never the same. Because by then 'Lloyd George' had come in, and that killed it, because you couldn't get no more members – there was no more young members, because 'Lloyd George' was payin' 'em if they was ill, so they wouldn't join.

But at one time o' day it was very strong, and I think it was about the only Ancient Shepherds round here: I never heared tell o' one anywhere else, except at Hunmanby. I know there was one there, because they wanted to join ours. You see, 'Lloyd George' had started then, and Hunmanby was going broke, and they wanted to join us, but our members wouldn't have it. Because we had such a lot o' members, and we hadn't many on the sick list, so there was plenty o' money behind us. And there was a lot still kept in it that'd lived in the village, but had left. We used to have two come to our house for t'Club Feast every year when I was a kid, and they used to allus leave their staff and their sash wi' me mother.

Club Feast Day

Because you couldn't go in the Shepherds' procession on Club Feast Day without a staff and a sash like these here. It was a green silk sash, with an orange rosette or an orange and white one – there was a few different kinds: and the officials used to wear white sashes, wi' a white rosette, but there was only about three of 'em, the chairman, secretary and treasurer. The sashes went over one shoulder, and they fastened wi' tapes: you'd be walking in twos, and one would have it over the one shoulder and one over t'other, so that they both slanted outwards – it looked better that way. And if there was a lad, and he wanted to walk wi' me, we had to change our sashes so they both slanted out – you couldn't have 'em both going one way.

Then everybody would have a staff, and that was green too, and on top used to be a brass shepherd's hook – I only came across this t'other day, and they'd been stoking bally fires wi' it! Of course, the boys would have a small staff, but if you was a big chap like me, you'd have a tall one – that 'un o' mine would be taller than me.

And we used to have a very big banner, wi' Latin on it, and there'd be two strong chaps carrying a pole at each end, and they used to have white gloves on that carried 'em. And they generally used to have two young lads to hold long tapes from the banner: and when the wind got hold of it, it used to nearly pull them kids off their feet, because it was a terrible big banner.

Well, at eleven o'clock on Club Feast Day, we all 'ad to meet at Bosville Arms, and that's where the procession started. At the head of the procession would be the banner, and behind that – I think – come the children, and then the band, and then all the men. They generally used to hire the Bridlington Excelsior Band, and that was one o' the finest bands they had round here. So we'd set off straight down Long Street, and down Eastgate, and up the hill to the church, and then we had a special church service from Mr Boot, that was vicar here over fifty years. And at one time o' day – before the 1914–18 war – after church, we used to walk right down to Thorpe Hall – that's the squire's house, a mile down t'road – and we used to parade round there and then come back. It was a wonderful sight, you know: but funny thing is, *nobody* had cameras in them days!

So procession ended up at Bosville Arms, and when we'd got back there we'd have a big dinner in the room off the yard – the old court-house. And then they used to have a drink-up, did men! But us lads'd be going on fairground, on the swings and roundabouts they'd got on one o' farmer's fields. Then, about six o'clock at night, sports would start: and there used to be some lovely prizes – in them days it used to be those big barometers were first prize in some things. They'd have cycle races, and obstacle races, and egg-and-spoon races for women, and they'd have a greased pig for people to catch!

And they had another game – climbing the greasy pole. You'd to get to the top to win, and I'd say it was about twenty-five to thirty foot high, and it was that greasy, there wasn't many on 'em got halfway up. But one year, I remember, there was a chap just come and got straight up it! Because there was cyclists came from all over for Club Feast: there was one lad, they called him Jack Bean, and by God he could ride a bike! They used to handicap 'im when he came, but they couldn't stop him winning. People would make a proper day off for Rudston Feast.

A noted fighter

And I'll tell you what they used to be in, one time o' day. If two lads would fall out during year, they'd put fight off 'til somebody's feast day. Like they had a feast day at Burton Fleming – we used to call it 'North Botton', then – they hadn't a club like us, but they had a feast day, and there was a fight there, that year when I went there. And then there was another at Rudston, when I was a young lad. I heared two chaps whisperin' to one another, 'I don't know wheer they're fightin', but they *are* fightin'.' And I met a pal o' mine, and I said, 'I hear tell there's a fight on, hast thee heared anything?' 'No, but I've seen two blokes going through big doors in old Laycock's yard.' So I says, 'Coom on', and off we went down Long Street. And th' old farmer's there, wi' a storm lantern in each hand, holdin' 'em up for these lads while they had this fight out! And we climbed up doors and looked over top, and watched 'em: and when it was ower, we saw 'em shakin' hands, and they walked up streets straight into Bosville Arms to have a drink together. It was settled!

Because there was a lot o' bare-fist fighting round here at one time o' day. My father often told me, he worked on a farm where their foreman was noted for a fighter. Well, one day they were leading corn, and this foreman were making stack when a chap come into t'yard, and shouted to him: and he heared foreman say, 'Well, I can't now, but if thoo can wait while dinner, we'll have it out.' And d'yer know wheer that man had come from – Birmingham! He came all that way from Birmingham up onto Yorkshire Wolds to fight this foreman, because he'd heared tell he was a noted fighter. And they fought in that yard, and afterwards foreman invited 'im to stop rest o' day, and to stop overnight, because they was both fighters. There was no quarrel between 'em: it was just that they was both fightin' men, bare-fist fighters.

MAY FAIR BLUE

Mrs Elsie Hilda Williams, whose reminiscences of Victorian Hay-on-Wye we shall hear next, is not only the oldest speaker in this book, but also one of the most remarkable. Born in 1891, daughter of the postmaster of Hay, she was one of the first women to gain a scholarship to University College, Aberystwyth, and subsequently dedicated her life to teaching, eventually in her own school at Hay.

Hay (or more usually the Hay, a memory of its Norman name, La Haie Taillée, the 'clipped hedge' which once helped to fortify its castle) stands just within Wales, and on a route-centre at the junction of three counties, Herefordshire, Radnorshire and Breconshire. So, long before its invasion by the second-hand bookshops for which it is now famous, it was first and foremost a thriving market town.

What do I remember best about Hay? Do you know, I think it was the Christmas markets, when all the traders came in with their drays full of dead birds, all laid out – full of turkeys and geese all decorated with holly and mistletoe. They came in very early in the morning, all covered in sheets, and then the sheets would come off and there would be these lovely decorations : but they were all gone by midday, because the dealers came up from South Wales and bought them.

There was always a weekly market on Thursdays, of course, when the people came in from the farms all round: that was what Hay really depended on, because the farm people did all their shopping here. And the May Fair was once a year: that was when people really 'went to town'! They had roundabouts and stalls, and the market people came in their best clothes: in fact, there was one particular shade of blue that we used to call

'May Fair blue', because nearly all the people seemed to be wearing it. It was a *very* bright shade of blue, and they all had their dresses and costumes made in it, and their long skirts: when the market women came in on horseback, they rode side-saddle, and they wore very full over-skirts, right down to their ankles, which they took off when they dismounted. They used to have big baskets, big panniers on each side of their horses, for the eggs and the Radnorshire butter: and if it was cold or wet, they'd have big hooded cloaks on as well.

For the children, at May Fair time, they had the 'ha'penny horses': that was a roundabout with little horses and cockerels, and the man turned the handle in the middle: that was for the tinies, and then you graduated to the 'penny horses', and they were bigger. Then there were coconut shies, and boxing booths, and sideshows of all kinds: there were always 'Fat Lady' shows, if I remember rightly.

When I was young, we wouldn't *dream* of going to Hereford or Brecon for amusement. You see, transport was so difficult, so we just couldn't get out, and we had to make our own amusements. No, we had great fun here in Hay. We had a dramatic society, and we always did a comedy a year, and a Gilbert and Sullivan: we actually had the impudence to do Gilbert and Sullivan every year! And we had an orchestra, too, purely among ourselves. We had a hockey team, we had football for the boys and men, and we swam in the Wye. And though I only half remember this, they had an archery club that used to meet in the field below the castle. Our population then was only about eleven hundred, so we didn't do too badly, did we?

Oh yes, and there was a Christy Minstrel company – Father ran that! They used to black their faces and sing 'darkie songs' – just to entertain themselves and their friends in the Hay. And the Volunteers, of course. They sent a contingent to the Boer War, five I think it was: and I distinctly remember them marching down Broad Street, with the *whole* town escorting them off. Five volunteers, with Hay Town Band in their red coats blowing away in front of them: one of them died in Africa, but the rest all came back.

Then we children belonged to the Band of Hope – all of us from the church Sunday school did. It was a social evening, you know: we all sang hymns, and the great thing was, we each had to prepare a programme of entertainments, with recitations. I remember reciting:

> Water bright
> Water pure
> Water for me
> The drink of the Lion, the Brave and the Free.

Of course, we all wore a little blue [temperance] ribbon, and we were taught that 'strong drink was a mocker' and very wicked. But as far as we were concerned, it was just a happy social evening, and a chance to show off.

There *was* a lot more drunkenness then than there is now, though: it was the only pleasure poor people had. It was nothing to see a drunken person, you thought nothing of it, and we had all the old cattle-drovers rollicking around every Thursday. But the best known character was this woman, and she came from a very poor background – in those days, if you were poor, you were *really* poor. And she used to get hopelessly drunk, but she had a beautiful voice, a really beautiful soprano voice. So from time to time the Salvation Army would get hold of her, and convert her: and then she'd sing about the streets with the Salvation Army for a week or two. But soon enough, she'd be up before the magistrates for being 'drunk and disorderly' again. It happened quite regularly. She'd be up before the justices, off to Brecon gaol, and when she came back she'd be converted again. Yet there was no vice in her, not a bit, and she was very popular. I remember as a small child seeing her being taken through the streets to the train, off to gaol: and all the town children were accompanying her to the station to see her off. And the Salvation Army never stopped trying!

Then I remember the Jubilee tea, Queen Victoria's Diamond Jubilee tea in 1897: we had it down the Warren, and I distinctly remember sitting on planks, down by the riverside. We had our tea brought to us, and there were sports in the river, with a board out and people diving into the Wye. Then we went round the corner to the Men's Duckings – that was where they used to duck offenders in the old days, and it was a very deep pool, where we children never normally went. There was a greasy pole stuck out of the bank there, and they tried to walk along it and dive from the end: but most of them just fell in! The food was brought round in paper bags, and we had a paper bag each: isn't it strange, that's what I remember most about the Jubilee, the paper bags and sitting on the planks!

EVERYBODY WAS SOMETHING

Squire-dominated or squireless, 'Club' nurtured or 'get along as you can', a village's social life revolved round its places of worship, each the centre of a mutually exclusive band of adherents. For though the Church of England had its vicar in every parish, it was only in parts of the rural south and in some estate villages that he ruled unchallenged: in most communities, he had to compete – often with scant success – against one or more Nonconformist chapels. Nor were the various persuasions of 'chapel folk' united in anything save their dislike of 'the landlords' church': and their most numerous party, the Wesleyans or Methodists, was itself divided into a number of rival factions.

Some people, admittedly, like Libby Low's family, were content to 'chop and change about':

My family were – well, we were everything. We used to go to three chapels on a Sunday. In the morning we'd go to the Wesleyan, and then in the afternoon we'd go to the Baptists at Hendregenny, and then at night we used to go the Wesleyans again. And at school, in Lent, we went to the Church of England – they'd take us in the dinner hour. Religious? no, we weren't *religious*: but when your mother said you'd go, you went.

The great majority, however, stuck firmly to 'the religion they were born with' – even if (as in Maggie Joe Chapman's family) this did not accord with 'the religion they married'.

Of course, the church or the chapel was everything to people then, you know. They always had a Sunday-school treat, and over in Swaledale we always had buns and milk: they were buns wi' currants in, and a farmer came with a back-can* full of milk, and we all had to take wir own mugs. We went and had a little bit of a do by the river, and ran races – we thought it was as good as going to London, was a do like that.

I always went to the church Sunday school: but it was rather funny in our family, because me mother was a big Wesleyan, but me father, he was a big church man. So we used to all drive down to Muker on a Sunday morning in a horse and trap, and then I went to church wi' Dad while our Dick went to chapel wi' his mother. They never fell out about their religion, but neither of them would ever give over going to their own place. Father never set foot in the chapel.

There *was* quite a bit of rivalry between church and chapel in them days, though. Church people was church people, and Wesleyans was Wesleyans, and there were the 'Prims', the Primitive Methodists, and they didn't mix. Church folk was 'lardy-dardies' [would-be genteel] and Wesleyans was 'good old Wesleyans', and the rest was just clingers-on. Of course, there'd never be no cards in a 'good old Wesleyan' house, no cards and no drink. Church people didn't mind so much.

Methodists were also in the forefront when it came to 'Sabbath Day Observance', as Mrs Mary Brader remembers from her girlhood in Saltfleetby, Lincolnshire:

Lots of people never even cooked Sunday dinner – especially among the Methodists, that was. And you couldn't read the newspapers. Where I lived, we had a little stand in front of the window with some newspapers on: and on a Sunday morning them newspapers was off, and Dad's hymn-book and Bible was on there. And some of the Methodists didn't cook Sunday dinner, because they did the work in the yard and they all went to chapel: they'd have cold meat and fried potatoes. And sometimes, when it was their turn, they took the visiting preacher home, and *he* had cold meat and fried potatoes for *his* Sunday dinner. And they never started work, neither Sundays nor weekdays, without family prayers.

If the Methodists – heirs of John Wesley's evangelical revival during the late eighteenth century – regarded 'church people' as disgracefully lax, they themselves were sometimes looked at askance by stricter, older-established 'chapel' denominations like the Congregationalists, Presbyterians and Baptists, who traced their origins to the Puritans of the Civil War period. The Baptists (so called because they reject infant 'christening' in favour of adult baptism by total immersion) are particularly strong in mid-Wales, where Mrs Mills (b. 1895) spent her chapel-centred childhood.

In them days, we used to have the chapel full, and it'd surely take eighty or ninety to fill it. Oh no, it wasn't a *Methodist* chapel, it was a Baptist. I never *heard* of a Methodist, 'til we came in this part of the world. And I suppose I might have been in a church once or twice in my life, for a wedding or a funeral – but I did never like church.

No, I always went to chapel every Sunday, *every* Sunday, when I was at Llaethdy. After dinner, I'd clean up and change, and beside that I'd got three mile to walk to chapel. Sunday school'd be two o'clock, and that'd go on 'til three; and three o'clock would be the service – a preacher possibly, and if they didn't have a preacher it'd be a prayer meeting – and that would end about four. And then the neighbours around, it'd be, 'Oh, you come with me to tea today': and next Sunday it'd be somebody else, 'You come with *we*, this time.' After tea, you'd help them to wash up, and it was back to chapel for half-past-six service. That would go on perhaps 'til half past seven, and after it'd be a choir practice, and *that* may go on 'til half past nine – and then I'd have three mile to walk home after, in the dark.

People used to say, 'Oh, I couldn't do that, I'd be afraid of a ghost.' Somebody'd persuaded 'em there was 'something to be seen' here and there. But it was nothing but nonsense. Nonsense. I don't think there ever was such a thing! I never had no fear of anything, was it dark or was it light.

They used to baptize people in the river Ithon, then: and I was one that was done. There was five of us done the same Sunday, by the minister of the chapel. Of course, I'd be about seventeen then: because I don't think there was any of that christening of young babies about here, in them days.

The minister'd stand in the river with you, and he'd receive you in, and talk and say a portion of Scripture. Then he'd dip you down in, 'til you were head and all under the water – you had to be completely under. Of course, you'd be wearing a kind of white robe for the baptism: you'd have taken your clothes you was going to put on after to the nearest house, and you'd go there and change. When you'd changed, you'd go into the service, and you was received into the chapel then. You weren't a full member, not 'til you were baptized.

All our family were members. And my grandfather, Richard Jones, used to go to Bwlch-y-Sarnau Baptist chapel, and they'd no music there of any description. Well, I think there was none nowhere, in them days: no organ, piano nor nothing. So Grandfather always used to have to go there to lead the singing: they'd expect him there every Sunday, to lead them.

There was an old man, and – well, he'd been a tramp. But he always called hisself 'Thomas the Preacher'. And in the summertime, he'd come around our way and call at the house: we'd give him a meal, and he'd ask 'em to put the pony in the cart – what I do call a gambo* – and take the cart out onto some grass so's he could stand on it and preach. And perhaps he'd have half a dozen come to hear him. But I did never interest myself in that. I preferred the chapel, and of course, I *still* go to chapel, every Sunday.

Outside the north-west and a few Catholic-owned estates, Roman Catholics were comparatively unusual in the English countryside – where church and chapel folk alike were still inclined to regard them with suspicion. But their number was rapidly being swelled by the descendants of Irish immigrants: among them Lizzie Grange, whose tale illustrates an ability (conspicuously lacking among some other denominations) to see the funny side of religious observance.

Father was a Catholic too, of course, but he never went, like. He used to say, he couldn't go to God and have his beer – so he preferred his beer! And I'll tell you a tale about him once. He always went to his Easter duties: well, he had to, else he was out of his church. And he used to go with me mother on the Sat'day night. Now in them days we did our own bit bread-baking and that: and the baking wasn't finished, and me father was impatient, because he was an impatient man. So Mam says, 'You go down, Jimmy, and I'll come down after yez, it'll not take many minutes.' But by the time the bread come out it'd be about twenty minutes.

So she goes to church, and she goes to confession. And she's sitting there and saying her prayers; she sits up, and looks, and she kneels down and says some more, and she sits up; then she turns round to the woman behind her.

'D'ye think there's anyone in the confessional?'

'Yes.'

So she said, 'Ee dear me, poor soul must have an awful lot of sins to tell. Ee dear.' So she started praying for this party's soul in the confession box. 'Ee', she says, 'it must be years and years and years since they've gone. They must be worse than what our Jimmy is.' And she started to say some 'Hail Marys'.

Then, all of a sudden, the confession-box door opens, and who walks out but *Father*! She said, 'If there'd been a hole in the floor, I'd ha' went down through it!' She nearly died.

And she says, 'Jimmy! I knows it's twelve months since you've been to confession, but you must a' done something drastic.'

'I'll tell you what I did, or what I would like to do anyway, but I couldn't get it done' – because this old priest was trying to get him to sign the pledge, that he wouldn't drink, you see. And he couldn't, and he told the priest.

'I cannot, I *cannot* do without drink.'

And of course this old priest had a tube. He was hard of hearing, and he had a tube in his ear, and a funnel on the end, and you had to shout through there. And Dad says, 'If there'd been a tap, nae joke, I'd ha' poured the jug of water down it!'

The heathen tombstones

Still rarer, and viewed with still greater horror, were the tiny minority of avowed atheists – their avowal being quite as bad as their atheism, especially when (as here in Maggie Joe Chapman's story) it was carved in stone for all to see.

There were more Wesleyans than church in Muker, but everybody was something: there weren't any heathens. Well, there were one or two, and I'll tell you a tale about them. Now there's something in Muker churchyard that's in no other churchyard in England, and that's a lot to say! There's some tombstones there, and the verses on them tombstones was being written down wi' visitors when I was a girl going to school. Because them that put those tombstones there was heathens, that didn't believe in God – and they said so in them verses. These stones were put down by the Brodericks, that lived out at Spring End by Gunnerside: they were monied people, and they had a lot o' property; but they were no believers, they were heathens. And some of them were buried in churchyard – I don't know why they buried 'em there, being non-believers: mind you, they'd buried one or two about the farm, as well – they weren't supposed to, but they did. So some of 'em were buried in churchyard, but the vicar wouldn't allow 'em to put any stones up: in them days the vicar had to be there when they put up stones, to see that they were fit.

Well, old Broderick had got these stones ready carven, but he couldn't put 'em down openly. So he had his men all ready wi' 'em, turned wrong way up so nobody could see what was written on 'em. Then he got the vicar interested in the east window of the church, and he said, 'Well, what does it look like from inside?' He got the vicar of the church to take him inside to look, and he kept vicar talking inside church until his masons had got stones dug in *outside*. And once they're laid, nobody can take 'em up, unless them that put them there gave 'em permission – that was the law. So vicar had to leave 'em, else they'd have been thrown out long ago, because them stones really used to vex the church people when we were girls. It was the talk of Muker for years!

(The tombstone – which obstinately remains in Muker churchyard to this day – reads:

> *I want the world to know*
> *That I know*
> *That there is no fame*
> *That all life is co-equal*
> *That deficiency in intellect is the why*
> *Of deficiency in action.*
>
> *That every thing is right*
> *That every atom vibrates*
> *At its proper time, according*
> *To the true results of the forces*
> *That went before*
>   *By the son, Luther*

'Old Man Broderick's' 'Christian' name would seem to indicate that his parents did not share his 'heathenism' – and it is to be hoped that they did not share his evident confusion of mind!)

8

CRAFTSMEN

THE CARPENTER'S APPRENTICE

Les Swansborough was born and brought up in London, and he has lived near Monks Eleigh, Suffolk, for a mere thirty-six years or so. So he is not precisely a 'country' voice, but his trades of carpentry and joinery are as much rural as urban, and his tales of his apprenticeship during the 1920s are so graphic that I cannot resist including a few of them.

When I left school, at fourteen, I had to have a job, and fortunately the chap that lived next door to us in London offered to set me on the right road at Pollard's, the big store-fitters. So I went there as shopboy, unbound apprentice and so forth, at threepence farthing an hour! I had to buy all my own tools out of that, of course. Well, I was there for about three years, under a marvellous old boy, really one of the old school: he was the type that didn't spare the rod and spoil the child. He was the wickedest old so-and-so there was. Things had got to be *right*, and if they weren't *absolutely* right, they were no good. For instance you were given a length of 'two-by-one', the cheapest wood they'd got: and you had to make a tenon on one end, and a mortice on the other. Then you cut off the tenon with a saw, and it should fit the mortice perfectly: it all had to be done by eye, of course. And after two or three attempts, if it didn't fit, there was always his straight-edge to help you along with it better. 'No, don't you use a chisel. Start again.' Like a fool, on one occasion I'd got it pretty good, though it didn't fit perfectly: and I took it to him, proud as anything. 'Well, does it fit?', 'Well, near enough', 'Near enough's no damn good, I want it right!' And out came the straight-edge! But you learnt, and eventually you could do it straight from the saw.

Richard Faulkner (1876–1946) 'general carpenter and wheelwright' of Llangunllo, Radnorshire, sitting (on a chair of his own making) outside the house he built himself.

Sandpapering, sandpapering oak counter-tops. I remember one in particular, the so-and-so: it was a twelve-foot oak counter-top for a draper's shop. 'Well boy, I want you to give that 'middle two' glasspaper all over. I'll be back shortly.' So I was left with this counter-top, and I rubbed and rubbed 'til my fingers were raw, and I thought I'd made a beautiful job of it. He still didn't come, so I thought, I know what's got to be done next – 'fine two' paper. So I gave it 'fine two', and I got down to 'one and a half', which was as fine as you went with oak. And that was lovely.

He came back, and proud as anything I explained what I'd done. 'Yes, yes, boy!' Then he got hold of his blue pencil. 'See that little mark there, and there's another one there.' And he marked them with his blue pencil, and I swear that blooming blue pencil went in half-an-inch deep! 'Now start back again with "middle two" and ... keep it flat, I don't want any hollows in it.' And, oh my God, the time it took me to rub those blasted blue pencil marks out!

And we used to make those beautiful mouldings, that you saw in the old-fashioned drapers' shops. You made wooden moulds to wrap your glass-paper round, and you rubbed them up, and all the edges of the mouldings had got to be razor sharp. And that used to annoy me, because you having got all those edges beautifully sharp, when *he* fixed them on the job, he'd get his glasspaper and he'd rub them round again! Well, I thought, I needn't have got a razor edge in the first place. But that's how it had got to be! This old man, he was real master of his trade, and he taught me a hell of a lot.

I stayed there about two or three years, and then I asked for a rise. 'Rise, yes, why certainly. We'll give you threepence *halfpenny* an hour, instead of threepence farthing.' So I thought, 'Blow you, chum', and I went and got a job in a little shop that had just started up, and that must have been one of the earliest 'do-it-yourself' shops, I reckon. That I stuck for a little while, and then I decided to go into the building trade. I'd no idea of anything about it, of course: I could handle wood, and I'd been to night school to learn what I could, but I knew nothing about building ways.

'D'you want any joiners?' 'Joiners? No, but we could do with a carpenter.' 'I can do that too.' 'All right then, bring your tools in Monday morning, and we'll see. But we can't pay you the rate.' So I didn't get full pay, but I got *tenpence* an hour, and that seemed marvellous money to me.

As I say, I knew nothing about building. And the first thing they said to me was, 'I want you to go up on the roof, and put a secret gutter round that chimney. The last bloke made a muck-up of it, and the plumbers wouldn't have it.' 'Oh God', thinks I, 'what the hell's a secret gutter? I've never heard of one.' But I was dead lucky, because when I got up the ladder, there was a plumber. Saved! 'I've come up to put a secret gutter round here,' I said, cool as you please, 'Suppose you show me exactly what you want, then perhaps we'll have it right this time?' And he showed me! I had no problems with secret gutters after that. You've got to pick things up where you can when you're learning a trade. And since then: well, I've never made a wheel, and I've never made a matchbox, but I think I've made everything else that can be made in wood.

GENERAL CARPENTER AND WHEELWRIGHT

Versatility was required, above all, of a carpenter working in the remoter rural areas. For he had not only to be able to make 'everything that can be made in wood' – from a waggon to a bread board – but also to turn his hand to building, decorating and engineering: indeed, to any task (save only 'blacksmith's work') that the community might set him. One such 'general carpenter and wheelwright' was Richard Faulkner, who until his death in 1946 served the tiny village of Llangunllo, set amid a bowl of hills in the border sheep-farm country – neither wholly Welsh nor completely English – of the Radnorshire district of Powys.

    There, in the house his father built by the banks of the little river Lugg, Richard's son Dick still carries on his father's trade. A well-known wit in a society where wit is highly prized, it was some time before he would consent to take my questions seriously. And when I asked, 'What did your father do when you were born?' – meaning 'what was his occupation' – he replied:

What did my father do when I was born? Well, he kicked me mother for a start. And then I think as there was no water left in the bucket, so they decided not to drown me. Mind you, we were a big family. We were nine, that lived: but I heard my elder sister say that we started off at about fourteen, but the rest of 'em died. I was the youngest, of course – you mostly are if you're the last. Anyway, eventually I went to school up the hill here, the primary school: I never went to any other school, except Sunday school a bit.

My father, he was a self-employed carpenter too. He used to travel quite a bit, when you consider the mode of travelling there was then. Mind you, we had an Overland car, that would convert into a lorry: an American make it was. I think we bought it off Sir Robert Green-Price [the local squire]. Father used to work as far as Leominster: then out to Beguildy, Llanbadarn, Dolau, maybe Presteigne. You asked what he did – it would've been easier to ask what he didn't do: he did everything.

One of the things I remember was the oil-engines – I don't know whether they *was* just starting off then, but they seemed to me to be. He used to be fitting them, putting in the shafting, and building the lofts – you had the engine usually down below, and the chaff-cutter, or whatever it was driving, up above in the loft. They used to use them to work sheep-shearing machines: I turned the handle on those many a time.

Then there were the horse-works, he used to do those. A horse-work is a metal cast – oh, about six feet in diameter – shaped something like a bell: and in the top of it there'd be a slot, in which you fitted a timber balk, say six by three, with ironwork to fasten it to a horse. Then the horse would pull the cast round, and that turns a smaller cog, which is on a flexible shafting – you could use it to power anything you'd use an oil-engine for, later on. They had something similar to turn the cider presses. Emlyn Lloyd, now, he had a *travelling* cider press: it was made of heavy oak. He used to haul it round the farms with horses: it wasn't on a cart, it had its own road-wheels. I been on that myself. I made cider many places with that: and by God, when the cider comes out – that's lovely.

But his main business was carpentry. He had a bit of a sawmill, here in Llangunllo, and he used to run a travelling saw-bench, run off a little oil-engine: a paraffin-engine, made by Naylors of Hereford. If a farmer wanted a bit of building done, he'd supply the timber from his trees, and we'd bring up this rack-bench and cut it into planks: then we'd more than likely do the building as well. But it wouldn't go quite as quick as that: the timber'd need to dry out a bit. Timber was better then than 'tis now: it had the time to season – maybe twelve months from sawing time to using time, or more than that. Any kind of wooden building my father could do: nothing stopped him. This chapel up here, he built the pulpit in there and the gallery, all in pitch pine. He could do anything.

He could indeed, as his ledger for the years from 1905 to 1910 clearly shows. During that time, Richard Faulkner made and erected: a granary; two barns; a bungalow; a large verandah at the Manor House, Knighton; three sheds; seven pigsties; two fowl houses; a goose coop; a porch and a kitchen. He installed two sets of 'horse-works', one oil-engine and several ventilators. He also manufactured large numbers of agricultural necessaries, including pig troughs; sheep racks; mangers; ladders; a grindstone frame and a dozen gates: all kinds of household utensils, including a mangle; a butter mitt; a bacon rack; a 'gambrel' for hanging up slaughtered pigs; an ironing board and two pastry boards: a new pulpit for one chapel; a pair of collecting boxes for another; and three coffins, two of them for children.

In addition, he did a considerable amount of house renovation (including plastering, masonry work, decorating and wallpapering); framed pictures; and repaired, not only furniture, but also a shotgun, two watches, a piano (which he completely restrung) and a birdcage. And he caught and sold nearly four hundred rabbits.

Nor was all this by any means the sum total of his activities. Because, Dick continues:

Most of all me and Father made carts: wheelwrights you'd call us, more than anything. Wheelwright, that's my real trade. My father could make all the kinds of carts they used round by here. They was mostly the heavy farm-carts, two-wheelers – a cart has two wheels, a waggon has four: but he made

Richard Faulkner's 'Lugg Valley Saw Mills', Llangunllo, c. 1926, showing Mr Faulkner (foreground) standing by his circular saw. Notice the large number of wheels; the 'gambo' awaiting repair by the shed; a trap (right) and part of the undercarriage of a waggon (extreme right, between two cart-tyres).

waggons as well, he made many waggons. I only repaired waggons: they were just about going out when I started. He made four-wheeled drays, too, for road work: the front wheels on a dray are smaller than on a waggon, and they'll turn in under on a turntable. A waggon's wheels are all four the same size, and they won't turn very much.

An average farmer round here, he'd have one cart, maybe two. Two wheels and a deep body, say for putting roots in: tipping gear it would have, too. He'd only have the one or two carts: 'cause, good God, money was short round here then. Very few round here would have a waggon: it would need a biggish farm to have a waggon, and a flat place, too – you wouldn't get them up our hills. When my father made waggons, they'd be for farmers lower down country. I remember one he made for John Morgan at Old Impton, down by Presteigne. That was a harvest waggon, you'd get the devil of a lot of hay on that: and the wheels was very wide – six inches wide, probably – so they didn't cut into the ground, see, same as a narrow wheel would.

Round by here they'd be more like just to have a cart, and then what we call a 'gambo'.* That had straight shafts, and it was slung fairly low. It was quite simply made, really: a kind of flat cart with a cart-stick at each corner, and things like gates – I think they called them 'cratches' – which you dropped into slots on each side, to keep the hay from falling off. They were mostly for lugging hay, rushes, fern – that kind of thing. Rushes for thatching, fern for litter, and hay – 'cause you can't lug hay on a cart, or not much of it, anyhow. Then you might use it for carting 'trowse'* for hedging. That's hazels or thorns, cut fairly straight, for 'glutting' a hedge: if the beasts have broken through a hedge, you mend it with trowse. If you do it well, it looks like the original hedge: only of course it doesn't grow.

So there's the carts, the gambo, the trap – for going to market: and then there's the 'wilkyer' – that's a Radnorshire word, its a 'wheelcar' really. He made quite a lot of those: in fact he probably made more of those than anything else. And I made quite a few, too, after he died. I think I made my last one in about 1950, and they were still using it not so many years ago.

Found only in Radnorshire and the immediately adjacent parts of Shropshire, Herefordshire, Breconshire and Montgomery, the wheelcar was a most ingenious vehicle. Basically a wheeled sledge (see p.117), it was designed for carrying hay or other light material both on steep hillsides – where an ordinary cart would be liable to overturn or run away; and also on roads and level ground – where an ordinary sledge would be tediously slow and unwieldy. Its main timbers were a pair of massive side members, linked by cross-pieces which formed the body of the vehicle: at their front or 'snout' end, these swelled into iron-shod runners, on which the front of the 'car' ran. Its centre and rear, however, was carried on two full-sized cart-wheels, whose axle was mounted above the body, in order to maintain a low centre of gravity: and rather nearer the back than the front, so that the vehicle would be inclined to dig in, and thus slow down, when descending steep hills. This it did, effectively, as a sledge, with the wheels locked solid by means of chains: but when ascending, or on the level, the chains were removed, and the car ran on both wheels and front runners. It could be hauled by either one or two horses, which were harnessed to it by chains rather than shafts. The driver therefore had comparatively little fine control over it, and (as everyone who has used one agrees) 'those wheelcars could be brutes to handle'.

Richard Faulkner made five of them between 1905 and 1910, when he also manufactured a gambo, two carts and five wheelbarrows and performed major overhauls of three traps, a waggon and a gambo, most of them requiring new wheels. It was 'wheelwrighting', indeed, which was the most skilled and exacting part of the Faulkners' trade, as Dick now shows.

Well naturally we'd have to have the timber before: it wants a couple of years to dry, anyway, before we'd come at it. We had no band-saw then, no band-saw at all. So we had to saw it all by hand – all the curved shafts. I've sawn many and many out by hand. Mind you, to keep a saw upright from one end to the other, and go round all the various curves, that isn't a simple job. We'd mostly use ash, for the body of the cart: but the wheels now – the stock was elm, must be elm. And as I said to you the other night, if we had to go back to making them again, now that the elm has died out, I just don't know what we'd use. Because, by God, elm is *hard* – it takes some splitting. But the fellies [felloes, the curved sections that make up the rim of the wheel] they could be either ash or elm: ash was a bit nicer to work with.

You start a wheel by making the stock – that's the hub, like. You get this piece of elm sawn out of a trunk: it would be sixteen inches in diameter, about that, for a cart-wheel. We had no lathe to turn it on. So we used to bore a hole down the middle with an auger, trap a spindle in it, and put the handle from the grindstone on it. And the minute I came home from school, I'd have to turn this old handle and my father'd go at it with a chisel. Why he did it that way, I don't know, mind you. Because he had an oil-engine then, but he just didn't use it. He *could* have had a lathe: 'course he could. I made one as soon as I left school. But before, I remember turning those bloody stocks for hours and hours.

There was quite a lot of fancywork on them, too: they weren't just lumps of wood. You had to have their faces true. You already had the ironwork: that'd be made first, and you'd make the stock to fit it – allowing a bit for the ironwork to be put on hot. Then you'd put your spoke-holes in: cart-wheels had five or six fellies, and of course for six fellies you'd have twelve spokes. You divide the stock up equal, all the way round, so as you'd get your twelve spokes in equally placed. We used to do it with dividers – there was no mathematics nor calculators. You had your dividers, and you went round the stock and round the stock, and if it ended up right, that was it.

Then you had your patterns. A wheelwright's shop was always full of patterns, and you had one to make the spokes out. Because they weren't just straight up and down: they was curved, a kind of oval pointed at both ends: then you had to fit the spokes individually. You'd use a kind of paint, just ordinary paint: and when you're cutting the mortice – the hole for the spoke – you'd offer the spoke up, and see that the paint got from the spoke onto the mortice: all the way round, top and bottom, then you'd know 'twas just the right taper. Then you'd mark that particular spoke for that hole: it was individually fitted. So you'd go round 'til you'd fitted the lot. Then you'd support the stock on something very firm, *really* firm: and you'd *belt* those spokes in with a hammer – a big sledgehammer now – until the hammer would *bounce*. It's got to bounce. It would really bounce back, it wouldn't go in another eighth. Or so you would think, *so* you would think. But you'd see later on as it would.

When you'd got all the spokes into the stock, you'd trim them up with a spokeshave, and you'd cut them off to a length: about four foot six they were for a cart-wheel. Then you'd got to cut your tenons and shoulders to fit them into the fellies: some had two shoulders, but most had just one, a back shoulder. Of course, the shoulders and joints had to be exactly the same distance away from the stock on all the spokes. So before you cut them, you'd use what they call a 'speech stick': it was just a piece of wood, that would screw into the stock at one end, and at th' other end it had a peg: now this peg touched the spoke just where the shoulder should be, just where the felly should go into the spoke. Then you marked at the end of this peg, so it was just the same distance on every spoke, and you cut your tenon there. So they were all dead true-fitting.

The spokes didn't come *straight* out of the stock, of course. Because the majority of cart-wheels have got what they call a 'speech' – they're dished, for strength I presume. The spokes would lean outwards, so the fellies were further out than the stock. They're dished.

You'd have cut the fellies already. Long before the days of band-saws, you would cut them roughly with a pit-saw, or whatever you had. But you wouldn't go quite to the line you wanted, so you'd finish off by adzing it out. You know what an adze looks like? Well, the adze was made so you couldn't go too deep, 'cause you'd bump the back of the adze agin' the timber first.

Then you'd put the felly to the spoke, and make a pencil mark where the spoke is going through, and cut the mortice in the felly. But when you go to offer the felly up, you'd find the spokes was in the wrong place: the points are further away than the shoulder, but it's the shoulder has got to go in first. So you'd have to *spring* them on. We used what they call a 'spoke drawer' – two hooks to pull each two of the spokes together, until you'd got them where you wanted them. Some of them had to be very strong! And when you got the spokes right, you knock the felly on: as soon as you'd got it on a reasonable amount, you could relax the pressure a bit. You'd fit every spoke up to its shoulder: then you could knock it back a bit, and fix the next one – all the way round.

Once you've got all your fellies on, you run your saw between each two of them, to leave a bit o' gap. Mind, you *must* get the gap between fellies wider on the outside than the inside: because the outside *gains* on the inside when the wheel's been closed up by the iron band [the cart tyre]. It's the law of the circle. So you'd got to leave a wedge-shaped gap: you could easily do it by eye.

Having done that all the way round, you knock the fellies off, and bore holes in the end for the dowels that join them together. Mostly iron dowels, they'd be, but the biggest cart-wheels had big oak dowels – I'd get oak dowels for them. The smaller wheels, we'd use half-inch-diameter iron.

Then you'd start again. Draw the spokes together, spring on the felly, put the dowels in. You'd have to paint the joint and the dowels now, of course – a red-lead kind of paint. Then, when you'd got the fellies on, you'd keep going round and tap each one, tap each one. 'Cause you can't do any more cutting once those dowels are in there: that's it.

Now you've got an axeing job. You'd put this speech stick back on again, what you'd used to get the spokes true, and then you'd pencil mark a circle the right diameter all the way round the wheel. Then you had to *axe* it down to that mark, axe it all the way round. I think I only cut myself the once. In those days you got so as you could almost do it as good as planing, see. It was a lovely job.

After this axeing round – and you may just plane it off a *little* bit, where it was rough – you'd take the wheel to the blacksmith. But usually before that, apart from cutting it to a true circle, you bevelled the rim a bit. The tyre was always a bit narrower than the inside of the felly – the side that's agin' the spoke. I don't know why that should be, but that's how it was done: the rim always tapered out.

Then you'd bowl the wheel up here to the blacksmith's – where Gib Lewis lives now, that was the blacksmith's. When he knew you was coming, the smith would get help – there was always plenty of old chaps about to give a hand. Then they'd heat the iron band all the way round: they'd have two sets of tongs each, and they'd keep turning it and turning it over the forge. The wheel was fastened down, like, on a concrete dish: there was a pin up through the middle of it, and a screw on the pin to hold the wheel down – because when the pressure came on it, it would hop up in the air, otherwise. Because the pressure would be very great. As I told you before, you may *think* all that hammer-bouncing had got the spokes in as far as they'd go. But by God, when you got that iron tyre on the wheel, and it was cooling, you'd hear the old thing go 'Bang', 'Bang'.

Once you'd got the band hot enough, you'd offer it up over the rim of the wheel, and tap it down – you'd tap it quite hard. It'd have to be between black-hot and red-hot: if you got it too hot, it'd burn the wheel. The real art of it was to get the metal just at its most expansion, without it being red-hot. Then, when the tyre was all tapped down right, you'd all throw buckets of water over it – lots of them. As soon as it was on, he cooled it down just as quick as he could. Then – Boy, you'd hear them spokes going in, terrific! The spokes really stuck and then, all of a sudden, 'Crash!' – he'd got to go further in: oh, it was quite noisy. The power was terrific, and that's really what held the wheel together. There was nothing else holding the spokes in – they weren't pinned nor nothing: there's nothing holding them in but the band.

THE CIDER MAKERS

A few pages ago, Dick Faulkner mentioned 'Emlyn Lloyd's travelling cider press'. Here it is in action, described by his brother John, with whom he farms at Cwmheyope, near Llangunllo. The interview was conducted, amid a fair amount of general hilarity, in the village pub, with Dick adding his comments from time to time.

You'd go round from October 'til about Christmas: my father and my uncle travelled it. We had two wheels on the cider press, and shafts on him, so the horses could move him about. We'd go from farm to farm, and set it up: and a few people from round about would come in with a couple of barrels, and have a day cider-making. They'd make six or eight barrels – that's six or eight hundred gallon – in a day, and that'd probably be for two or three different places. And they'd be two or three days on the same farm, sometimes.

The apples would be picked ready: and they'd bring 'em in and crush 'em. They goes through this chawling machine first. Have you ever seen a root pulper? Well, the chawling mill's very similar to that, only apart from the thing that claws 'em up, there was two cement rollers on it, and they were crushed as well as pulped. That was powered by one horse: it went round and round in a ring, and drove a spinny-jinny, like. They'd put a dozen or fifteen bags of apples through, then the horse would stand for a time. When the apples come out of the bottom of that mill, they're what we called 'pomace': and they did add some water at that stage, while they were being crushed. So they wanted some water handy – they needed a brook handy.

Well, this pomace dropped onto a little platform, and then they used to shovel it into another machine, the press. They had a cloth, and he fitted on a frame about two foot six square; that was like a box with no top nor bottom, with handles on. They'd put the cloth on top of this frame, and shovel the pomace in, and the weight would pull it down: and when it was full, there was a proper way to fold this cloth – they'd fold him in, the four corners all the same. Then they'd rise this frame, and put two little laths through it, to hold it onto the one underneath: and they'd put another cloth on, and fill that. They used to fill about a dozen cloths, one on top of the other: those cloths was made of a kind of coconut matting.

So they'd go up about four or five feet with these dozen cloths. Then they'd put a square of timber on top of all that, the same size as the cloths was, and they'd screw this old timber down on top of 'em, to 'queak'* it – 'queaking', that's cider makers' talk for pressing! There was three handles on this screw, and you'd come down a long way just by turning them with your hands. But when that got very difficult, you'd put in some old ash poles, and get behind and push. Push one so far, then push another, like a capstan on a ship. There was two of these screws on either side, on a double press, and you'd do a quarter of a turn on each screw, one after the other.

Well, you'd press it down until it was nearly dry. All the juice would seep out of the bottom, onto a table with six-inch side pieces, and a little bit of a spout for it to pour from. There'd be a half-barrel under, for it to run into, and they'd carry from that into the barrels. Of course, they'd be adding water all the while: every chance you had, you put water in. The dirtiest

Cider-making with a travelling cider press at the New Inn, Talgarth, Powys, on Brecon Fair Day, November 3rd, 1957. Left: Hugh Morgan (owner of the press) prepares the 'cloths' of crushed-apple 'pomace' for pressing. Below: The timber pressing beam has been screwed down as tight as possible by hand and now the cider makers are using ash poles for extra leverage on the handles. The cider pours into the half-barrel (centre right) and water from the pump is added.

water you could find: *tap* water would be no good, and they always reckoned pool water was better than brook water. Then you put it in casks, and leave it open, fermenting: the stronger it was, the quicker it fermented. You don't stop it up until it's finished fermenting: and they used to reckon to put some beef in it, too, years ago.

DF: Then you put the rats in, and it makes *rat*tling good cider! Have *I* seen 'em put rats in? Boy, I've seen the time you couldn't *stop* the b——s going in!

JL: When they'd got these old presses right down at the bottom, and it'd almost all run out, it used to be a favourite habit of everybody's then to come out with a cider jar, and pop that under the spout for the real last run in. They'd cork that down straight away, to *stop* it fermenting. And that was kept 'til about Christmas, and it'd come out like wine – it was real sweet.

DF: One thing I remember. If you was making cider and you had this old pot under there, there was no need for Epsom salts!

JL: A lot of the farms would make cider then: the bigger places would make five to ten big barrels, and they *were* big barrels. And very often they'd not drink it 'til it was a twelvemonth old – or two years old, some places. They'd drink it summer and winter, because there were men on the farm then that would prefer cider to tea. They'd have cider for breakfast, boy!

Travelling cider presses were common on the Welsh borders until a very few years ago, and some may be travelling there yet. Certainly I know of at least two still operating in a stationary role, and very good cider they make.

Jokes about rats in cider are, I suspect, as old as cider itself: but raw meat in cider does seem to do some good. At the time of this interview, we'd recently made some that was not doing at all well, being both cloudy and unpleasantly sharp. So I followed John Lloyd's advice, by adding a lump of raw, fatty meat: and within weeks our cider had cleared and improved out of all recognition. It is now greatly in demand.

THE SEDBERGH CLOGGER

Myles Bainbridge is a well-known figure in Sedbergh, a small Cumbrian town on the western side of the Pennines. For, though the bovine tuberculosis that crippled him as a child kept him from the family business of farming, he has not let it interfere with his hill-walking: and even now, at eighty-three, he can still be seen ascending the steepest fells on two sticks, and at a pace which makes 'able-bodied' people half his age turn pale. But that is merely his hobby, practised in the intervals of making and repairing clogs, a trade he began in 1915 and which he still continues from the basement of his house. Here, then – interwoven with anecdotes about 'Kaiser Bill', George Bernard Shaw and others, and with a cautionary tale about a 1914 war 'clog-profiteer' – is the story of the man who must surely be Britain's longest-serving clogger.

My name's Bainbridge, but my family came from Middleton-in-Teesdale way. They were all farmers, and my grandfather went to the farm there when he was a baby in arms. So Bainbridges have been there for two or three generations. But now they've built another reservoir and covered that farm – there's only the outbuildings left above the waterline. It was just above Mickleton-in-Teesdale, where the road goes over to Brough, over what they call Wenaby Moors. That's where Kaiser Bill came to shoot in 1911: me brother told me about it. Because they swept t'road all the way from Wemmergill Hall – that's just above Mickleton – to Brough: it was a moorland road. Well fancy, he'd never notice whether road had been swept! But they swept the road specially for his horse-carriage, and they said the horses were white wi' lather when they got to Brough, he'd pressed them that much. He'd been shooting on Lord Strathmore's estate – that was the Queen Mother's family, the Bowes-Lyons.

He had a deformed arm, the Kaiser, they say: so he had to have a gun made specially for him. And of course Wenaby Moors was noted for grouse, they always got big bags o' grouse there: me brother had the job of leading cartridges to the moor, in big bags on each side of a horse. So I expect he might have led cartridges for the Kaiser! And he used to go beating for them too – but *he* didn't get the money, the boss got the money, his uncle. They had to do those jobs, because they were tenants of the Strathmore estate.

I suppose my father would've been born somewhere about the 1840s. And me mother used to tell me that he'd had his education from a travelling schoolmaster, because they didn't have a proper school up there. This schoolmaster used to come round, and he used to teach them in the farm outhouses – that must have been in summer, because you'd think in winter they'd have to be in the house. They had to pay this master, and I don't suppose they'd get much education from him. I think he'd come two or three days a week, because he'd have another place to go to: he'd come on Monday, and he'd teach 'em so much and set 'em something to do, and he'd be back on Wednesday: then he'd be doing t'other farms, and he'd come back on Saturday for his last day.

Tuberculosis milk

So I was born there in 1900, and when I was very young we shifted to a farm in Rosedale (on the North Yorkshire Moors). I suppose *I* should have been a farmer: I always fancied being a gamekeeper, or a shepherd, or some kind of farming – because I liked walking, you see. But I couldn't do that, because I've been handicapped all me life almost. I had what they call bovine tuberculosis, and it rotted the bone away and made me one leg shorter than the other. It just came on gradually, when I was about five or six: it just began to hurt, and then I began to limp just a little bit, because I couldn't be putting weight on the one leg. It'd be as long as th' other when I first started, but I couldn't bide to put weight on it. So I used to go about on this same stool here – leaning on this stool – that was th' only way I could walk when I was six years old, because the pain was terrible.

And it was neglected, you see. Because it was nine miles to the nearest doctor, and even then he wasn't a qualified doctor – he was what they called a quack-doctor. And he come, and he put a black plaster on the bottom of me foot, thinking to draw it out, like: he thought it was rheumatism or something. He used to measure me leg against t'other one with string!: and it was beginning to get a bit shorter then. But it never got no better – it got worse: of course, he didn't know what trouble was. Anybody that wasn't a newly qualified doctor didn't know about this bovine tuberculosis then, or at least not about here.

So at last we went to a bone-setter in Pickering, and he said, 'Oh, that's no good: it's past me. He'll ha' to go to hospital.' It had swollen up something terrible by then: I was in a pushchair, and if you went over a pebble or something I used to shout, because a lightning pain went through it. So I went into hospital, and after three days they operated on it, and then they did another operation, and I got shot of all the pain then: though I've had a bit of trouble with it since. It ran when I was thirteen, and then when I was fifty-eight it started again: but it's better now, and I think it must've stopped rotting. Though that toe's no good now, it goes where it likes. But if it hadn't 'a been for modern medicine, I'd had to have lost me leg, I'm sure.

I'd got it from drinking tuberculosis milk, of course. Well, now there *isn't* any tuberculosis milk, but I'll bet you in them days *every* farm had tuberculosis cows. Because they used to keep more stock than they had hay or fodder for: and they used to let 'em stay out in cold wet weather, to save their hay. Well, they used to get consumption, you see. I had an aunt who I *knew* had consumptive cows, because I've helped to bury them. They used to slaver a lot, and their skins all go tight: usually a cow's skin'll lift up if you get 'old of it, but these used to be all tight and show their ribs. But *now*, you see, they're all vet-tested.

Apprentice clogger

Well, after I'd been to hospital, there was a time when it didn't hurt so much: and I could get to school a bit. But by that time we'd shifted from Rosedale back to Bowes, agin' [near] Barnard Castle, and I'd three mile to walk to school: and of course I missed a lot. If it was a bad morning, or wet, maybe I wouldn't go. So I wasn't much of a scholar, and I couldn't take to farming, because I was lame. And I had to do some job when I left school, so me mother decided I'd be apprenticed to a clogger and shoemaker: that was the one job I could do.

I was apprenticed to a man here in Sedbergh – that was in 1915 – and I was supposed to do me time for seven years, but I only did two. Because when I first come, he said, 'You'll have to sign an indenture': but first, I had to be examined by a doctor. And I *was* examined, but that was the last I heard of the indenture – I suppose it was going to cost so much to get the solicitor to make one out that he decided not to bother: and I never heard no more about it, though I was supposed to be tied for seven years.

Was I paid? Well, I was paid one and six a week! I started at seven, and went on 'til seven at night: and I had a half-day Thursday, but it didn't start until three in the afternoon, didn't 'half-day' – I had to go back after dinner 'til three o'clock. And I had to try and live off that: but Mother used to send me five shillings a week, and me grandfather had a little butcher's shop here, and I used to get a little bit of rolled beef from him, and I'd make it last as long as I could.

Then, in about 1917, I had a chance of this job at Kirkby Stephen for more money – about thirty bob a week, I think. So I had a bike, and I went! First I went to live in digs with the foreman, but I didn't like it so well, so I went to live with the clog-sole maker instead. It was a big shop where I went to – there was five of us doing nothing but clogs, as well as this clog-sole maker.

That was a hard job, making clog-soles by hand: it was such a hard job, making 'em by hand, that nobody would follow t'trade – and I didn't blame them, either. The wood's pretty tough to cut, and you're bent over all day long cutting: and unless you could make 'em quick, it wasn't worth it; because i' them days, you was only getting about six shillings for making a dozen pairs, and that's twenty-four soles. The wood was in a block when you started, wi' just a bit chipped out: and the rest's all to cut out wi' the different knives. Oh, it's a hard job, because there's such a lot to cut off – there'd be a great swill full o' chips at night. Sometimes soles'd be made of beech, but there was alder as well, and sycamore's a good wood too: and birch – silver birch – makes good clog-soles, it has a brown vein in the wood.

But it was a hard job, and by the time I went into clogging a lot were buying their soles factory-made, from Hebden Bridge or somewhere. And the only reason *this* clog-sole maker was doing it was because he was exempt from t'war as long as he stopped in his job: but if he shifted his job, he'd 'a been called up. So the boss had him where he wanted him, and he didn't pay him a lot: he paid him more than us, though, about two pounds a week. But look at the hours he worked – from eight in the morning until seven at night!

So the boss had the only clog-sole maker in Kirkby Stephen, and the other cloggers couldn't get soles while t'war was on. And didn't the boss exploit it! He charged 'em plenty, and he made his fortune: because there was five of us, and you can imagine what a lot of clogs we made. And when he found out t'others couldn't get clog-soles, he had all t'run of trade from all the country for miles around, and he could charge his own prices. And the clog-soler's soles were good, mind, they were absolutely perfect: if a customer had a difficult foot, and the clog had gone out o' shape a bit, he'd make sole to fit t'upper!

But the boss himself didn't know much about trade – I think he must have inherited it: and he didn't seem to care how things were done. Well, as soon as t'war was over, t'others in Kirkby began to get machine-made clog-soles, and his trade really began to drop off – because the people he'd exploited were getting their own back, you see. So there wasn't the work to do for us all – and things had got to such a pitch he didn't want us all, and I got the sack.

Independent clogger

Well, I went into Lancashire then, to try and get a job, but I couldn't get one. You see, t'war was over, and the chaps was coming back to their jobs. And of course, they were slackening off – the wartime boom was tailing off, and nobody was wanting men.

So I came back here to Sedbergh, and I've been working here ever since: that would be 1923 or 1924. I'd saved up twenty-four pounds when I was at Kirkby Stephen, and I set up me own shop in the street here. And the first week, I took twenty-three shillings, and there were some weeks after that I didn't take a lot more. Because there wasn't really room for me here – there was nine other shoe-and-clog-shops here then. Well, there was some that worked at home, in a hut at home, repairing shoes and clogs: and there was one man that had three working for him. So there was really no room for me, but I had to do something.

I used to buy machine-made soles for the clogs, and I used to buy leather from travellers. There was plenty o' travellers, and they used to come from Preston, and down in Lancashire, and there was one come from Newcastle: they had samples, maybe a bend or two in a car back. Then, if they were getting near th' end of their journey, they'd let you have this sample: and if they'd had it for a sample, you could rely on it being about as good as there was in t'bale! Because I never bought a whole bale – that was twenty-five hides – but I sometimes bought as many as about seven sides – that was the length of a cow, like.

Now when I started for meself, I used to make some men's clogs for nine and elevenpence, but I generally got about ten and six or ten and elevenpence – but now, t'last pair I made were twenty-five pounds! There used to be hundreds wore nothing but clogs round here: I have some customers still that won't hear tell of anything else but clogs for everyday, though they'll mebbe have something else for when they're dressed up. But there *was* some as'd never wear clogs, chemists and shop people and that.

Most farmers, and that, would wear them all year round. Do you see that sign?

Clogs are cool for summer's heat
Clogs are warm for winter's sleet.

Well, that's what I had up in my shop, and it's quite true. Because, for one thing, clogs don't close round your foot so tight, like a shoe does: and when a shoe bends, it puts pressure on your foot, doesn't it? A clog doesn't bend, so your foot has plenty of room, and circulation goes freely: and then wood is such a good insulator, it's inclined to encourage warmness. And it lifts you up out of the wet: so many people would have clogs instead of wellington boots, if they could get 'em. A lot o' people fairly hate wearing wellingtons, but it's often all they can get nowadays. Me brother-in-law, he was a farmer, and I made clogs for him for over forty years – he never wore anything else until he was very old, and then he started wearing boots, 'cause he didn't do much work then. And once he wanted them soling in haytime, in the hot weather: so I said to him, 'What's your hurry, can't you manage with your boots for a bit?' But he said, 'No, I can't: because when I'm forking hay up to t'stack, I can reach a bit further in my clogs.' Because, you see, the sole didn't bend on a clog, so he could spring up a bit farther!

Duck toes, clasp clogs, and pattens

There was two kinds of clog-sole people wore round here. These is round toes, and these is duck toes, what some people call 'Lancashire toes' – they come to like a wedge-shape at the front. Most people in Sedbergh had the round toe when I started, but o' course at Kirkby Stephen the men's was ducks, nearly all: so when I came from Kirkby and set up for meself, I did duck toes, and t'others in Sedbergh that did clogs eventually had to do same as me. A duck toe looks smaller when they're on your feet, you see: if you wore a duck toe on one foot and a round toe on t'other, you'd think round-toed one was a size bigger.

And I once had a farmer and his wife come in: and he'd been in Lancashire farming until he come up here, and he'd always had round toes. And when he come to me, I had both, and I said, 'Try some ducks': and when he got 'em on, he said, 'Aye, they look tidy, I'll try 'em.' And then his wife come in a month or two later, and *she* wanted a pair o' clogs: and she said, 'I don't want any of them duck toes you sold me husband. I did sauce him, coming back with them narrow toes.' *She* thought 'twas a change for the worse. But I persuaded *her* to try them: and she tried on one of each, and she says, 'Well, they do look tidier.' So *she* took duck toes in th' end, after she sauced him.

But t'others in Sedbergh went on doing round toes for quite a time, but in the end they *had* to do ducks. Because a farmer's wife would go to them and say, 'Haven't you got any o' them narrow-toed ones. My neighbour has some, and I like them.' So they had to get them in.

The men's clogs round here was all lace-ups: men wore some clasped clogs in Lancashire, but mostly for Sundays and Saturdays – they'd have a fancy pattern on the front. But women *always* wore clasped clogs: they were very handy, because they just had the one brass clasp to fasten 'em: and you get down wi' one hand and do 'em, and you could unfasten 'em wi' one hand. And so they were very handy for a woman that was getting a bit stout. Then there were t'children's clogs: they were usually clasps, but they had button-bar and buckle-bar clogs as well, and they was all sorts o' colours – red was the most popular. And the women would wear red in latter years, but going back a bit, before the last war, there was hardly any women wore colours, it was always black.

And of course clogs was very good for hanging clothes out in wet weather, or going out to feed calves and pigs through puddle 'oles and all that: because when they come in, a clog with irons on bottom didn't leave a great pazzick-mark* on the floor. They'd only walked on the irons, so it dried up almost immediately.

And another thing I just remember was pattens: I just remember one pair, and that would be in about 1916 – a lady on Back Lane had some, and I remember taking them to her just after we'd put some irons on. They was just a piece of wood, the shape of a clog-sole but a bit flatter, and they had two straps, wi' buckles: they'd put a shoe on, shove it through one strap, and then fasten t'other over the shoe. That was for washday, or for hanging out t'washing: but they weren't worn for wearing's sake, though when snow and slush was on I suppose they might've worn 'em to t'shop, to keep 'em out o' t'wet. But they'd more or less gone out altogether by my time.

Beatrix Potter wore clogs, you know. Have you heard of her? She had a cottage in the Lake District, and one morning she was off for a walk, and it was rain and fine drizzle. So she had her cloak on, and these clasp-clogs clatterin' away along t'lane: and she meets a tramp, and he says: 'O missus, it's a horful morning for the likes of us!' That's true, you know, because she told it herself at th' Women's Institute.

And George Bernard Shaw used to come round here, too. He used to come here to a girls' school, Balliol School, for a holiday in the summer months: they were writers and that, and they were members of – what do they call 'em? – the Fabian Society. Well, I don't know whether he wore clogs, but I *do* know he used to want his socks knitted different for the left and right feet. There was a man here in Sedbergh, Mr Douglas, and he used to knit socks, and he said Bernard Shaw wanted 'em lefts and rights. 'How d'you make 'em lefts and rights?' I said. And he says, 'Well, in th' inside of one foot you take so many stitches out, so it makes less room.' 'When he's got them, how does he tell which is which?' 'Oh, he has a button stitched on th' outside of the left 'un!'

THE BASKETMAKER

Frank Bigg (who lives, by a remarkably happy chance, in the hamlet of Wicker Street, near the picturesque Suffolk village of Kersey) is the last surviving member of a long line of East Anglian basketmakers. And though driven out of full-time trade during the hard times of the 1930s, he has never ceased to practice the craft to which he was apprenticed, and still does so in his retirement from bus driving. When, that is, he is not ringing the bells of Kersey church, 'sweet-pickling' bacon, or cultivating such delicious but 'uncommercial' old varieties of apple as Darcy Spice, Norman's Pippin, or Doctor Harvey's.

For many of us brought up in the age of plastic, basketwork has about it a faint aroma of folksiness and 'craft shops' – or, at best, of shopping baskets and bicycle carriers. In Mr Bigg's youth, however, such things were the mere knick-knackery of a craft which played a vital part in many trades and industries as well as in everyday life: and which, as he remembers here, produced everything from oyster baskets to the ton luggage skips for the 'Queen Mary'.

I was apprenticed to basketmaking as soon as I left school, at fourteen. That was in 1929, and there was nothing much else to do in the country, at that time: times was so bad that most of the farmers had trouble keeping their own heads above water, and they wouldn't take a boy on. And then, of course, basketmaking had been in my mother's family – the Parsonsons – for generations. I think my great-grandfather was in the trade – he was a Sudbury man. In fact he was a Freeman of Sudbury, and the Freedom's still in the Parsonson family. Anyway, at that time my grandfather and my uncle *and* my brother were all basketmakers. Grandfather started his own business around about 1890, in Colchester: he had a shop at Colchester, 21 North Hill. He'd been apprenticed to the trade, and he'd first gone to Colchester as foreman of the basketmaking side of a coopering and basket business. Then, when the people he worked for packed up, he'd taken on the basketmaking business himself, and he carried on until he died, about 1936: after that my uncle took over.

I've still got the old chair-seat Grandfather used to sit on when he was making baskets – he'd sit on it on the floor: and I've still got his measuring stick, his yardstick. I've heard him say that was made from one of the shafts of a little wicker pony-cart, like Queen Victoria's children used to ride about in. Well, if you look, it's not a *yard*stick now, because there's nine inches broken off the end there. That was because he once had an apprentice who wasn't doing as he was told, so Grandfather broke that nine inches off on top of his head! He'd broken his rule, you might say!

Well, he never broke his rule on me, but I was properly apprenticed, even though I was family. It was a six-year apprenticeship, and I had to sign proper indentures. I did that, because there was a little money left in our village of Milden, that was left by some charity or other to pay for young lads to be apprenticed. I lodged with my uncle, of course, and I started at two shillings a week, to buy my clothes and that: and then the Milden money paid for my keep. Then it gradually went up, and when I finished my apprenticeship at twenty I got a man's wage. It wasn't very much though, because by then basketmaking was getting bad – we just couldn't compete with the cheap foreign stuff coming in.

You'd start your apprenticeship by just watching, and then you'd go on to trim up other people's work. After that you'd start on the cheaper types of basket: you'd start by making the bottoms, and you progress on from there.

You soon got accustomed to it. You'd all be sitting on the floor, with your legs straight out in front of you: you've your shop board to sit on, and you had your lap board, what you used to make your basket on. Then, if you was repairing big laundry hampers, there'd maybe be one inside and one outside it. If you were mending the bottom of it, you'd turn it upside down, and you'd have one pushing through from the outside and one from inside.

Of course, we never had a fire to work by, because that would dry the stuff out so quick: and if the osiers get a little bit too dry, they'll snap. You could always tell when they *were* getting too dry, because they'd start to squeak when you bent them: and Grandfather used to shout – 'Get them wetted, they're in agony.' You had a bath standing in the shop, and you'd brush them all over with water again. Your feet used to get cold, but your hands were on the go all the time, so they never got really cold: and they used to get quite hard on the edges, from knocking the osiers down, knocking one row into another.

We worked six days a week: we used to start about half past seven in the morning, and if we were busy, we'd go on 'til about seven or eight at night. Or if we weren't quite so busy, we'd maybe go and work in the garden for an hour in the afternoons: or we might pick Uncle's apples on a summer evening.

But it wasn't boring work. You could talk while you were working, you could sing, you could do what you liked, as long as you kept on working. And different people used to come in for a talk, or maybe they'd be interested to sit and watch you, watch the baskets growing.

I still do a bit of basketmaking for people, so I've still got most of my tools – and I still sit on Grandfather's old chair-seat! This here's what we call a shop iron, for knocking the rows of basketwork together: and that's a shop knife, for cutting the stakes with, the main framework of the basket. Then there's trimming-up knives, and your picking-up knife that you just give the osiers a snick with when you're bending then, so'll they'll bend without breaking. Now these are what you call bodkins, for sticking your stakes into the bottom frame: you get all sizes from tiny ones to these great big ones, for big hampers. And these are shears, for cutting off the top of the stakes: I shouldn't be surprised if these are smith-made. These little gadgets are for splitting the osiers, when you needed them very thin, for horse-sieves or something: you could split them into three or four. And here's a set of shaves, adjustable shaves for making different thicknesses of osiers, for whatever you wanted – chair-seats or whatever.

Osiers

We worked pretty well entirely in cane and osiers. The cane was imported from abroad, but the osiers – they're a kind of willow – generally came from round about Colchester. People used to plant them if they had a low or boggy place on their land, and while they were growing they'd be a shelter for pheasants. Of course, my uncle had his own osier beds for a time, out near Layer-de-la-Haye.

They were easy enough to plant. I remember my uncle got the 'sets' for starting a new bed, and they were just like little sticks. You just stuck them in the ground, about three feet apart in rows, and about four foot apart from row to row. Then they'd just grow: you didn't want to take any trouble with them, as long as the ground was right. It would need to be next to a stream, so it would flood over some times of the year: and there'd need to be plenty of springs, plenty of moisture in the ground. You'd cut them off every year, and the older they got, of course, the bigger the stump got, and the more osiers it had on. When they'd been going for a bit, there'd probably be twenty or thirty sticks on a stump. You could cut them year after year, but they'd reckon the first year's growth was the best and the strongest: if you get them over-yeared, if they get *too* old, the outside is inclined to be a little bit too brittle.

You can cut them any time after the leaves have dropped. We used to cut them about the end of January or February time, so that the old stumps they were growing on would have a good start for the next year's growth. It was a sort of coppicing, really. But, of course, you couldn't peel them when you first cut them, because the bark'd be too tight: you had to wait until the sap began to rise again. So, after we'd cut them, we'd tie them in bundles and stand them upright in a special ditch that was dug out, a wet ditch. They'd stand there until they began to shoot again, and get buds and little hairy roots on: that would be about May time, and then you could take them home and peel them, because then they'd peel easy. From about May, we used to have a chap go out to the beds and get us so many bundles every week, as many as we needed.

They all had to be peeled by hand. Well, you had a 'cleaver' to pull them through: it was a split piece of wood, with an iron on either side of the split: you wedge the osier in the split, grip the end, and pull it through, and the skins come off quite easily. There are lots of different types of osiers: some had nearly black skins, and some more a golden colour, and some almost red. I think they reckoned the black skins were about the strongest. When they were peeled, of course, they were all more or less white, and we'd use those peeled white osiers for the most expensive sort of baskets, shopping baskets and that kind of thing. For other baskets we might use 'buff' osiers: those are boiled with their skins on *before* they're peeled, and the buff colour comes from the dye in the skin. Uncle used to buy those from Somerset, because you needed to boil them in tanks big enough to stand them in, and we didn't have any of those. Then, for the very cheapest sort of baskets, we didn't trouble to peel them at all, and we called those 'browns'.

Oyster baskets, shrimp peds and barn-fans

We made just about every kind of basket you can think of: everything from shopping baskets and bicycle carrier baskets to the big skips they used to use on building sites. But quite half our work was done for the fish trade. We used to make all the baskets for what they called the 'Colchester-Pyfleet native oysters' – the beds were down at Brightlingsea. They were *the* oysters, you might say, and they were sent all over the world in our baskets. We had the contract for them, and we used to make perhaps three hundred in the course of a season: we made them to hold anything from twenty-five to a hundred oysters, according to what the orders were. They were more or less rectangular baskets, with a little lid, and we made them with just the rough unpeeled osiers, as cheap as ever they *could* be made: they used to work out about a shilling each, all round. Because they'd just be needed for the railway journey, and then they'd probably just be thrown away.

Then we used to make what they called 'shrimp peds', for the fishermen about Tollesbury and Mersea to send out their shrimps in: I suppose they'd hold about a bushel of shrimps. And we made sprat skips, without lids: they just used to load the sprats into them, straight from the boats, and they'd be sent off to market like that, or perhaps used for hawking round the streets on a barrow: so they were what you might call 'returnable'. And another thing we made plenty of were 'dockers', to wash the fish in when they came out of the holds of the smacks: the fish would be dumped in, and they'd pour water on 'em. So dockers were mostly uprights, less than an inch apart, with just horizontal bands at the top, middle, and bottom to hold 'em together. I expect they make most of those sort of things in plastic now.

We made all kinds of baskets for the farmers, too. We made a lot of sieves for horse feeding: in fact, we've got an old trades directory that calls Grandfather a 'horse-sieve maker and basketmaker'. The bottoms were made from split osiers, and they were used for sieving the chaff for the horses, and for feeding it to them: they'd give them 'a sifting' each. Then there were the big chaff hampers for carrying to the cattle, they'd hold maybe two bushels: and the apple-gathering baskets we called 'peck cobs', because they'd hold about a peck of fruit. Then there were chicken hampers, for sending chickens by rail, and I can just about remember Grandfather making a 'barn fan'. That was a shell-shaped basket, flat and turned up at the back: it was for sorting corn seed in the barn, so you didn't damage any of it: it was hammered so close, you couldn't see daylight through it.

Then we used to do quite a bit of chair seating. Mostly, unless we were very slack, my aunt did all the cane seating, but I did all the rush seating. They reckoned I had about the best knack for it – my brother, he always got in a muddle with rush seating. I still do quite a bit now, but you can't get the same quality of rushes: we'd always use the real saltwater rushes from Holland.

From the 'Queen Mary' to the carry-cot

But mostly, yes, you *could* say we were in the 'packaging industry'. We made nearly all our baskets to order, and we hardly ever kept any stock except, if we were slack, we'd maybe make an odd dog-basket or a linen hamper, and put it in the window, just to show off our wares. Then, of course, we'd repair a lot of things. We used to repair a lot of laundry hampers, because at that time the London and North Eastern Railway had a big laundry at Colchester, and all the stuff from the railway hotels used to be laundered there.

And we'd sometimes have to repair the hampers the commercial travellers used to carry their samples in, or theatrical hampers. We'd suddenly get someone come down in a panic from one of the theatres: 'Our hamper's got damaged on the rail, can you repair it before Friday?' Then we'd repair the old wicker baby-carriages, and once we had a wicker sidecar for a motorcycle to mend.

You'd be surprised at some of the things we used to have to make. One year when I was there, we were asked to make an osier frame for a model bottle, about ten feet high: that was for Daniell's the brewers, and they used it on their float in Colchester carnival. And during the last war, after I'd left, my brother made panniers for the airborne troops: they were just like big hampers, and they were the lightest and strongest things to drop by

*Frank Bigg (right) with his aunt and uncle,
and a basket-framed bottle they made for
Daniells' Brewery entry in Colchester carnival,
c. 1935. Behind Frank is a bundle of osiers.*

parachute. Because if a wooden crate happened to drop on its corner, it would probably split open: but these panniers wouldn't split, they'd got some give in them.

The *biggest* things we ever made regularly were the ton cargo skips for the 'Queen Mary' liner, after she was launched in 1934. They were huge: about three foot six square at the bottom, and more or less the same shape as a bucket: they'd hold about a ton of luggage, and they'd be slung on board with ropes, from a crane. Actually, the contract went to Lord Roberts's Workshops for Disabled Ex-servicemen; that was in Colchester, too: but they'd got no one capable of making them, so the Workshops asked my brother and me to do them. We made four or six in a month, and we had to use cane uprights about an inch diameter – they'd have to be well soaked, or you couldn't bend them.

And then, you know, my uncle made the very first carry-cot that ever was used: I think he *invented* the carry-cot. Well, there was a lady lived at Colchester, and her son was in the army, and his wife had just had a baby when they had to be posted to India. She came in one day and said, 'My daughter-in-law's got this baby a few weeks old. Have you any idea how they can carry it from the train to the boat? We wondered if you could make a wicker cot, so they could carry the baby in it?' So my uncle said, 'I should think we can: we can put a handle on either side.'

So he made it: the handles turned down on either side, and he left room for the baby to be wrapped up for travelling. The people were absolutely thrilled with it, but he never really thought any more about it. And the next thing we knew, there was a photo in one of the London papers – I think it was the *Daily Mail*: it showed a porter carrying the baby across one of the London stations in his basket, and it was labelled 'The Latest Mode of Travelling'. This was in about 1930 or 1931, and nobody seems to have thought about anything like it, previous: but after that, it didn't seem so long until these carry-cots were everywhere, and then they started to make them in this fabric-stuff. They'd had wicker cradles before, of course, but not with big handles for carrying.

Yes, basketmaking was a good trade to be in, in lots of ways: but in my time there was never any money in it. A lot of farm chaps got more than we did, and the miners got a lot more. I remember once Uncle had a man working for him, from Morpeth in Northumberland. He was an ex-miner, and he had to come out of the mines because he'd got some sort of a disease. So he was under a government training scheme, and they used to pay Uncle so much a week to employ him. Well, he could make the baskets all right, but he said he couldn't earn enough at it. He was only earning about twenty-five shillings a week, and reckoned that would only keep him in beer-money for Saturday night and Sunday. So he said he'd rather go back down the mines, and *that* was in the days when they reckoned mining was very, very bad.

And things got worse and worse. When I first finished my apprenticeship, at least we did keep pretty busy most of the time: but just before the 1939 war we couldn't get the work, because the foreigners were sending in baskets cheaper than what you could make them. Well, I'll give you an example. Just before I left, we had to make bicycle front baskets for eleven shillings and sixpence *a dozen*: that was elevenpence ha'penny each, *and* we had to deliver them to the shop. We did that more or less to keep the place going, because there were no other orders coming in.

My brother Felix, he stayed on, and he kept up basketmaking until he died. But I left in 1938, and I never went back, not professionally: though I still do a bit of basketwork, as a hobby you might say. Because you can't forget a trade you've really been trained in.

9

RECIPES, REMEDIES AND BELIEFS

RECIPES

This final chapter collects together some of the recipes, remedies and beliefs that I have come across during my travels. Others (which it would have been a pity to tear from their context) appear elsewhere, especially in the section on 'Them old horse chaps'. First then, a few recipes from the 'household book' now used by Mrs Vinie Bigg of Wicker Street, Kersey, Suffolk. It was compiled by her father when he married her mother in 1916, drawing on his mother's recipe book, which was in turn based on her mother's collection... 'so Heaven knows how old some of them are'. Most presume the availability of one of the great 'six-pail coppers' – metal cauldrons with a capacity of six bucketfuls of liquid, set into a brick-built fire-box – that stood in Suffolk 'back 'ouses' (p. 18): but the quantities can be scaled down for more modest utensils. I have done so myself with the apple wine recipe, and the result was both good and very strong – hence, presumably, the 'Amen'.

Apple Wine
Bruise 2 bushels [say 80 pounds] of apples, and put them in 1½ gallons of cold water, add 1 ounce of white tartar, 7 pounds of honey and 1 grated nutmeg. Boil together as long as any scum rises. Then strain into a tub. When lukewarm, ferment with 1 ounce of compressed yeast, stirred with a little of the wine. Leave 2 or 3 weeks. Remove the head, draw the liquor clean off and turn into a barrel or stone jug. It may be bottled in a few weeks. 1 pint of rum will improve the wine, and this should be added when the fermentation has ceased. Amen.

Parsnip Wine
To make parsnip wine, which, however, is best made in March. Scrub clean and slice the parsnips, allowing 1 gallon of slices to 1 gallon of water. Boil together till the parsnips will pulp, but are still whole. It will take 2 hours or more. Then strain the liquor and return to the copper. To every 1 gallon of this allow ½ ounce of root ginger and 3 pounds of Demerara sugar. Boil

again for ½ hour. Slice 1 lemon for every 1 gallon of water into a tub and pour over the wine boiling hot. When lukewarm, ferment with a slice of toast covered with thick yeast. After standing 1 week turn into the cask and bottle in 6 months' time. Do not bung the cask till the slow fermentation has ceased or it will burst.

Dandelion Wine
Use 3 quarts of flowers to 1 gallon of water. Simmer the flowers 20 minutes then strain them and put 3½ pounds of sugar, 1 lemon, 2 oranges to 1 gallon. Boil the sugar and rinds of oranges and lemon in the liquor ½ hour. Let it stand till cool, then put it in the cask with the oranges and lemon cut in thin slices and a little yeast. When it has done working, cork it down and bottle in 12 months. Some do bottle it at 6 months but it is best at 12.

Harvest Drink
Boil ½ ounce each of dried hops and root ginger well bruised in 1 quart of water for 25 minutes. Add 1 pound of Demerara sugar, 5 quarts more water and 1 ounce citric acid in powder. Boil again 5 minutes and strain and bottle still warm. It will be fit for drinking when cold. To thoroughly cool a bottle of this drink, wrap it up in a wet cloth and hang it on a tree or any place where there is a sharp draught. The cloth must be kept wet until the drink is wanted.

A Tonic
Squeeze the juice of 6 lemons on 5 eggs in a basin that will just hold them, for 3 or 4 days until the shells are all dissolved, then strain and add ½ pound of sugar and 1 pint of rum. Take a wine-glassful fasting in the morning. See the eggs are well covered with the juice.

REMEDIES

May as well begin with the collection of Mrs Violet Wade, who was born in 1897 near Doncaster in West Yorkshire, but now lives at Rudston in the East Riding. She still uses many of them, but: 'It's a job getting some of 'em made up now: because there's two penn'orth of this and two penn'orth of that, and it doesn't always give the ounces.'

Dutch Drops
Two-pennyworth of medicated turpentine
,,　　,,　　of aniseed
,,　　,,　　of balsam of sulphur
That's for bad backs: a few drops on a teaspoon wi' some sugar, and get it down you. That's good stuff.

Cough cure

Ipecacuanha wine, 20 minims
Spirits of nitrous ether, 20 minims
Liquor of ammonia acetate, 1 dram
Camphor water, ½ ounce

To be taken every four hours. [The first and last ingredients are expectorants to bring up the phlegm, and the second and third induce sweating.]

For a loose cough

Ipecacuanha wine, 10 minims
Ammonia carbonate, 4 grams
Tincture of squills, 50 grams
Infusion of senega, ½ ounce

To be taken three times a day. [Mainly expectorants.]

For a chest cold

Two-pennyworth of liquorice
    ,,   ,,   of marshmallow
    ,,   ,,   of chlorodyne

Put in a medicine bottle with cold water, take one tablespoonful three times daily. [This marshmallow is not the sweet, but a substance made from the root of the marsh mallow (*Althaea officinalis*). According to Gerard's *Herbal* (1597) this is also useful against 'Shortness of Breath, Wheesing, Excoriation of the Guts, Ruptures, Cramp, Convulsions and the King's Evil'.]

For a cold in the chest

Two-pennyworth of laudanum
    ,,   ,,   of oil of peppermint
    ,,   ,,   Spanish
    ,,   ,,   of ipecacuanha
    ,,   ,,   of oil of almonds
    ,,   ,,   of paregoric

Break the Spanish – that's what they call liquorice now – in bits, add ½ pound of black treacle with ½ pint of boiling water. That's one of the best, and we'd go and get the ingredients from the chemist and make it up ourselves: but you couldn't get the laudanum now. [Laudanum is a tincture of opium in water and alcohol.]

For double pneumonia

'Vinegar and onions, boiled together: thicken with oatmeal for a poultice, and put poultice on back and front, as hot as possible.' It's an old 'un, that.

For the nerves

1 ounce of phosphate acid
18 grams of quinine

That's good, for anyone that's nervous. [Or constipated.]

For the back

Oil of juniper
Spirits of wine [brandy, more or less]
Red lavender
Turpentine
Laudanum

One dram of each shaken in a bottle – take twenty to thirty drops on sugar. *That* was a pretty strong 'un!

Not so violent, however, as the 'cure' once inflicted on Mrs Wade's husband, Arthur.

A drastic cure

I'll tell you something what happened to me, when I was eleven year old. We went to a farm where they were thrashing, and us lads were cutting some turnips for 'em in one o' them turnip-cutting machines. Well, you know the handle that turns it, one lad sat on it: and there were some turnips fast [stuck] inside, and I put me hand in to shift 'em, and this lad swung on the handle. And the blades came round, and pinched a piece clean off that thumb!

And I set off through the village to home. I had to go right through the village, to this side: and I dropped once, and I gorr up again, and I fainted when I got nearer hoom. And a young lad that was wi' me ran to tell me mother, and she came and got me hoom. Now me grandmother was living i' them days, and she said: 'Bring 'im in lass. Now tha 'old 'im, and I'll do it.' And she got an owd pint pot, and she had it half full o' turpentine, just raw turpentine: and she shoved ma thumb straight in! And they say I screamed: well, I guess I shouldn't know *what* I was doing.

Doctor said to me afterwards: 'You're lucky to be here: they might have had you fastened up [in a coffin] by now, with the shock.' But d'you know, it growed up again, so you can't tell no difference now: only thing is, the nail's that strong, I can take little screws out with it!

Now for some more remedies against:

Colds and chest complaints

MARY: For colds, we used to get a teaspoon of blackcurrant jam in a cup, and boiling water put on – and that was your hot drink. There was no such thing as an aspirin.

CISSIE: But I can remember when they started with 'Veno's Lightning Cough Cure': the store had that, and we thought it was wonderful, because it had a nice taste.

MARY: For whooping cough, we'd have the juice of an onion, or of a turnip, and the moist soft brown sugar. And they used to say that if you took a child to a very high hill, where the wind was fresh, that would help with whooping cough. Or, the return air of a pit – that had been through the mine, and was coming out.   [ELLIOTT SISTERS, Ovingham, Northumberland]

For a cold, they'd make peppermint tea from these peppermints that used to grow in the garden. Never hear nothing about that now. Or they'd say, 'I'll ha' to make you a basin of onion gruel, and you can goo to bed.' That was a thick onion gruel, boiled in the saucepan. That'd make you sweat, you see, and you'd sweat that cold away.   [BILL PARTRIDGE, Lindsey, Suffolk]

Mrs Flinton, daughter of the miller of Burgh-on-Bain, Lincolnshire and wife of 'the engine-man', is a lifelong sufferer from asthma:

For pneumonia, there was only linseed poultices. We had a fire in the bedroom and we took the pan and steamer up, and my sister Fanny was sat up wi' me all night. She used to put one poultice in the steamer, and take th' other out and put it on me, and she did that all night. You mixed up the linseed with water, and put it on some rag: and you'd get it real hot in the steamer, then slap it on the chest.

And I was a bit better the next morning, when the doctor came. But he took one look at me, and he said to Mother, 'Have you one o' the boys at home? Well, get him on his bike, and send him for a bale o' cotton-wool, because I want this girl wrapping in cotton-wool from head to foot, as quick as you can do it!' So Leonard went to Barkwith and got this sheaf o' wool, and Mother wrapped me up in it, from me neck to me knees. And I had to stop in it while I come to get up, and then they took some of it off. But they left it on all round me chest, and I could only pick a tiny piece of it off every day: and it was summertime!

The Mother o' Burgh

Mrs Cook used to live up here, and we called her the 'Mother o' Burgh'. She was the midwife, and she'd go out for all babies, and she used to lay out corpses, too. And if anyone was ill, and you'd get Mrs Cook to 'em, I'll bet she'd cure 'em. She used to use herbs, and different things out o' the garden, and she'd soon tell you what was the matter wi' you. Everybody went to Mrs Cook, and if she hadn't got what would cure you, she'd tell you what to get yourself. You didn't run to the chemist's for everything then. For asthma, she told Mum to give me honey and vinegar, or teaspoons o' goose grease with sugar on it. And when I'd gotten to the last, and I couldn't breathe, they'd mix some mustard and gin, and that would make me vomit. Many's the time Mother would have to run for Dad to carry me and me brother outside in our chairs, because we both had asthma, and we were nearly black for want of breath. And now look what they've got for asthma! I've got one of these new drugs now, and it's cleared me: I never was clear all me life, but I am now.

Better inside than out

When somebody'd got a bad chest or a cold, they'd get some goose grease and brown paper and slap it on your chest all hot. Well, there was a man here one day, and he'd got a bad cold, and the woman of the house where he was working told him to get this grease, and rub it well on his chest before he'd go to bed. Next morning, she said,

'Well, how is your chest, Bert Jenkins?'

'Oh, better.'

'Well, how much did you put on, and how did you do it?'

'I did swallow it.'

'You were supposed to put it on outside, not swallow it.'

'Well, if it would do good outside, it's sure to do better inside.'

[MRS MILLS and RON MILLS, Velindre, near Hay-on-Wye]

Herbal cures

Feverfew

There was feverfew for earaches. Me mother used to warm it up and put it on your ear for earaches. She'd pick the young shoots off, heat 'em up, and put 'em in a little bandage round your ear.   [FRANK BIGG, Kersey, Suffolk] [Feverfew (*Chrysanthemum parthenium*) is a febrifuge, putting fever to flight and curing headaches – try crushing a few leaves and sniffing them if you feel one coming on. But I've found no reference in the herbals to its use against *ear*ache.]

Lilies

You know them flowers what we call the lilies – they come big white flowers. Well, when I was a young bloke, them old people used to take all the petals off, and put 'em in whisky or summ'at. And if you cut yourself, they'd take one out o' the jar and put one on the cut, and that'd soon heal up.

[BILL PARTRIDGE, Lindsey, Suffolk]
[According to Culpeper's *Herbal* (1653), the lily is 'excellently good . . . for it expels venom to the exterior parts of the body'. Preparations derived from it

were used against dropsy, scalds, ulcers, plague-sores, 'swellings of the privities' and to 'give speedy delivery to women in travail'. The antiseptic effect of the whisky must also have helped to cure the cut.]

Celandine

It's a delicate subject, but one old lady we knew used to use celandine roots for piles. The little yellow flower that comes in the early spring.

[MRS VINIE BIGG, Kersey, Suffolk]

[This is the lesser celandine (*Ranunculus ficaria*) also called 'figwort' and 'pilewort'. 'The latter age use the roots and grains for the piles, which being often bathed with juice mixed with wine, or with the sick man's urine, are drawne togither and dried up, and the paine quite taken away' (Gerard's *Herbal*, 1597).]

'Sennygreen'

My grandmother, she had all kinds of things for sick animals. At the back of our house at Llaethdy there was a place built on – an oven you may say – and it had a slate roof: and used to be things growing on there called 'sennygreens'. And any animal bad, she'd get some o' that and put pig's lard with it, and I don't know what else, and she'd make it into an ointment. Any animal that had got cuts or sores, this is what would be put on it.

We never heard talk o' no *vet*. I never seen a vet on the place. Grandmother always made her own things – and she always kep' em to herself!　　　[MRS MILLS, referring to Llaethdy, near Newtown, Powys]

[Sengreen or houseleek (*Sempervivum tectorum*), also called 'healing leaf' and 'thunder plant' was originally planted or encouraged on roofs – particularly those of kitchens and ovens – as a protection against fire and lightning. By extension, it was later used against burns and cuts, in people as well as animals.]

If you'd got a bad cut, you'd take some of these things that grow on the tiles, with squashy leaves: you'd get one of those, and wash it, and smash it all up, and mix it with lard to make a poultice. Wonderful healing stuff!

[MRS EDITH WATKINS, Radnorshire and Herefordshire]

Tobacco

Men always used to chew tobacco. They reckoned that would keep their teeth healthy – that would keep the germs off their teeth. It was what they called 'Franklin's pigtail'.

One place I was at, they used to get two or three ounce of this old Franklin tobacco, boil it up with a drop of water in a pot, and that was a good medicine for killing worms in sheep or cattle. You drenched [dosed] 'em with that, with a horn or a small bottle – but if you gave 'em too much, you'd see 'em tumble over for a bit: they'd stagger like as if they were drunk.

And if you'd got a young dog, it might get distemper at twelve months old. Well, you got a pinch o' Franklin tobacco, and push it down his throat with a bit of stick – make sure he do swallow it. And that'll stop him getting worms or distemper. Or if you've got a horse that's scouring [having diarrhoea] a lot, if you can get a half inch of a fag and push it down his throat, that'll stop it.   [RON MILLS, Velindre, near Hay-on-Wye]
['Tobacco', says Culpeper, 'helps to expel worms in the stomach and belly, and to ease the pains in the head, or megrims, and the griping pains in the bowels.']

Brought up on laudanum

The following tale, told by Mrs Flinton, is proof that drug addiction is no strictly modern phenomenon. Laudanum – a tincture of opium in water and alcohol, generally brandy – was once freely available in chemists' shops.

At lambing time, Dad always got a big bottle of laudanum, and one of sweet nitre, and one of rhubarb, and one of turpentine. Then if any o' the sheep was bad, he'd mix up a dose and give it 'em.

Well, we used to have a maid that lived with us, and when she was a baby she was more or less brought up on laudanum! Her mother used to go to work in the farms, you see, and she used to give her a drop or two of laudanum and take her in the pram, so she'd sleep while she came home. Well, Dad had got this big bottle of laudanum in, and it kept *going*, and he couldn't think why. So Mother put it away, out of sight.

And she couldn't get no work out o' this maid at all, after then. 'Really, Edith', she said, 'I don't know what's comed over you! You were such a good girl for work.' 'Well, Mrs Smithson,' says Edith, 'Put the laudanum back, then I can work.' 'You'll poison yourself.' 'I shan't, me mother brought me up on it.' So Mother says to Dad, 'Wheer's that laudanum bottle – then I might get some work done!' And when that laudanum came back, then Edith could do all the work there was to be done: but she got really beat wi'out it.

Bone-setters and wart-charms

VW: Bone-setters are very good. When I was only about four, I should say, I must have fallen and put this wrist out. I couldn't hold anything in this hand at all, it just went limp. So Mother thought I'd broken it, and she took me to the doctor: and he just got hold of it, and messed it about, and he said, 'Oh, it's all right: there's nothing wrong with it.' But I couldn't hold anything at all with it, so she took me to a bone-setter at Doncaster: I shall always remember the name, it was 'Grandage'. And she just got hold of it, and pulled, and set it back – and it was in, and it was quite all right after that.

Her father was in the same line, and it ran in the family. Her father was a well-known bone-setter in Doncaster. But they hadn't gone to any college or anything like that – they just knew how to do it.

I couldn't say whether we paid her or not, I don't remember. But I've heared 'em say they won't take money, because it's bad luck. Whether it's summ'at that originated from the olden days, I do not know.

AW: I can tell you a remedy. You can do it yourself, if you have warts. I've proved it, because I had warts all over the back o' me hands, and me fingers. You've got to *steal* a bit o' fat bacon – nobody's got to see you take it – then you've to rub your warts with it. And then you get a leaf off a tree, and however many warts you have on your hand, make as many holes in that leaf, and bury it. And as the leaf dies and withers, so will your warts.

I did that. I pinched bacon at my wife's father's house, and none of 'em never knew – I hope they don't come back! And I could tell you the exact place where I buried that leaf: but I won't! And where I buried the bacon, too: that was in a different place, of course, it had to be: and nobody had to see you bury them. Well, I did that, and all me warts disappeared!

VW: I've one better than that, for warts – dandelion root. You get the milk from the bottom of the roots, and rub it on your warts, and they'll go. That's wonderful stuff, dandelion milk.

[VIOLET and ARTHUR WADE, Rudston, East Yorkshire]

BELIEFS

We have now reached the shadowy borderline between 'remedies' and beliefs. Many beliefs were held because they worked – though that is not to say that they worked because they were held. Arthur Wade's warts really did disappear, and so did those of the Gwernyfed bullocks; green did appear to bring death to Lizzie Grange's family; and lightning really does strike oaks more often than other trees. It is worth noting that green is the colour of the fairies – and also of putrefaction; that oak-trees were once sacred to the thunder-god; and that knives were once made of magical iron: but if you are one of those tedious people who demand 'scientific' explanations – the sort of person that goes about crossing conjurors – you have come to the wrong shop.

Storms and stars

I din't care for it the mornin' when that thundered. 'Cause, oh, that *did* storm: an' I was that frightened. So I thought meself, 'Daise, you mun't be frightened, the Lord'll be wid yer.' An' I get on with me journey. An' though that kept flitterin' and flutterin' around, and crackin' over'ead, I din't take the slightest bit o' notice of it. An' jest as I got to that gate, I 'eard such a clap, and that lightnin' came whistlin' down, and *rain*! So I thought meself, 'Thank Heavens I'm back.'

Dad always used to say, 'When there's a storm comin' on, *git further out*, don't stop under the trees, nor under a 'edge.' Oak trees is the worse, 'cause of the draught: they draws the lightnin'. And when we was kids, Dad always used to tell us the weather by the stars. When there was a lot in a group, he used to say, 'That's fine weather'; but when they was dotted about, it wasn't so good. An' another thing what e' used to say: 'Always look for Jack and his Waggon [the Plough], and if 'e's dipping, you must take your coats.' That'd be in the winter. And the Seven Sisters [the Pleiades], if they was clear, he'd say you'll be all right for fine.

But Mother was bad when there was storms: she used to say, 'I'm a-gooin' in the coal-hole.' An' she used to git all the towels and dishcloths and cover the mirrors up: then we 'adn't got no towels. She'd put the silver away, and the knives: she'd put them under the tablecloth. Knives are funny things. Some people I know in Coventry give me that knife there, an' I says, 'Now I gotta give you a penny, else that'll cut the friendship.' That's what they say. And you mustn't pick a knife up if you drop it; you gotta git someone else to pick it up.

The lightnin' seems worse now than when we was kids, 'cause it's all blue, now. It was yellow then, and you wouldn't mind that – the lightnin' wasn't so strong. But it's terrible today. I think it's 'cause there's too much electricity in the air nowadays. An' I think people git struck when they've got a bit of steel on: a safety-pin, or a pen – like you got – or shoelaces. Now me, I 'ave all me 'airgrips out if I'm gooin' outside in stormy weather. I 'ad a handful o' grips the other mornin'. Well, you never know!

[DAISY RECORD, Hunton and Harrietsham, Kent]

Cauls and churchings

CISSIE: It could bring bad luck on the house, if an unchurched woman or an unchristened baby was brought into it. But if a baby was born with a cowl [caul] over its head, that would be thought *very* lucky, and the caul had to be kept and put away.

MARY: After I'd had my child, I couldn't go out until I'd been 'churched'. I could go out in our yard, of course, but I couldn't go into anybody's house, it wasn't allowed. I had to go to church, to thank God for the safe delivery of the child: that would usually be about a month after it was born. But before you did that, you couldn't go into anybody's house: it was unclean, and it was unlucky.   [ELLIOTT SISTERS, Ovingham, Northumberland]
[The caul – part of the foetal membrane which sometimes clings to a newborn baby's head – has always been considered a powerful talisman, particularly good against drowning.]

Mother's superstitions...

'Course, me mother used to like her fortune telled. I think, with being Irish, she was a bit superstitious – and *I* am. I'm very superstitious about *green*: I wouldn't wear green, and Mother wouldn't either. She reckoned that always a death follows green. And that's happened to us, three times in the family.

I always remember when mother lost a baby, a little 'un about a year and a half: she had a cold, and then pneumonia. And there was an old neighbour was a dressmaker, and she said to me mother, 'Get some material, and I'll make the bairns some frocks, for Easter: I won't charge you anything, but get the material.' So me mother got *green* material – and our Katie never had hers on, because she died. And after that Mother would never have green.

The next time was me grandfather. I got a green coat, and somebody give me mother a green frock. And that week me father comes back, and tells us Grandfather had died on the tram. 'Well', she says, 'that's green.'

And the next time was when me mother was ill – she was fillin' with water, because she had Bright's Disease. And our Norah was going into Newcastle to get a new coat, and our Annie was going with her. So me mother said, '*Do not* bring green, 'cause if you bring green, you'll go flaming back with it!' So when they came back, Mother says, 'Are you getten' your coat, then? What colour are you getten'?' 'I dorsn't tell you.' 'Don't tell me it's green!' And it *was* green, and a week after that me mother died.

Then, if a knife dropped, me mother'd pick it up and say there was a man coming: and she didn't like knives crossed, she'd say it was a sign of a row. And another thing was, for a bad throat: you'd take your left stocking off, and tie the foot of it round your throat – it had to be the left foot.

And we used to laugh at her superstitions about shoes. Father used to cobble all our shoes, and of course he used to put the shoes on the table to cut his leather. 'Jimmy', she'd say, 'don't put the shoe on the table.' And if he went out of the room to sharpen his knife on the step, he'd come back and find the shoe on the floor. He used to go mad: he said, 'A bloody Catholic, and you don't like shoes on the table: and you a bloody Catholic.' [*My* mother also disliked shoes on the table – because, she said, it presaged the laying-out of a shoed corpse there.]

But this one day, when Dad was at Greenside pit: it was on a Tuesday morning, and he was on first shift. And he says, 'Mother, I'm not goin' the dee [today].' She says, 'What are y' not going for?' 'I don't know, but I've got a feelin' I don't want to go the dee.' And he wouldn't go.

And when the men came from first shift, they told him there was a man sat in his very place – the place where me father used to sit to get his bait [eat his lunch] – and the top fell down, and that man was killed! And that was the only day Father didn't go to work.

[LIZZIE GRANGE, Prudhoe, Northumberland]

I'll tell you another legend about mines. When a miner was going to work in what they call first shift – what they used to call 'in-by' – in which he'd probably leave home about one o'clock in the morning. If he met a woman on the way, he wouldn't go, he went back home: it was very unlucky to meet a woman on the early shift, but I don't think it would matter during the day. Or no one would ever have got to work!

[CISSIE ELLIOTT, Ovingham, Northumberland]

The conjuror

They had some bullocks on here, at Gwernyfed, and they was plastered in warts, hanging in warts: and they couldn't get no cure for 'em – they had things from up the vet's and all. So somebody said, 'Why don't you go and see old Meredith, the conjuror, up Lumpenvane [?Llwynpenfaen]' – he was an old council-man, that used to go round seeing what pot-holes there was in the road and reporting 'em. So they went to see him, and down he come on this old black horse of his – I can remember his riding th' old black pony about. And these bullocks was in the field, with warts as big as your fist all over 'em. Meredith stood in the gate and just looked at 'em for a minute; then he got on his horse and went for home, and didn't say a word to nobody. But in two or three days' time, every one o' them warts was dropping off the cattle. He cleared the lot up! Oh no, they didn't pay him: you mustn't pay him.

But if this chap didn't like anybody – if he'd fell out with 'em – he could go up to their place and stand about the gate or look around there, and he could put things to 'go th' opposite way'. Perhaps he'd *look* at a cow or summ'at, and you'd find that cow dead. So you'd got to keep in with him! And he wasn't the only conjuror about here: there was old Enoch from Boughrood, too.   [RON MILLS, Velindre, Hay-on-Wye]

GLOSSARY

The ingredients of horse medicines are mainly based on Martindale's *Extra Pharmacopoeia* [*EP*].

The derivations of the dialect words are principally drawn from the *English Dialect Dictionary*, published in 1898, when many of them were already declared to be obsolete! By and large, the areas in which they survive conform to the settlement patterns of the races whose languages make up modern English. Thus, Scandinavian-based words are found in the northern and eastern regions settled by the Viking armies during the ninth century: and specifically Norwegian (as opposed to Danish) examples occur mainly in the Pennine dales, infiltrated by Norsemen from Ireland a hundred years later. French-derived words, a legacy of the Normans, come from the south and east: and Old English (Anglo-Saxon) survivals from the south and, particularly, the west, the area farthest from either Scandinavian or French influence.

AETHIOPES MINERAL. Black mercuric sulphide, used in horse medicines mainly as a laxative [*EP*].

ANISEED. Spice used in horse medicines as a 'carminative' (wind producer) [*EP*].

ARVE (also harve, horve, worve, etc.). Command to a plough or cart horse to 'turn left'. Derived from Old Scandinavian 'horfa', 'turn', it is used in Yorkshire, Lincolnshire, and Nottinghamshire, the areas of heaviest Viking settlement. The opposite ('turn right') is 'gee back', and it is said of an obstinate or single-minded person that they 'will neither gee nor harve' ['George', Lincolnshire: Bill Denby, Yorkshire].

AVELS. The sharp spikes or 'beards' on barley-corns [Bill Partridge, Suffolk].

BACK-CAN. Churn-shaped tin can, curved on the inside to fit the back and equipped with carrying straps: it had a capacity of six or eight gallons. Used in the north Pennine Dales for carrying milk from cows kept on outlying pastures or in field barns [Kit Calvert, Wensleydale, North Yorkshire: Maggie Joe Chapman, Swaledale, North Yorkshire].

BAIT. A packed meal taken to work: in widespread use [e.g. 'Jim Bush' and 'Gib', Radnorshire, Powys: Lizzie Grange, Northumberland]. Also, to feed [Bill Partridge, Suffolk] or to rest ['George', Lincolnshire] a horse. From old Scandinavian 'beita', 'pasture'; or 'beit', 'food'.

BANNOCK. Strictly, 'a cake of oatmeal or barley, mixed with water and baked on a griddle' [*EDD*]. Now also used, particularly in the northern English counties, for cakes and scones made with flour. From Old Gaelic 'bannach'?

BALKS, THE. A loft for storing hay or straw in a field barn, situated immediately below the roof and often directly above the cow-byre. Used in the northern counties, where 'balks' are 'beams' or 'rafters' [Kit Calvert, Wensleydale, North Yorkshire].

BEEVER (also baver, bever, etc.). A packed meal or snack. The word was once used very widely in south-east and south Midland England: up until 1890 Eton boys had 'beer, bread and salt laid in the hall, under the name of "beever"'. But according to Bill Partridge and Mrs Vinie Bigg, it was applied in Suffolk only to the substantial packed meals eaten during harvesting. From Old French 'beivre', 'a drinking'.

BOX. Trunk or other container used by domestic servants and 'living-in' farm labourers for their clothes and personal possessions. General [e.g. Ted Bateson, East Yorkshire: Edith Watkins, Radnorshire, Powys].

BRAY, TO. Northern dialect word for 'to beat, whip, strike, etc'. A survival from medieval English.

BUSHEL. A bushel is a pre-decimal dry measure of *capacity*, used for corn, apples, coal, etc. and its weight varies according to the nature of the material measured. The capacity of a bushel once varied from county to county, or even within the same county: so that in Cheshire, for instance, a bushel of barley weighed 60 lb, and of oats 45–50 lb; whereas in Devon barley was 30 lb to the bushel, and oats 36–40 lb. Probably the only way to establish the exact weight of Bill Partridge's bushel ('To be a farmer's boy') would be to obtain a *Suffolk* bushel measure, and fill it with stones from a field in Lindsey!

CAD-YARD. Word used only in Lincolnshire for a 'knacker's yard', a place where animal carcasses are cut up and boiled down. From Danish 'kjød', 'meat', via Lincolnshire dialect 'cad' ('offal', 'bad meat') ['George'].

CAMRON. Curved wooden rail, notched at both ends, from which pigs and other animals were hung by their hind legs after slaughter. This was elsewhere called a 'cammerill' or 'gambrel', but the Northumbrian form 'camron' (used by the Elliott sisters) is closest to the original, the Old British or Welsh 'cambren' – i.e. 'cam', 'bent'; 'bren', 'stick'. No doubt the word was handed down from the large Welsh-speaking British community which survived unconquered in Northumbria until the seventh century.

CHARLOCK. A weed (*Sinapis arvensis*) that commonly grew as 'rubbish' among corn. Known as 'ketlocks' in south and west Yorkshire, but as 'brazzocks' (from Latin 'brassica'?) in the north and east of the county [Bill Denby, Yorkshire].

COULTER. Knife-like blade fixed towards the front of a plough, to make the first, vertical, cut in the soil: this is then sliced horizontally by the ploughshare and turned over by the mouldboard. Proper adjustment of the coulter is an absolute prerequisite of satisfactory ploughing.

COUNTRY. Often used by older people (as it was once used generally, e.g. by Jane Austen) to mean 'county' or 'district' [Bill Partridge, Suffolk: 'George', Lincolnshire].

CREET. Kent and Sussex dialect word for the 'cradle' framework attached to a scythe when mowing corn. From Old English 'crete', 'a baby's cradle' [Alf Friend, Kent].

CREWE. Northern and north Midland word for a small yard or pen for cattle or sheep. From Old Welsh 'creu', a pen or sty? ['George', Lincolnshire].

CURRICK. Apparently 'to cause diarrhoea in horses' ['George', Lincolnshire].

DERRIS ROOT. Used, powdered, against lice in horses' coats.

DEW. Used by Bill Partridge (Suffolk) with the sense of 'moaned' or 'complained'. It is obviously a 'strong past' form [cf. 'hew' for 'hoed'] but of which verb?

DIDIKOIES. A Romany word meaning, precisely, travellers with some (but less than half) gypsy blood. Used in southern England for all kinds of itinerants save pure-bred gypsies [Will Forman, East Kent].

DRAGON'S BLOOD. Mysterious ingredient of horse medicines. Perhaps originally a preparation made from Herb Robert (*Geranium robertianum*), one of whose dialect names was 'dragon's blood': according to Culpeper's *Herbal* (1669), this was 'held in great esteem by farmers, who use it in diseases of their cattle'.

DUTCH OVEN. Small cylindrical tin oven. Meat etc. is hung on hooks inside, and the oven placed in front of an open fire.

FENUGREEK. Spice (*Trigonella foenumgraecum*) used in horse medicines, perhaps mainly for its smell, which is attractive to horses.

GAFFER. 'Grandfather' (grand'fer); 'a respected elderly man' – and hence 'the boss', 'the master'.

GAMBO. Type of small cart found in central and south Wales and the adjacent English border counties, where it is used for carrying light loads in hilly areas. It consists simply of a flat platform, supported on members continuous with the shafts, and running (in order to maintain a low centre of gravity) on comparatively small cart-wheels. The platform has no fixed back, front or sides, the load being held in place by a 'cart stick' at each corner and detachable ladders or 'cratches' slotting into either side. The design (which resembles that of primitive carts still to be seen in Mediterranean countries) is clearly an ancient one, and may even date from Roman times [see Dick Faulkner, 'General carpenter and wheelwright'].

GATHMAN (garthman). Lincolnshire dialect word for the stockman, who supervised the 'garth' or yard where cattle (generally bullocks) were fattened. From Scandinavian 'garthe', 'enclosure' ['George'].

GENTIAN. The herb *Gentiana luteia*, used in horse medicines to stimulate appetite.

GIRD. Scottish and northern English word for a child's iron hoop, originally made from the bands used to 'gird' wooden barrels or tubs [Elliott Sisters, Northumberland].

GLEANING. Picking up the ears of corn left in a field after the harvest had been gathered: these would then be ground for bread or, latterly, fed to pigs or chickens. Usually done by women and children, gleaning was a privilege traditionally granted to 'the poor of the parish'. Thomas Tusser:

> Corn carried, let such as be poor go and glean
> and after, thy cattle, to mouth it up clean.

GREASY. 'Greasy legs' or 'greasy heels' is a chronic skin infection of horses, especially Shires and other heavy horses. It can be caused by lack of exercise, damp stables, or grazing on wet land, and therefore attacks mainly in winter.

GREEN COPPERAS. Crude ferrous sulphate, used in horse medicines to counteract anaemia [*EP*].

HALES. Lincolnshire and north-east Midland word for the handles of a plough. From Scandinavian 'hali' – the tail of an animal? ['George': Lincolnshire].

HARTSHORN. An ammonia liniment used in horse doctoring [*EP*].

HELLEBORE, WHITE. The dried and ground root of the American plant, *Veratrum album* (as opposed to the native Green and Stinking Hellebores), used in horse medicine. While it acts as a tonic in small quantities, excessive amounts can cause convulsions and death [*EP*].

HERDEN (also harden, hurden). Strictly, very coarse sackcloth made from the refuse ('hards') of flax and hemp: but used in northern and western England for any kind of sackcloth or hessian [Edith Watkins, Radnorshire, Powys].

HEUGHED (pronounced 'hewfed'). In the northernmost English counties, a heugh, heaf or heft is 'an accustomed pasture or dwelling'. So 'heughed' sheep are those hereditarily accustomed to one part of an unfenced moor, from which they will not normally stray. From Old Norse 'hefta', 'to restrain' [Maggie Joe Chapman, Swaledale, North Yorkshire].

HICK, TO. To lift by jerking: a Yorkshire and Lincolnshire form of 'to hitch' ['George', Lincolnshire].

HOOLY. 'Wholly' therefore: 'very', 'entirely', from Old English 'hallice': now apparently used only in parts of Suffolk [Bill Partridge].

HORKEY. Uniquely East Anglian word for a post-harvest celebration. Said to derive from the cry of 'Hark ye', signifying that harvest was over [Bill Partridge, Suffolk].

HUCKING. Word used in western English counties for 'haggling' or 'bargaining' – hence 'huckster' ['Gib', Radnorshire, Powys].

JUNIPER BERRIES. Used in horse medicines against flatulence and colic [*EP*].

KNAG-RAKE. Yorkshire dialect word for the very large wooden rake used for gathering the last remaining hay left in a field after carting and stacking. From Norwegian 'knagge', a wooden peg? [Kit Calvert, Wensleydale, North Yorkshire].

KYLE. Word used in Northumberland and north-western England for a small pile of hay: several kyles would later be gathered into a 'pike' (q.v.). From Old Scandinavian 'kile', 'a cone shape' [Elliott sisters, Northumberland].

LAITH. Northern word for an outlying field barn, including a 'mew' and a 'shippon' (qqv.). From Old Norse 'hlatha', 'a barn' [Kit Calvert, Wensleydale, North Yorkshire].

LEEP, TO. Northumbrian and north-western for 'to scald', 'to boil quickly'. From Old Scandinavian 'hleypa', 'to scorch or curdle' [Elliott sisters, Northumberland].

LOFRUMS. Knitted footless 'waders', made of unwashed and undyed wool (and therefore waterproof) worn over Swaledale men's trousers in the days before wellington boots. Derivation uncertain, but probably connected with old Danish 'lothbraekr', 'shaggy woollen trousers', as worn by the Viking hero, Ragnar Lothbrok: they protected him against snake-bites, and had to be removed before he could be killed in King Aella of Northumbria's adder-pit. Or else, just possibly, from the Manx 'loghtyn', literally 'mouse brown', but also conveying something made of homespun, naturally coloured material. Many of the Norsemen who settled in Swaledale in the tenth century came via Ireland and the Isle of Man [Maggie Joe Chapman].

LUNGE REIN. Long rope used during the early part of a horse's training. One end is fastened to the bridle, and the other held by the trainer, who encourages the horse to run round him in circles: thus it gradually becomes used to being controlled [Alfred Tinsley, 'The gentleman's groom'].

MADDER. Herb (*Rubia tinctorum*) used in horse medicines as a laxative, and 'for opening and cleansing obstructions in the liver and gall-bladder' [Culpeper].

MAYWEED, STINKING. Plant (*Anthemis cotula*) known as 'Dog Daisy' or 'Stinking Nanny' in Yorkshire [Bill Denby] which commonly grows as 'rubbish' among wheat. 'The worst wede that is' [Fitzherbert's *Boke of Husbandrie*, 1523]. 'An unprofitable weede among corne, and raiseth blisters on the hands of the weeders and reapers' [Gerard's *Herbal*, 1597].

MEW. Northern and south-western version of 'a mow', i.e. a loose heap of mown hay kept in a barn. By extension, the part of the barn where the mew stands [Kit Calvert, Bob Metcalfe and Maggie Joe Chapman, Wensleydale, North Yorkshire].

MEYTHER (also moither). East Anglian word for a girl or woman [Jim Spooner, Suffolk].

'MINER'S COUGH'. Silicosis, a lung disease which attacks miners.

NAB. Northern dialect for a headland: literally 'a nose' [Sam Robson, East Yorkshire].

PAZZICK-MARK. Cumbrian word for a wet mark on the floor. Probably related to 'puzzy', 'puzzicky', i.e. 'close', 'damp' (of weather) [Myles Bainbridge, Cumbria].

PIKE. Northern word for a large conical (i.e. peaked or 'piked') pile of hay, made in the field – especially when bad weather threatened to soak the lying crop. Such temporary stacks would later be carted (perhaps on a 'pike-bogie') to the permanent stack in or near the barn [Kit Calvert and Bob Metcalfe, Wensleydale, North Yorkshire: Elliott sisters, Northumberland]. Also 'to pike' – to clear the edges of a field with a scythe, before or after a horse-drawn mowing machine [Bob Metcalfe].

PINEHOUSE. Yorkshire and Lincolnshire word for a place where animals were shut up to fast before slaughter: usually attached to the slaughter-house. From dialect 'to pine', 'to starve' [Ted Bateson, East Yorkshire].

QUEAK, TO. To squeeze, press down (e.g. apples for cider). A medieval English word apparently now used only in 'cider-makers' talk' on the Welsh borders [John Lloyd, Radnorshire, Powys].

SALTPETRE. Used in horse medicines as a diuretic.

SCARRYING. Lincolnshire and East Anglian dialect word for breaking up ploughed land with a horse-hoe, cf. 'scurry', 'to stir up' ['George', Lincolnshire].

SCOOTS (also skoots). Word used on the east coast of England, from Suffolk to Northumberland, for various species of sea birds. It usually meant guillemots, but could also apply to razorbills, puffins, cormorants or *scoter* ducks. Given the rapid flight of all these birds, and the word's occurrence in the more Scandinavian-influenced parts of Britain, it seems more likely to have been derived from Old Norse 'skiota' – 'to shoot, move quickly' (cf. skoot off) than to be connected with 'scouting' (i.e. reconnoitring) which is derived from Middle French 'e[s]couter' – 'to listen' [Sam Robson, East Yorkshire].

SEEDSMAN. The deputy foreman of a large farm, who was once responsible for selecting and sowing seed ['George', Lincolnshire].

SET. North Yorkshire and north-eastern dialect word for a 'trouble', 'difficulty', 'fuss', or 'disturbance' [Maggie Joe Chapman, Swaledale, North Yorkshire].

SHIPPON (also shippen). Northern and western word for a cow-byre, or the part of a barn used as such. From Old English 'scypen', 'a stall or fold' [Kit Calvert, Wensleydale, North Yorkshire].

SHIRES, THE. The former administrative divisions of northern Northumberland, viz. Hexhamshire, Norhamshire, Islandshire, Bedlingtonshire and Bamboroughshire [Elliot sisters, Northumberland].

SKELL-BOOSE. Yorkshire Dales word for the wooden partition between the shippon (q.v.) and the rest of the barn. From Old Norse 'skilja' – 'to separate or divide'; and Old English 'bos' – 'a stall for a horse or cow' [Bob Metcalfe, Wensleydale, North Yorkshire].

SKETTINS. East Yorkshire word for part of the edible offal from a slaughtered bullock: probably connected with 'sket' or 'skit' – 'excrement' [Ted Bateson].

SLACK. An Old Norse word, 'slakki', for a shallow valley, used in the north Pennine Dales [Kit Calvert, Wensleydale, North Yorkshire].

STADDLE-STONES. Mushroom shaped stone pedestals, used to raise ricks, granaries, apple-stores, etc. several feet above ground level, in order to keep out damp and rodents – which, it was hoped, would be unable to negotiate the overhang of the 'mushrooms'. From Old English 'stathol', 'foundations' [Alf Friend, Kent].

STANK, TO. To dam a stream in order to produce a 'stank' (or pool) for washing sheep etc. From Old French 'estanc', 'pool, lake' (modern 'étang') via Middle English 'stank' [Mrs Mills, Radnorshire, Powys].

STUVVER. East Anglian word for a mixture of clover and hay used for feeding horses, especially in winter. From Old French 'estover', 'something necessary' [Bill Partridge, Suffolk].

SULPHUR, BLACK. Used as a mild laxative and a parasiticide in horse medicines.

TALLY. In hop-picking, the means used to record the amount of hops gathered by a picker or group of pickers: also, in East Kent, a five-bushel basket into which hops were poured for measuring. The original tallies were flat sided sticks, with notches cut across their edge for every five bushels picked: these were then split (French, 'taillé') down their length, one side being kept by the 'tallyman' and the other by the picker. Payment due could thus be checked by comparing the two halves [Will Forman, Kent].

TARTAR EMETIC. Antimony potassium tartrate, used in horse medicines against flukes and other internal parasites [EP].

THIRD LAD. In East Yorkshire, the waggoner's senior assistant: the foreman was presumably 'first', the waggoner 'second', and his assistant 'third'. In most parts of the country, however, the waggoner's senior assistant would be, more logically, 'second chap'.

TREE OF PARADISE. Also called 'wood laurel' by some horsemen. Probably spurge laurel (*Daphne laureola*) which was once also used as a cure for cancer in humans.

TROWSE. Midland and Welsh border word for boughs, brushwood etc. used for repairing gaps in hedges. Perhaps from Old Norse 'tros', 'leaves and twigs' [Dick Faulkner, Radnorshire, Powys].

TUMBRIL. Word used in East Anglia for any kind of cart [Bill Partridge, Suffolk], but elsewhere specifically for a dung cart, or for a movable wheeled feeding trough ['George', Lincolnshire].

UNYOKE, TO. Lincolnshire dialect for 'to uncouple horses from a cart, plough, etc.' A survival from the days of oxen, which pulled from a 'yoke' laid across their shoulders – whereas horses pull from a collar, or on shafts ['George'].

WARE. In the north, any kind of pottery or earthenware, e.g. 'a ware jug' [Elliott sisters, Northumberland].

WOOD-CUT. Lincolnshire word for a 'timber-tug', a horse-drawn vehicle consisting basically of two axles linked by a massive centre pole, used for carrying one or more complete tree-trunks ['George', Lincolnshire].

WINDROWS. Parallel lines into which drying hay is raked before gathering or cocking.

SOURCES OF ILLUSTRATIONS

P. 91: Thomas Bewick, *A History of British Birds*, 1826; p. 216: by kind permission of Mr Frank Bigg; pp. 114, 203: Welsh Folk Museum, Cardiff; pp. 99, 111: by kind permission of Mrs Maggie Joe Chapman; p. 96: courtesy of the photographer, Mr Peter Crawley; p. 70: by kind permissin of Mr Bill Denby; pp. 77, 118, 119, 177: Beamish North of England Open Air Museum, Co. Durham; pp. 192, 197: by kind permission of Mr Dick Faulkner; pp. 135, 137: by kind permission of Mr Will Flinton; p. 146: by kind permission of Mrs Lizzie Grange; pp. 16, 59, 125, 126, 131: Suffolk Record Office, Ipswich; pp. 21, 40: photos by Frank Parkinson, Parkinson Collection, Museum of Lincolnshire Life, Lincoln; pp. 38, 46, 74, 133: Museum of Lincolnshire Life, Lincoln; pp. 87, 92: by kind permission of Mr Sam Robson; p. 143: courtesy of South Eastern Newspapers Limited; p. 107; Henry Stephen, *The Book of the Farm*, 1852; p. 180: by kind permission of Mr Arthur Wade; p. 51: Castle Museum, York.

INDEX